D1501463

FUTURE-FOCUSED HISTORY TEACHING

The life cycle of real learning

Key Charts

Basic principles of history education

PRINCIPLE	DESCRIPTION
Purpose	A mission of fostering judgment in human affairs gives history education a coherent and useful purpose to guide instruction.
Relevance	Historical knowledge is suitable for educational purposes when it imparts principles and concepts relevant to the future.
Importance	Superficial and trivial learning can be limited by emphasizing more-important knowledge over less-important knowledge.
Scale-to-detail	Superficial and trivial learning can be limited by appropriately matching the level of factual detail in a history course to the scale of the course.
Cognition	The transfer of school learning to life beyond school is most likely to succeed when relevant and important knowledge is learned in multiple contexts over an extended period of time.

Cognitive learning strategies for education

STRATEGY	DESCRIPTION
Emphasize key knowledge	Relevant and important principles and concepts are essential to the transfer of learning from school to life beyond school.
Teach knowledge in multiple contexts	When students learn knowledge in multiple contexts, they see how it applies in different situations, which increases the likelihood that students can apply their learning to new situations arising in the future.
Teach knowledge over time	For knowledge to be retained into adulthood, knowledge should be reinforced over an extended period of time through spaced learning (distributed practice).
Avoid excessive content	Effective transfer of school learning requires deep study of a limited number of important principles and concepts, and deep learning is not possible in an overstuffed curriculum.

Kinds of historical knowledge suitable for education

KNOWLEDGE	DESCRIPTION
Principles of history	Timeless and universal principles of historical knowledge describe how the world works and are applicable to the future.
Events with continuing effect	Historical developments that exert significant, continuing impact in the contemporary world are likely to continue to affect students' lives into the future.
Foundational concepts	Foundational concepts of history and geography are necessary for understanding historical events of the past, present, and future, and they provide situational awareness of the world around us.
A big picture	A big picture of human development though time can tie together the three kinds of historical knowledge described above. It is the source of principles of history, provides multiple contexts for students to learn the principles, can inform judgment by placing events in historical perspective, and can satisfy human psychological needs to know who we are and where we came from.

Criteria for weighing historical importance

CRITERIA	DESCRIPTION
Amount	The number of people and amount of land affected by a historical event.
Change	The extent of change prompted by the event.
Duration	The duration of the event's consequences.
Proximity	The proximity of the event to the learner in time, space, or culture.

FUTURE-FOCUSED HISTORY TEACHING

Restoring the Power of Historical Learning

Mike Maxwell

Maxwell Learning

First published in 2018 in the United States of America
by Maxwell Learning LLC, Mancos, Colorado

ISBN 978-1-7321201-0-5

Library of Congress Control Number: 2018903129

This work of scholarship is intended for educational use and is meant to benefit society
by informing the public about matters of important public interest. Under provisions
of the fair use rule of the Copyright Law of the United States, sources quoted in this
book are employed in a transformative capacity for purposes of comment and criticism
meant to assist in illustrating the author's concept of future-focused history education.

FIRST EDITION (PAPERBACK)

FRONT COVER: Ángel y Diablo
Mexican folk art representing two sides of human nature,
which is the chief source of principles of historical knowledge.

Contents

ix

Figures

Figures in **bold** are reproduced at the front of the book.

To Sue,
who made everything possible

and to Katy and Gus
with apology for the messes my generation
left for your generation to clean up

PART ONE
THE PROBLEMS

When the past no longer illuminates the future,
the spirit walks in darkness.

–Alexis de Tocqueville, *Democracy in America*, 1840

A conflict at the heart of history education

This book is intended for people who value history and believe that historical learning should be less a pointless exercise in temporarily memorizing trivial facts for the next exam, and more a quest for important knowledge from the past that can inform judgment in the future. Any society that has developed the capacity to destroy most life on earth needs all the good judgment it can get, and there is no better place to seek it than in the long record of human experience.

Unfortunately, a conflict at the heart of history education prevents it from functioning effectively: History is about the past, but education is about the future. By history, I mean the record of human experience compiled by historians, and by education, I mean the kind of formal schooling that most people will receive during their years in school and college. Historians and educators have very different jobs to perform. The role of historians is to describe events from the past; the role of educators is to prepare students and society for the future.

This conflict between past and future does much to explain why history occupies an inferior position in the schools relative to other fundamental realms of knowledge such as mathematics, language, and science. More important, it explains why society finds it so difficult to learn from history.

If you stop to think about it, you will notice that school subjects other than history are based on imparting general principles of how the world works that can be applied in the future, principles like addition and subtraction in mathematics, grammar and punctuation in language, and photosynthesis and gravity in science.

General principles are the king of knowledge because they possess the extraordinary capacity to carry knowledge of past experience across the boundary of time into the future where this knowledge can help people to function effectively in their lives. Furthermore, general principles are universal in nature; they have proven valid in the past; they remain valid in the present, and they are likely to remain valid into the future anywhere that humans are present. It might be said that disciplines of all kinds exist for the express purpose of developing, systemizing, and imparting their sets of general principles.

History is unique among school subjects in that it identifies no general principles derived from its subject matter. They aren't found where principles of intellectual disciplines are normally identified: in textbooks, curriculum standards, and programs of instruction such as Advanced Placement courses.

What sort of knowledge does history education provide? Because educators have relied on historians to set the agenda for history schooling, history education looks very much like history: a large collection of one-time events from the past. Without principles useful in the future, history is unable to fulfill the purpose of education the way other school subjects do, and the cycle of historical ignorance can repeat indefinitely. As Santayana said, "Those who cannot remember the past are condemned to repeat it."

In our society, we may learn *about* history but we seldom learn *from* history. If history schooling is to fulfill the mission of education—and if society is to learn from history—history education will have to undergo a fundamental shift in orientation from a focus on isolated events of the past to a focus on knowledge relevant to the future.

Educators commonly try to compensate for history schooling's lack of subject-matter knowledge useful in the future by emphasizing skills knowledge instead: critical thinking skills or the job skills of professional historians. Other core school subjects also have their critical thinking skills and professional practices, but in these other disciplines, general principles constitute the foundation of learning, because knowledge of how the world works is a necessary prerequisite to critical thinking. In history education that foundation is missing.

The truth is, history has been supplying humans with useful principles of knowledge for at least 2,400 years, since the time of Thucydides in Greece and Sun Tzu in China. In earlier times, history could involve more than the act of describing past events; it could involve the ambition to derive from events principles useful in the future, an ambition that the history profession has largely abandoned. This loss deprives historical learning of the power possessed by other intellectual disciplines.

In addition to supplying general principles of knowledge, the historical record can be a source for several more kinds of knowledge that are also relevant to the future.

If historians wish to concentrate on the role of describing events of the past, that's their business. Then the task of providing future-focused historical learning falls to history educators, who bear the professional responsibility to impart important knowledge of the world that can help students and society to function effectively in the future. For that's *their* business.

Mike Maxwell
Villa Santiago, Mexico 2010-2014
Montezuma County, Colorado 2014-2018

General Principles or Recurring Dynamics?

Following the original publication of this book in 2018, it became clear that some historians will remain uncomfortable with the idea that general principles can be derived from the subject matter of history. Such people might find it easier to support the sensible concept of future-focused history education if the term *recurring dynamics* of history were substituted for the term *general principles* of history.

Recurring dynamics of history are similar to the general principles that define social studies fields other than history, and no one can reasonably doubt their existence: We need only look to major events of our time—the problem-plagued US invasion of Iraq in 2003, the Great Recession of 2008, and the COVID pandemic of 2020—to recognize contemporary instances of often-repeated dynamics of the past.

About the structure of this book

Insofar as practicable within a single volume, this book adheres to the cognitive learning strategies identified in Chapter 6: Impart important principles and concepts in multiple contexts over an extended period of time.

The heart has its reasons, which reason knows not.

–Blaise Pascal, *Pensées*, 1669

CHAPTER ONE

An encounter
with the power of history

The author explains why he wrote this book.

I'm growing old now. Like you, I always knew it would happen—on an intellectual level at least. But on an emotional level, I never really believed it. Not sure that I do yet. It's a funny thing how emotion can trump reason. I discussed this idea one day with Molly*, a bright young professor I met when I returned to college to obtain my teaching license.

Molly argued that reason was the greater force in history, while I held out for emotion. We came from different backgrounds that represented opposite poles along the reason-to-emotion continuum: Molly had earned a PhD in history, and I had been in a war. She went off to teach history at an Ivy League university, and I went off to teach history in a small working-class community in southwest Colorado.

It was the war that got me interested in history. Like other teenage boys in the late 1960s, I was plucked from my hometown, issued a new wardrobe, and sent on an all-expenses paid trip to Southeast Asia courtesy of Uncle Sam. I didn't have a clue what a kid from Ohio was doing on the other side of the world, living in a hole in the ground and carrying a fully automatic weapon. That's when I started reading history, the history of America's involvement in Vietnam.

I read about the chain of events that led from the French colonial occupation of Indochina to me hunkered down on a hilltop somewhere east of Laos eating my C rations. And I learned about something else from reading the history of Vietnam: I learned about a thousand-year-long

---

*Name changed for privacy.

5

pattern of tenacious Vietnamese resistance to foreign invaders, who included the Chinese, the Mongols, the French, the Japanese, and now the Americans.

Learning this history was almost like a religious experience; it removed the scales from my eyes. It reminds me now of the words of the former slave ship captain who wrote "Amazing Grace"—I once was blind, but now I see. I could see that history was available for the taking, and it possessed an awesome power to enlighten. I was now in a position to think my own thoughts and reach my own judgments about the war in Vietnam, and I concluded that the American war effort was no more likely to succeed than previous invasions of Vietnam. As it turned out, history proved me right.

This wasn't the first time that I had experienced an emotional response to learning some history. The first time was when I was maybe five or six years old, and I gained a primitive understanding of the concept of historical chronology. One day it occurred to me that knights must have come before George Washington, and he must have come before cowboys. The past wasn't just a jumble of events, after all—it followed a sequential pattern; it could be *intelligible*.

The sense of empowerment I felt at that moment was not unlike the feeling I experienced years later upon learning about the history of Vietnam. In both cases, I felt as though I had acquired important insights into how the world works.

I don't know how common it is for people to get excited like this about learning a little history, but I'm pretty sure millions have shared with me a very different emotional response to historical learning. Return with me now to those less-than-thrilling days of yesteryear when I was a student in junior high school, seated at my desk on a warm spring afternoon. Sunshine and freedom are beckoning from just beyond the open classroom window when all of a sudden the teacher utters those five dreaded words: "Take out your history books."

Instantly, my world goes dark and shrinks to the size of a shriveled-up pea. "Open your books to page 357," the teacher intones. The book is thick and gray with dark blue lettering; it has graffiti scrawled on the edges by previous captives. The act of opening the book releases soporific vapors redolent of the old and the boring, which render futile any further attempt at concentration. Impenetrable blocks of text swim before my eyes, threatening existential annihilation. I look at the clock: 45 minutes until the bell. Then everything goes blank.

Does this scene from my youth (with some grown-up embellishment, of course) feel at all familiar to you? I have no way to prove it, but I suspect that this sort of negative reaction to history learning is far more common than the joys I recounted earlier. (It's worth noting that both of those happy occasions occurred outside school.) This junior high episode reflects my general experience with history education through my freshman year at Ohio State, which, if anything, was even bleaker.

Undergraduates at that time were required to take a series of three introductory-level history courses set in a hot, creaky third-floor auditorium. The historical content consisted of an endless succession of European wars and kings with Roman numerals after their names. The instructor was a disembodied battery of television sets distributed around the room. Machines administered and graded exams. It was like living death.

A notice from the draft board and the possibility of actual death in a distant land delivered me from these dreary circumstances and taught me that historical learning could involve more than tedious memorization of pointless facts. History had the power to enlighten! After I returned to civilian life, history continued to exert its pull until I acquired a history degree in my early thirties, and midlife found me standing in a classroom facing 28 teenagers and a fearsome responsibility: to teach them about the world, no less.

As a history teacher, I tried to do all the right things. I assigned my students research projects, simulations, and source-analysis activities; my students examined important events from the past, essential questions, and big ideas. But no matter what I tried, I couldn't shake the feeling that my history teaching wasn't effective—that my students weren't leaving school with knowledge that would be useful later in life. Their learning seemed to fade quickly, leaving behind little more than half-remembered facts and vague traces of historical events. My teaching wasn't conveying the power of history.

What's more, other history teachers didn't seem to be effective either. Don't get me wrong; there are wonderful history teachers out there who make history interesting to their students. But that's not the point, is it? Education is supposed to provide knowledge useful in the future, and I saw no evidence that history teachers had found a way to provide their students with a meaningful understanding of history that would be useful in life. My nagging internal doubts were reinforced by external evidence, including decades of nationwide testing that showed American students scored much worse in history than in the other core subjects of math, language, and science.

I was frustrated by the huge chasm that separated history education's potential from its practice. I knew from firsthand experience that history possessed an awesome power to enlighten, but on a national level I saw political leaders making terrible decisions that no one with even a rudimentary understanding of history should make. All the while, I knew that my profession—and I personally—wasn't helping citizens to acquire the kind of useful historical understanding that might limit such costly ignorance in the future.

Yet I didn't see educators talking about such matters—which only heightened my frustration. Leaders in the history-education community appeared to be consumed with matters like writing voluminous content standards, promoting extensive factual memorization, glorifying high-stakes testing, and devising various instructional fixes meant to divert attention from history education's fundamental lack of relevance.

It seemed to me that history educators were whistling past the grave-yard, and society was squandering a vital national resource. I felt that I had to try to do something about it, so when I left classroom teaching, I gave myself a new full-time job—to find the answer to one simple question: How can history education be made useful?

I figured that writing a book would be the best way to pursue this goal, but such a plan had serious flaws. In the first place, I didn't know if an answer to my question existed, and if it did exist whether I would be able to find it. Furthermore, I had never written a book, and I didn't know if I could express my thoughts effectively or if anyone would care to read what I was thinking anyway. Plus, the whole thing promised to be a lot of work. Given these entirely rational reasons not to write a book, why did I proceed?

I had little choice in the matter. My belief in the power of history was so strong, and my frustration with history education was so intense, that I was compelled to undertake a quixotic mission to set things right—even if nobody would ever read what I wrote. In the final analysis, this book was born of gut-level feelings that demanded release.

Once again, emotion had trumped reason.

Nothing in education is so astonishing as the amount of ignorance it accumulates in the form of inert facts.

–Henry Adams, *The Education of Henry Adams*, 1907

CHAPTER TWO

Basic problems of history education

Five problems prevent history schooling from fulfilling the purpose of education.

The year is 1995. A quarter century has passed since I returned home from the war in Vietnam, and now I'm the father of a sweet little girl in the third grade. One day she brings home from school a study sheet for her upcoming exam on the Age of Exploration. She is expected to know the names of several explorers and the names of Columbus's ships and other factual details. Missing from the study sheet, however, is any mention of why European explorers came to the New World or what resulted from their visits.

Disheartened, I go out and rent a copy of Ridley Scott's film *1492: Conquest of Paradise*. Together, Katy and I sit on the couch and watch excerpts from the film as we discuss the causes and consequences of Columbus's voyage. I tell her I don't care if she misses the names of Columbus's ships on her test. Katy is only in the third grade, but already she is learning that history is more about memorizing trivial facts for an upcoming exam than understanding why people behave as they do.

Fast-forward another fifteen years. By now I have retired from classroom teaching, and my wife and I are living in Mexico, where she is working as a literacy specialist. Due to my feelings about the state of history education, I know that I should be using this time to try to do something about it, but I don't have a clear vision of the problems or how to fix them, so I have been finding other ways to occupy my time (primarily involving the consumption of Mexican cuisine).

On this particular afternoon, I'm sitting at my computer when I happen across the Virginia Department of Education (VDOE) website, where I see a selection of seven sample questions from the state's recent standardized assessment for high school students enrolled in World History 2: 1500 to the Present. The first question is reasonable; it asks students to interpret a diagram about world religions. But the next two questions grab my attention.[1]

Each of these exam questions expects students to connect a name from history to a historical concept: Thomas Hobbes to absolute state power and the Mahdi Rebellion to European imperialism, but the questions are unconcerned about the concepts themselves. My reaction is visceral: *Oh my gosh, history education is still stuck in the third grade!*

Now, I have a history degree from a reputable university, and I taught world history in high school for a dozen years, but I didn't know the answers to these questions. (And I probably didn't say *gosh*.) My next response was also emotional: I swore to write a book blasting the kind of history education that insults the intelligence of third graders, let alone high school students. That was the day when my procrastination ended, and I got to work on this book.

WHY DOES EDUCATION EXIST?

My allergic reaction to those two Virginia exam questions provoked me to write a book, but I didn't know what I was getting myself into. I didn't even know why I found the Virginia exam questions so upsetting. As the author Doris Lessing said about growing up under the apartheid system in Rhodesia, it's one thing to know you're uncomfortable; it's quite another to understand why.

As I labored to figure out the source of my discomfort, I came to understand the nature of my task. I had taken on the job of (a) trying to comprehend on a rational level the reasons for my gut-level feelings about history education, and (b) trying to translate these thoughts into intelligible language that could communicate with potential readers, an undertaking that has consumed more than seven years of my life and has felt for the most part like sweating blood.

My first order of business was to understand why I was upset by the Virginia assessment questions. As I tried to make sense of my feelings, I found it helpful to drill down to first purposes—to seek the fundamental reason behind a given educational undertaking. Before I could understand what was wrong with the Virginia exam questions, I would need to know the purpose of education itself.

Education is a social institution, I mused; so it must exist to fill a societal need. What is that need? Early in the history of our species, our Paleolithic ancestors needed to teach their children about important features in the environment so they would be equipped to survive in a challenging world. Children needed to know about two essential realms of knowledge: the *physical* world of plants, animals, weather, and tools, and the world of *human behavior*, which dictated relationships within groups and between groups—relationships that determined whom to love and nurture and whom to fear and fight. The purpose of education was to teach children how to function effectively in their world. It was a matter of survival.

When language developed, people could widen their range of knowledge by sharing information with others. When writing appeared, much later, it became possible to transmit knowledge over long distances and multiple lifetimes, and society enlisted teachers to acquire important knowledge accumulated by the larger culture and pass it on to children, who were unlikely to encounter this knowledge from contacts with immediate family and friends.

It's easy for us to lose sight of the purpose of education amidst all the trappings of modern-day schooling—the standards, assessments, textbooks, theories, lesson plans, worksheets, grades, technologies, interest groups, commerce, politics, reforms du jour, college applications, student loans, and so on—but schooling exists today for the same reason it has always existed: *to impart important knowledge of the world that can help students and society to function effectively in the future.*

As obvious as this conclusion might seem, it wasn't until I pinned down the purpose of education that I was able to figure out what was wrong with the Virginia exam questions. The Hobbes and Mahdi questions were like my daughter's third-grade question about the names of Columbus's ships; they quizzed a student's ability to memorize names, *but the names did nothing to explain how the world works*—they did nothing to help students function effectively in the world. Knowledge that lacks a useful function is termed *inert* because it doesn't do anything. But it's better known as trivia.

It's not that Thomas Hobbes and the Mahdi Rebellion are themselves trivial—far from it. If students were to study either of these subjects in sufficient depth, they might gain very useful understandings of how the world works. Hobbes was concerned with how society might be made less brutal and better able to ensure the well-being of its members. The Mahdi Rebellion against British rule in the Sudan demonstrated the perennial human desire to break free from external control.

Both topics dealt with timeless imperatives of human nature and the question of what constitutes a good society, but the Virginia exam questions didn't ask students about important matters like these. The Virginia questions didn't ask for any intellectual understanding at all; they merely called on students to match names.

The Hobbes and Mahdi questions demonstrated that *history education is trivial not because of its subject matter but because of the superficial way the subject matter is treated.* If Virginia's test designers had wished to emphasize important concepts rather than superficial name recognition, they might have asked a question something like this:

> From the 1800s through the 1960s, peoples in Africa and Asia often struggled to obtain freedom from outside control. Examples include the Opium War in China[2] and the independence movement led by Mahatma Gandhi in India. What force in history were these people resisting?

This alternate question calls for the same answer choice as the original Virginia exam question—European imperialism—but the two questions place very different demands on teachers and students. The alternate question expects students to be familiar with an important historical concept, while the Virginia question expects students to have memorized large quantities of factual detail, which requires extensive superficial instruction that steals time away from learning about the important historical concepts.

The Iron Law of Superficiality[*] states: "All other things being equal, as the number of topics increases, time per topic decreases; as time per topic decreases, the level of superficiality increases." Superficial instruction doesn't leave enough time per topic for students to learn about events in sufficient depth to gain useful understandings of how events illuminate the workings of the world. Consequently, the Corollary to the Iron Law states: "Superficial learning is trivial learning."

The two Virginia exam questions that I stumbled across on a winter's day over seven years ago proved to be the key to unlocking two of history education's basic problems, the *scale-to-detail* problem and the *importance* problem. These problems work together to produce superficial and trivial learning.

---

[*] The Iron Law of Superficiality and the Corollary to the Iron Law are timeless educational maxims that I just made up.

PROBLEM 1: THE SCALE-TO-DETAIL PROBLEM

The *scale-to-detail* problem arises when the level of factual detail in a history course is too great for the scale of the course, which results in instruction that includes more topics than can be covered in sufficient depth to produce useful learning. According to historian William H. McNeill, "Each scale of history has an appropriate conception and amount of detail, just as each scale of map has an appropriate projection and amount of detail."[3] The scale of a history course is a function of the geographic extent, time span, and range of subject matter covered by the course.

The scale of the history survey courses offered in secondary school and college is typically quite large, covering subjects from politics and economics to science and society that have occurred over a large geographic area over a long span of time. If the course also includes a high level of factual detail, the course will include too much information to produce anything other than superficial learning. This kind of history schooling is often characterized as "a mile wide and an inch deep."

The Virginia history program provides a case in point. It was based on a set of extensive content standards that called for students to memorize large quantities of facts. The world history standards, for example, expected students to memorize two things about each of seven Enlightenment-era thinkers, one of whom was Thomas Hobbes. Students were expected to know the name of a publication authored by each man and a snippet of each man's thinking that averaged about nine words in length.[4] The Virginia Department of Education recommended that teachers use flash cards to help students memorize these superficial facts.[5]

Surprisingly, however, the Hobbes question that appeared on Virginia's standardized assessment didn't ask about the Hobbes information specified in the state content standards.[6] Likewise, the Mahdi question asked students about two events not covered in the state standards.[7] Apparently, when students sat down to take the state's 60-question, multiple-choice standardized assessment in World History 2, they would need to know virtually every fact of history that occurred anywhere in the world over the past 500 years. If students could be tested on anything, they would need to know everything.

Do you suppose that the Virginia Department of Education deliberately chose to test students over topics not included in the state's content standards out of meanness? Or was the VDOE simply unable to keep track of all the factual detail that it expected Virginia students to memorize? I suspect the latter, which points up the kinds of problems that can result when instruction is based on extensive, often trivial, factual detail rather than on important historical concepts.

PROBLEM 2: THE IMPORTANCE PROBLEM

Both the *scale-to-detail* problem and the *importance* problem stem from the same source: Curriculum designers don't make hard choices about what to include and what to exclude from history courses, so everything gets thrown into the pot. The *importance* problem arises from a failure to weigh the relative importance of historical topics, which violates the commonsense principle that a school curriculum should emphasize more-important knowledge over less-important knowledge.

Pressure always exists to add more facts to history courses. In a period of just 25 years, the Cold War ended, the Soviet Union disintegrated; China and India returned to world prominence; the World Trade Center toppled; the US fought wars in Kosovo, Kuwait, Afghanistan, and Iraq; world economies underwent the Great Recession; and the Arab Spring uprisings altered the complexion of the Middle East. All of these events have found, or will find, their ways into textbooks and history courses, swelling an already overstuffed curriculum.

In addition to the march of history, other forces have added content to history courses in recent years. The array of subjects considered suitable for instruction has expanded, and various interest groups have pushed to include their favored topics. One might assume that US history courses, which operate on a much smaller scale than world history courses, would be less prone to content inflation, but such is not the case. Curriculum designers have simply increased the level of detail to generate a volume of content comparable to world history courses, if not greater. In the absence of countervailing forces to filter out less-important material, the balloon just keeps filling up.

REAL LEARNING VERSUS PRETEND LEARNING. Students can't be expected to learn and remember every fact of world history—or every fact of less-broad school subjects for that matter—so why would the people at the Virginia Department of Education place students in the untenable position of needing to know virtually every fact of world history? One can only assume that the *scale-to-detail* and *importance* problems weren't on their radar—that the VDOE was simply adhering to the time-honored tradition of indiscriminately stuffing large quantities of pointless facts into history courses.

Traditional history instruction of this sort demands the kind of Bucket O' Facts instructional approach that would devote an average of nine words each to the beliefs of seven Enlightenment thinkers and would have students memorize this superficial content through the use of flash cards.

I'm drawing a distinction here between two very different kinds of historical learning. One kind takes the time to truly understand the thinking of a man like Thomas Hobbes or the dynamics of an event like the Mahdi Rebellion with the intent of understanding how these historical developments can illuminate human behavior and the workings of the world. This is *real learning*.

The other kind of learning involves memorizing large quantities of inert facts for an upcoming exam, facts that are likely to be forgotten shortly after the exam is over because they weren't learned in sufficient depth to be meaningful. This is *pretend learning*. Pretend learning abounds in American education, where it may be extolled as "rigorous" due to the extensive amount of factual memorization involved, whereas in reality it's a counterproductive waste of time and educational resources.

Pretend Learning   vs.   Real Learning

| Superficial knowledge that fails to explain how the world works and is useful only for passing an exam. | Knowledge of how the world works that is retained in memory and can be applied in life beyond school. |

PROBLEM 3: THE PURPOSE PROBLEM

Education exists to impart important knowledge of the world that can help students and society to function effectively in the future. Once I recognized this as the first purpose of education, it became the key to unlocking two basic problems of history education: the scale-to-detail and importance problems, which combine to produce superficial and trivial learning. Recognizing first purposes also proved to be key for uncovering additional basic problems of history education.

After identifying the first purpose of education, I naturally wanted to know the first purpose of history education within the broader framework of education, and here I ran headlong into a third basic problem of history schooling: the purpose problem. It seems that historians and history educators have yet to determine the first purpose of history education. If you listen to its defenders, historical learning has nearly limitless purposes; it appears to be the snake oil for curing all of society's ills. This is a partial list of lofty reasons that various people have advanced for the study of history:

> History helps us understand human behavior, world issues, the impact of individuals and groups, the working out of God's purposes, how societies came to be as they are, the significance of the past in shaping the present, how to assess evidence and conflicting interpretations, and how to recognize long-term consequences of actions.

> History provides identity, empathy, collective memory, instructive examples, a moral sense, social glue, comparative perspectives, a wide range of models and alternatives, a guide to public action, and the materials of future wisdom.

> History improves judgment, improves reading and writing skills, solves big problems significant to our understanding of ourselves, solves small problems resulting in incremental progress, is essential for good citizenship, is a means for cherishing the past, is useful in the working world, and is a species of moral illustration.

> History helps us to appreciate other cultures, helps us negotiate an ambiguous world, supports common understanding and dialogue, enlarges our sense of human capacities, promotes pride in national achievements, promotes patriotism, promotes tolerance, and promotes open-mindedness.

> History prepares us for private lives of personal integrity and fulfillment, provides a common political vision, provides a framework for the other humanities, presents possibilities for choice, makes us less ethnocentric, is a weapon against false ideologies, removes provincialism and egotism, develops critical thinking

skills and historical thinking skills, develops worthy
human beings, and gives pleasure.

So many reasons to study history amount to no coherent reason to
study history. Fritz Fischer of the University of Northern Colorado was
chair of the National Council for History Education when he observed,
"Much of the public and even many professional educators do not have
a clue about the nature or purpose of history."[8]

Professor Fischer doesn't paint a terribly flattering picture of history
educators, but I wonder how many professional historians "have a clue
about the nature or purpose" of history education. When it comes to
the purpose of history schooling, there is plenty of cluelessness to go
around. This awkward truth was underscored several years ago when a
group of international historians and scholars met in the Netherlands
to discuss the future of history education. The official report from
that conference noted that participants "diverged significantly" on the
purpose that history teaching should serve. Attendees frequently cited
two competing purposes: education for citizenship and education focused
on the discipline of history.

> Some argued that history should inculcate civic values
> and ideals of citizenship (from local to national to global).
> Others argued instead that history should be taught as
> an intellectual discipline inculcating historical conscious-
> ness and introducing students to rigorous methods of
> inquiry, but not as a tool for civics education.[9]

This disagreement over the basic purpose of history education is
reflected in American education circles, where the National Council for
History Education favors intellectual discipline, emphasizing "history's
habits of mind,"[10] while the National Council for the Social Studies
believes history should be "education for citizenship."[11] These two
positions represent a conflict between an inward and an outward focus
for historical studies: Should history schooling hold up a mirror to the
history profession, or should it open a window on the world?

It's an unresolved dispute with a long history. Attendees at a 1905
session of the American Historical Association advocated teaching
historical thinking and historical methods to first-year college students,
but after World War I prompted anxieties about the strength of democratic societies, universities adopted a new emphasis on education for
citizenship.[12]

If historians and history educators can't agree on the purpose of history education, the public can hardly be expected to figure it out. Without a coherent purpose to guide instruction, history education is a rudderless ship adrift at sea with no destination in mind. It's exceedingly difficult to succeed at an endeavor when you don't know what that endeavor is trying to accomplish.

PROBLEM 4: THE IRRELEVANCE PROBLEM

Education exists to impart important knowledge of the world that can help students and society to function effectively in the future. School subjects other than history supply knowledge useful in the future by teaching students about general principles of knowledge that describe how the world works, principles such as addition and subtraction in mathematics, spelling and grammar in language, and photosynthesis and gravity in science.

History is unique among school subjects in that it doesn't identify general principles derived from its subject matter. Apparently, this is not a mere oversight, but a precept of the history discipline. A popular college guide to historical methodology sums up the distinction between history and the social sciences: "While the historian attempts to reconstruct individual events in all their uniqueness, social scientists attempt to discover general principles that can be used to understand many events."†

The guidebook's authors don't mention why history—unlike the other social studies fields and virtually all productive human endeavors—chooses not to identify general principles drawn from its field of study. Is there a rational explanation, an inherent limitation of the history discipline perhaps, or is history's singular reluctance simply the result of tradition?

Whatever the reason, general principles of historical knowledge are not found where the principles of intellectual disciplines are normally identified: in textbooks, curriculum standards, and formal programs of instruction such as Advanced Placement (AP) courses.

I conducted full-text electronic searches of nine widely adopted curriculum materials in the field of history: three textbooks used at the high school and college levels, three sets of state curriculum standards, and three Advanced Placement history courses. Although these materials identified "principles" of numerous other fields, principles of history were nowhere to be found.[13] This search verifies that principles of history are not part of the official curriculum taught to students in American schools.

---

† Conal Furay and Michael J. Salevouris, *The Methods and Skills of History*, Second Edition, 2000, Harlan Davidson, Inc., p. 246.

General principles useful in the future constitute the foundation of learning in core school subjects such as mathematics, language, and science. By contrast, history schooling is based on teaching students large collections of one-time events from the past, most of which have little relevance to the present or future. In the absence of principles useful in the future, history is unable to fulfill the purpose of education the way other school subjects do, and society is deprived of its only formal, systematic opportunity to learn from the past.

Figure 1. Unlike other realms of knowledge, history education lacks principles relevant to the future

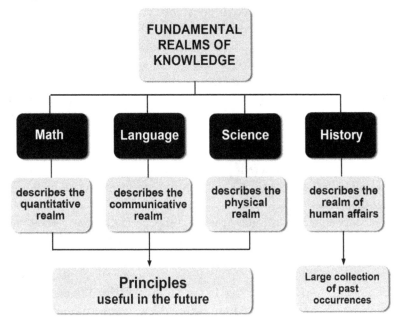

Although the history community is reluctant to acknowledge principles of history, it readily accepts the related concept of "themes" in history, such as trade, warfare, religion, government, and technology. Themes and principles of history are related in that both recognize recurring patterns in history, but themes are essentially categories of interest rather than principles that describe how the world works. If science functioned more like history, science might identify themes such as physics, chemistry, biology, geology, and so on, but science wouldn't then take the next step to identify useful principles within these categories that can be applied in life, such as Newton's laws of motion, Darwin's theory of natural selection, or Einstein's theory of relativity.

If mathematics were taught in school like history is taught, students might learn facts such as the name of a man from ancient Greece who invented a formula involving right triangles (Pythagoras), and the name of another ancient Greek who used mathematics to calculate the circumference of the earth (Eratosthenes), and that Isaac Newton and Gottfried Leibniz invented calculus, and that NASA engineers used mathematics to plot a course to the moon. If mathematics were taught like history is taught, students would learn these kinds of disconnected facts about mathematics, but students wouldn't learn the principles of addition, subtraction, multiplication, and division that can help them to live their lives and contribute to society.

This is not to say that principles of historical knowledge never surface in history classrooms. History teachers who wish to impart knowledge useful in the future may take it upon themselves to include principles of history in their instruction. In my classroom, I mentioned principles such as *government actions tend to produce unintended consequences, leaders try to get their way by appealing to the emotions of their followers,* and *leaders often justify foreign invasions by claiming to be helping the people they invade.*

Students who engage in source-analysis activities might learn the principles that *bias is everywhere* and that *comparing multiple sources is a good way to approach the truth.* But even when principles of history do occasionally appear in history courses, they are unlikely to be identified as such or to form a coherent program of instruction, whereas principles of knowledge constitute the core instruction in math, language, and science courses.

History educators commonly try to compensate for history schooling's lack of subject-matter knowledge useful in the future by emphasizing skills knowledge instead: critical thinking skills or the job skills of professional historians. Math, language, and science also have their critical thinking skills and professional practices, but in these other disciplines, principles of knowledge constitute the foundation of learning because knowledge of how the world works is a necessary prerequisite to critical thinking. In history schooling this foundation is missing. (The role of thinking skills in history schooling is addressed in Chapter 4.)

THE POWER OF HISTORY. Looking back on my time in Vietnam, I now recognize how I came to discover the awesome power of history. It was when I read histories of Vietnam that described a thousand-year-long pattern of tenacious Vietnamese resistance to foreign invaders. I took this pattern to be a general principle that could be applied to my particular situation, the American war in Vietnam. And this principle informed my judgment about the war, which I concluded was unlikely to succeed. A recurring pattern from history had revealed a general principle that informed my judgment about the future.

I was just a young GI with a high school diploma, but three history books apparently supplied me with better military intelligence than the top-secret briefings and advanced degrees of the best and brightest experts of the Kennedy and Johnson administrations.[14] Today I realize that the principle of history I recognized in Vietnam—that people resist external control—wasn't limited to the Vietnamese people; it's a universal principle that has held true throughout much of history across much of the world, from the ancient Greeks to American colonists to Vietnamese peasants. History, in fact, possesses general principles applicable to the future much as other disciplines do.

But when I became a history teacher, I didn't know about such timeless principles of history, because the history profession and history educators don't officially recognize them. So my teaching consisted mostly of recounting one-time events from the past that had little or no relevance to the lives my students would live in the future. Because my teaching lacked principles of history, it lacked the power of history.

PROBLEM 5: THE COGNITION PROBLEM

Education exists to impart important knowledge of the world that can help students and society to function effectively in the future. For knowledge to be useful in the future, it must be conveyed in a manner that is understandable and meaningful to the learner so that the knowledge can be retained in memory long enough to be applied to new situations arising in the future. A conscientious teacher may go to great lengths to develop terrific lesson plans, but if these lessons are presented in a manner that is incompatible with the way human minds work, all that effort will go for naught.

The National Research Council has identified the transfer of learning from school to life beyond school as "the ultimate purpose of school-based learning."[15] The process of acquiring and using knowledge is called cognition, and findings from cognitive science indicate that learning transfer is difficult to achieve.

It's most likely to occur when general principles are learned in multiple contexts over an extended period of time.[16] This is how we learned to read, write, and do our sums in elementary school, but this is not how most knowledge is taught in school beyond the primary grades. The prevailing approach to history instruction—superficial coverage of large quantities of inert facts—can't produce the deep learning needed to render knowledge usable in the future. (The vital role of cognition in education is discussed in Chapter 6.)

Figure 2. Five basic problems of history education

PROBLEM	DESCRIPTION
Scale-to-detail	The level of factual detail is too great for the scale of the course, which results in excessive content that produces superficial and trivial learning.
Importance	Insufficient distinction is made between more-important and less-important knowledge, which results in excessive content that produces superficial and trivial learning.
Purpose	Without a coherent purpose to guide instruction, history education is directionless and ineffectual.
Irrelevance	Unlike other school subjects, history lacks principles of knowledge that describe how the world works and that are applicable to life in the future.
Cognition	When instruction is incompatible with the way human minds work, schooling is ineffective, and learning is wasted.

THE DISTURBING REALITY OF HISTORY EDUCATION

Cognition (*how* students learn) combines with superficial content coverage and the lack of general principles (*what* students learn) to yield the disturbing reality of history education: There is little point in teaching a school subject that offers little knowledge usable in the future. What, then, is the point of history education as currently practiced?

It appears that the main point of history schooling is to require students to temporarily memorize inert facts for the next exam, facts that may be forgotten shortly after the exam is over.[17] This simplistic approach to instruction results in pretend learning—as opposed to the far more demanding task of (a) learning important knowledge, (b) retaining it in memory, and (c) applying it in life—which is real learning.

Figure 3. The life cycle of real learning

Real learning doesn't stand much of a chance under our prevailing Bucket O' Facts model of history instruction, which is most concerned with getting facts into the first oval where they may be retained long enough to be recalled on the next big exam, whether that's a unit exam, final exam, Advanced Placement test, or state standardized assessment. The teacher did his job, the student got her grade, and the college admissions office will get the transcript. The textbook sellers sold their textbooks, the assessment vendors vended their assessments, and the test-prep merchants peddled their test-prep materials. All is functioning as expected in the land of American education.

Who cares if historical knowledge never makes it into the second and third ovals and is never heard from again? Who cares if learning never fulfills the purpose of education by imparting knowledge usable in the future?

Shouldn't we all care?

Life is too short, time too valuable,
to spend it on telling what is useless.

–Voltaire, letter to Abbé Dubos, 1738

CHAPTER THREE

Who is to blame for the trivia game?

A key player in the education–industrial complex is identified as the culprit.

The natural state of history education is trivia—if trivia is defined as facts, information, and knowledge that are unimportant because they're not useful to people in living their lives. History education naturally flows to trivia, like water naturally flows downhill.

History has its origins in stories told around the campfire by our prehistoric ancestors, and historians maintain this storytelling tradition. The English word *story* comes from the Greek word *historiā*. Over thousands of years, the historians' stories have been collected into the historical record, and history education has traditionally attempted to transmit as much of this record as possible to students, a natural inclination much like water flowing downhill, but an inclination that produces a flood of information too great to be assimilated by human minds and too superficial to be of much use.

When we want water to serve our needs, we intervene to direct the flow of great rivers into reservoirs and pipelines that bring water into our homes and businesses in a quantity that can be put to productive use. The previous chapter identified five basic problems of history education that represent history schooling's failure to adopt commonsense measures to channel historical knowledge away from inert knowledge and toward productive uses.

Why haven't educators dealt with these basic problems before now? Two plausible explanations come to mind. Perhaps history educators are so rooted in the received tradition of telling myriad stories about the past that it doesn't occur to them to step back and ask the essential question: Does this kind of schooling fulfill the purpose of education by imparting knowledge useful in the future? That's one possibility. The other possibility is that it's not in anyone's perceived interest to ask the question.

Leaders in the history-education community have developed reputations and livelihoods based on working within the existing system, and they might not welcome different approaches that could upset the apple cart. Experienced teachers have spent years developing lesson plans consistent with existing educational practices; they might not welcome the prospect of redoing their work, so they, too, have an incentive to accept things as they are. Habit and self-interest militate against altering the status quo.

Some teachers may have nagging doubts, like I did, about the usefulness of history schooling as presently practiced and would jump at the chance to alter the status quo if it meant their students could leave school with important historical understandings useful in life. But if these teachers are anything like I was, they don't see a promising alternative, so they keep plugging away within the existing system, trying to add value to their instruction where they can.

THE EDUCATION-INDUSTRIAL COMPLEX

In his farewell address to the nation in 1961, President Dwight Eisenhower warned of a burgeoning military-industrial complex that could unduly influence the actions of government and harm America's core interests. The education-industrial complex is even larger. Multiple levels of American government spend more than a trillion dollars annually on education, a figure that exceeds military spending by over $200 billion.[18] With so much government money in play, it's not surprising that an education-industrial complex has grown up around the field of education to take advantage of its money-making opportunities.

Educators routinely collaborate with the education industry to develop products ranging from textbooks and standardized exams to Advanced Placement courses. Profits from these enterprises can fund lobbying efforts and campaign contributions meant to influence government policies and spending priorities. Education products are meant to be used widely within the existing educational environment, so these products must be consistent with current practice. In the case of history schooling, this means that the education industry delivers mountains of products that legitimize and promote the teaching of trivia.

The education industry, like educators, has reason to maintain the status quo. These are two of the key players in the education-industrial complex; the third player is government, which makes the decisions about where education dollars are spent. What follows is an account of my attempt to determine which of these three players is the culprit ultimately responsible for the trivialization of history education.

IS GOVERNMENT TO BLAME?

As government has responsibility for deciding how taxpayer dollars are spent for educational products and services, perhaps government is the party most responsible for the trivialization of history education that results from this spending. Since this book was prompted by a standardized assessment from the state government of Virginia, I began my search for the trivia culprit there.

When I didn't know the answers to two of the first three sample questions from the Virginia standardized assessment in world history, I phoned five practicing history teachers to see what they knew about the subjects of those questions: Thomas Hobbes and the Mahdi Rebellion. Four of the five teachers were currently teaching world history in high school, and the fifth had taught it previously. They were geographically distributed from North Carolina to San Francisco, from a small rural school in the Midwest to a big urban school in Houston. Their history-teaching experience ranged from a few weeks to 29 years.

As it turned out, none of my five teacher colleagues knew anything about the Mahdi Rebellion. They didn't recall ever hearing about it. Hobbes was a somewhat different matter; most of my colleagues recalled hearing the name. Joel, a second-year teacher from Iowa, suspected that Hobbes was a philosopher of the Renaissance (pretty close), and he recalled teaching his students something about Hobbes from the textbook during the previous year, but he couldn't remember what. As Joel put it, "The textbook mentions everyone: this philosopher, that philosopher, this philosopher."

Fred, a 15-year teaching veteran from Oregon, was the star of our group. Although he was no longer teaching about Hobbes, Fred had taught about Hobbes in the past, and he was able to identify one of Hobbes's major positions, support of absolute monarchy, but he got another position wrong; he thought Hobbes was opposed to the social contract.

My little survey found that licensed professionals paid to teach history didn't think that Hobbes and the Mahdi Rebellion rose to a level of sufficient prominence to be included in their world history survey courses. Between us, we had nine college degrees and 63 years of collective history teaching experience, yet all of us together didn't possess the knowledge expected of a single Virginia teenager when taking the state's standardized assessment in world history.

It didn't make any sense. Why would the people at the Virginia Department of Education want to turn history education into a giant game of trivia? I wanted to know, so I rang them up to find out. The two VDOE officials with whom I spoke were wary of commenting on the greater purposes and practices of history education, so I was unable to plumb the depths of their motivations.[19] I did learn, however, that Virginia places greater emphasis on history education than do a number of other states—specifically those that never got around to implementing statewide history assessments—probably because Virginia takes considerable pride in the state's notable role in American history. Furthermore, when designing its academic standards, Virginia involved multiple stakeholders in an elaborate, multilayered development process.

It seemed to me that the Virginia Department of Education was trying to be responsible and do things right, and the two VDOE officials didn't strike me as evildoers bent on trivializing history schooling; they seemed like normal people trying to do their jobs. Furthermore, the VDOE was merely carrying out orders issued by the Virginia legislature, which became the next suspect on my list.

But it was hard to pin the blame for trivializing history schooling on the state legislature, since it was responding to a federal mandate that required all states to implement academic standards and assessments under the No Child Left Behind Act signed by President George W. Bush in 2002. Now here was a promising target for blame. The federal government is everyone's favorite whipping boy, and Bush was an unpopular president by the time he left office.

But that seemed a bit of a stretch too. The Bush administration was trying to establish accountability over the large US educational system. The Bush people hoped to produce positive educational outcomes for all students, including those traditionally disadvantaged in American society. My dear departed mother wouldn't think it nice of me to beat up on people for trying to attain such responsible and humane goals, so my search for the trivia culprit continued.

IS THE EDUCATION INDUSTRY TO BLAME?

"The market for testing products and services is booming and could continue to surge over the next few years," began a report in *Education Week* that appeared at about the time that states were beginning to implement the then new Common Core State Standards, designed to replace the content standards of individual states with a single set of nationwide standards in language arts and math. *Education Week* cited a projection that the market for standardized testing products would reach $4.5 billion within a year.[20]

The American education industry is big business, with the kind of clout that big money can buy. According to *Education Week*, industry giant Pearson spent more than $6 million lobbying at the federal level over a decade, and a charter school operator in Pennsylvania was the biggest contributor to the successful gubernatorial campaign of Tom Corbett, who later visited one of the company's schools and called it a model for the state.[21]

The education industry has branched out beyond traditional products like tests, textbooks, and instructional materials to encompass newer offerings such as online learning programs and charter schools. Private contractors also supply nonacademic services to schools, including transportation, food, and custodial services. The College Board, a private company, operates the Advanced Placement program, which supplies entire curricula for a wide range of school subjects, a program that has been termed "the juggernaut of American high school education."[22]

Anyone who doubts that extensive factual coverage remains a focus of history schooling in America need look no further than the Advanced Placement history program, which is the closest thing America has to a nationwide history curriculum. Each of AP's three history courses requires students to learn hundreds of discrete historical developments, hundreds of supporting examples, and sets of historical themes, historical thinking skills, and periodization schemes, plus students are typically expected to absorb thousand-page textbooks.[23] (The AP program is examined in Chapter 8.)

Textbooks, those venerable guides to the content and structure of history courses, have probably contributed more to the trivialization of history education than any other single factor. Sam Wineburg of Stanford University has written, "Textbooks dominate instruction in today's high school history classes,"[24] and James Loewen has cited research showing that history students spend more time with their textbooks than students of any other subject.[25] Nowadays, the availability of online resources might be cutting into the textbook's dominance, but its influence remains formidable.

History textbooks have grown bigger and more expensive over the years as the scope of their coverage has expanded beyond the political events of Western civilization to include more global history, economic and social history, and histories of women and minorities. High school history texts can now approach 1,400 pages in length, seven pounds in weight, and over $250 in cost.[26] Some states have imposed weight restrictions on textbooks to protect children from back injuries.[27] In an effort to lighten backpack loads and save money, some schools have opted to replace paper textbooks with e-textbooks. While the physical form of the book may be different, the historical content remains pretty much the same.

Chester E. Finn Jr., a former assistant secretary of education, is president of the conservative Thomas B. Fordham Institute in Washington, D.C. Several years ago, the Fordham Institute conducted a study of high school history textbooks, which Finn described this way:

> The writing and editing are done with one eye on the marketplace, the other on sundry interest groups....[They are] fat, dull, boring books that mention everything but explain practically nothing. There's no thread, no priorities, *no winnowing of the important from the trivial.* (emphasis added)[28]

Diane Ravitch is another former assistant secretary of education and a longtime critic of American education policies. She and Pasi Sahlberg of Finland's Ministry of Education point to what they call the Global Education Reform Movement or GERM, which they criticize for adopting a corporate-driven approach to education that emphasizes such things as test-based accountability and data-driven administration.[29]

Ravitch says international test score comparisons show that a dozen years of GERM policies haven't succeeded in the United States: "The billions invested in testing, test prep, and accountability have not raised test scores or our nation's relative standing.... [these policies] are manifest failures at accomplishing their singular goal of higher test scores."[30]

The education industry is looking like a very good candidate for our trivia culprit, but we have one more suspect to consider.

ARE HISTORY EDUCATORS TO BLAME?

Standardized assessments, such as those administered in Virginia, are usually produced by the education industry, but they are based on subject-matter content standards that are usually developed by groups of educators. When educators across the country began to develop content standards in response to the No Child Left Behind legislation, a set of national history standards was already in place to serve as a guide. The country's first and only National Standards for History, issued for both US and world history, were funded by the federal government and developed by a collection of historians and educators assembled by the National Center for History in the Schools based at the University of California, Los Angeles (UCLA).

When controversy surrounded the original release of the national history standards in 1994, a revised set of standards was issued two years later.[31] The revised standards for world history include 46 main content standards, 121 "standard components" and 631 "elaborated standards," plus 36 "standards in historical thinking." The comparatively modest US history standards expect students to master 589 standards of various kinds. Here are two of the elaborated world history standards and what they declare "students should be able to do":

> Describe the institutions and economics of Ashanti, Dahomey, Benin, Lunda, and Kongo in the period of the Atlantic slave trade.

> Evaluate the interplay of indigenous Indian, Persian, and European influences in Mughal artistic, architectural, literary, and scientific achievements.[32]

In addition to their arcane subject matter, these two standards contain a minimum of 10 and 12 subrequirements, respectively. Other elaborated standards include up to 30 or more subrequirements. If one were to add up all the standards and their embedded lists of requirements, the National Standards for History expect students to learn, by my rough estimate, somewhere in the neighborhood of six thousand facts about US history and nine thousand facts about world history.

Consider for a moment how much time it would realistically take for teachers to teach and students to learn anything useful about each of these facts in a real-world classroom setting. When faced with loopy expectations of this magnitude—issued by the nation's highest authority on history standards—a conscientious history teacher doesn't know whether to laugh, cry, or assume the fetal position.

How did this travesty occur? The answer involves the multitude of contributors involved in the project—some 400 people from 33 organizations distributed among 20 boards, councils, committees, panels, forums, task forces, and focus groups—many of whom wished to see their favorite areas of interest included in the standards. The history standards were the product of a groupthink process that sought to gain, in the words of Chester E. Finn, "the approbation of innumerable constituencies within the education and history communities whose blessings [were] thought desirable."[33]

Ruth Wattenberg, who represented the American Federation of Teachers during the standards-development process, objected to the overwhelming number and complexity of the standards, but "these criticisms were completely overshadowed by the general euphoria," according to Linda Symcox, assistant director of the project.[34] Classroom teachers, who might have injected a note of reality into the proceedings, were shunted aside, according to historian Paul Gagnon, while "scholars compiled pretentious wish lists of historical knowledge mastered by only a few PhD's and prescribed them for middle and high school students."[35*] Then this fantabulous cornucopia of factual plenitude was presented to America as the model for all history teachers to follow.

By 1998, standards had been developed for all core school subjects, and the bad news was starting to roll in. That year, Mid-continent Research for Education and Learning (McREL) released a study titled "Awash in a Sea of Standards." After examining 116 sets of standards at the state and national levels, McREL researchers determined, "If American educators were to adequately cover all of the knowledge identified in the current set of standards for the core subject areas, it might take as much as twenty-two years of schooling (literally!) within the current structure."[36] That is to say, students would need to attend school through the 21st grade before receiving their high school diplomas at the tender age of 27—but only if they skipped all the electives.

Unless designers of the national history standards and their counterparts in the states had discovered the secret to expanding the available volume of reality, the Iron Law of Superficiality ensured that these standards would amount to recipes for trivia.

NAMING THE CULPRIT

Who is our trivia culprit, then? Is the education industry—with its drive for profits, its trivia-infused assessments, textbooks, and Advanced Placement courses, its lobbying and political contributions—is the

---

*It is academic historians ensconced in colleges and universities who largely determine what is taught in our schools. They teach the teachers.

education industry responsible for the trivialization of history education in America? Any industry that reaps billions of dollars in revenue from sending trivia-laden products into classrooms can't be held blameless for the trivial learning that results, but the education industry is not ultimately responsible.

We live under a capitalist economic system in which the goal of business is to make money, and the trivial learning that results from industry products is merely a by-product of industry efforts to generate profits; the waste of student brains is merely collateral damage. Each of us needs to earn a buck to keep the wolf from the door, and if the education industry saw a way to turn a buck by selling useful historical learning, the industry would be more than happy to profit from this endeavor as well.

Is government the culprit? It was the national Congress that passed education laws that mandated standards and assessments in all 50 states. Departments of education in the states force schools to administer trivia-laden assessments, and local school boards tax their citizens to pay for expensive trivia-laden textbooks. National, state, and local governments sign the checks that pay for billions of dollars' worth of trivia-delivery devices. Multiple levels of American government across the country appear united in a conspiracy to force trivial learning down the throats of history students.

But wait a minute. Why would government be so intent on pushing trivia? Did government wake up one morning and decide that the United States needed a lot of overblown standards and overstuffed textbooks in order to provide Americans with a trivial education? It didn't happen that way. Government turned to educators for expert advice, and government accepted what educators gave it.

Those overblown standards over there were developed at UCLA; this overstuffed textbook over here bears the names of respected academic historians; inappropriate assessments abound because history educators haven't summoned the intestinal fortitude to identify the essential knowledge needed to create useful ones.

The trivial nature of history education rests squarely on the shoulders of history educators, who can't even agree on what history education is for.

History is now strictly organized, powerfully disciplined, but it possesses only a modest educational value and even less conscious social purpose.

–J. H. Plumb, "The Historian's Dilemma," 1964

CHAPTER FOUR

Hard times for history education

Trivial content is crippling history education, and thinking skills can't save it.

Trivial history education isn't good for students, it isn't good for society, and it certainly isn't good for history education itself.

Among fundamental realms of knowledge taught in school, history occupies a deeply inferior position relative to mathematics, language, and science. Unlike these other core academic subjects, history is not included in mandated nationwide testing, it lacks common state standards, it doesn't receive federal grant funding, and it is missing from college entrance exams. Furthermore, students score only about half as well in history as they do in math, language, and science on the National Assessment of Educational Progress (NAEP), termed "the nation's report card."

Figure 4. Comparison of core school subjects

	Language	Mathematics	Science	History
Percent proficient on NAEP Assessments[i]	31.5	32.7	31.3	16.3
Federally mandated nationwide testing[ii]	YES	YES	YES	NO
Common state standards[iii]	YES	YES	YES	NO
ACT College Placement Test	YES	YES	YES	NO

	Language	Mathematics	Science	History
SAT College Placement Test	YES	YES	NO	NO
Federal Grant Funding	YES	YES	YES	NO
Agenda of the Nat'l Center for Education Research	YES	YES	YES	NO
Doctoral degrees awarded in 2015[iv]	2,155	1,820	30,346	1,145

i NAEP = National Assessment of Educational Progress[37]
ii Common Core State Standards in language and math and Next Generation Science Standards
iii No Child Left Behind Act and its successor, the Every Child Succeeds Act
iv Doctorate Recipients from US Universities: 2015, National Science Foundation, 2016.
Science figures include science and engineering. Language includes languages and letters.

These objective measures of societal value indicate that society places far less value on history education than it does on learning in the fields of mathematics, language, and science. Why is this? One likely answer is that history isn't considered as valuable in the marketplace as are the other subjects. Language and math skills are necessary to commerce and scientific progress. Science and its technological offspring are key drivers of economic competitiveness, productivity, and growth. Historical knowledge offers little in the way of comparable economic benefits.

History's perceived lack of value in the marketplace doesn't tell the whole story, however. It doesn't explain why American students are only half as proficient in history as they are in math, language, and science on national assessments of student learning. These consistent results indicate that historical learning is far less effective than the other kinds. Perhaps society finds little to value in history education because it's simply ineffective at performing the basic educational function of suppying usable knowledge.

So long as history instruction remains characterized by trivia, it's likely to remain a marginal school subject whose role in education may continue to decline until it ultimately suffers the same fate as Greek, Latin, and rhetoric, subjects that were once at the core of schooling but came to be seen as irrelevant and faded away.

Fear of history education's decline and eventual demise is palpable among leaders in the history education community. Linda Salvucci was chair of the National Council for History Education when she told an interviewer, "Public officials and society at large have devalued the study of history....History must not be allowed to become some optional or occasional add-on to the 'real' curriculum."[38] A 2012 report from the American Historical Association found "the systematic teaching of history had all but ended in elementary schools across the country."[39]

A position statement issued by the National Council for the Social Studies said, "The last decade of the twentieth century and the first decade of the twenty-first have seen the marginalization of the social studies curriculum, instruction, and assessment at all grade levels."[40] Even two-time Pulitzer Prize–winning history author David McCullough weighed in: "Because of No Child Left Behind, sadly, history is being put on the back burner or taken off the stove altogether in many or most schools, in favor of math or reading."[41]

Like McCullough, many people link an accelerated decline in the fortunes of history education to passage of the No Child Left Behind Act in 2002, which required states to conduct standardized assessments in language and math and to a lesser extent in science—but not in history. Congress has since replaced NCLB with the Every Child Succeeds Act, which maintains a similar nationwide testing regime. In education circles, it's a truism that what gets tested gets taught. Two-thirds of public school teachers polled in a survey agreed, "Disciplines such as art, science, and social studies are being crowded out of the school day [and] the main reason is state tests."[42]

The marginalization of history extends to higher education as well. Addressing the American Historical Association in 1977, former AHA president William H. McNeill observed that history courses were no longer compulsory in colleges and universities, with the result that "college students became free to avoid history—and did so in such numbers as to exacerbate the job crisis for our junior colleagues."[43]

Richard J. Evans of Cambridge University noted that the number of bachelor degrees awarded in history at American universities declined by 63 percent in the 15 years from 1971 to 1986 as "students began to look for subjects they considered more relevant to the present."[44] And in late 2018, the AHA observed, "Of all major disciplines, history has seen the steepest decline in the number of bachelor degrees awarded."[45]

The beginning of the decline of history education in America can be traced to 1957, when the Soviet Union launched Sputnik into orbit. Alarmed that the United States was falling behind in science and technology, the nation's educational priorities shifted. Science and mathematics education were seen as keys to meeting the Cold War threat posed by the Soviets, a threat later replaced by the challenge of intensified global economic competition. Perceived as essential skills for pursuing technological and commercial advantage, math, language, and science became the central components in the school curriculum, while history, with no discernible practical use, was left to languish.

The fortunes of history education appeared to revive somewhat in 2001, when Congress passed the Teaching American History Grant Program, which spent millions of dollars over the next decade on teacher workshops, a website, and other initiatives. Funding declined in the later years of the program, until Congress ceased to allocate funds in 2012.[46] While the federal government no longer provided grant support to history or the social studies, it continued to award lavish grants to the STEM subjects of science, technology, engineering, and mathematics.[47]

The "general euphoria" that accompanied the writing of National Standards for History in the early 1990s has been replaced by a general malaise that has descended over the field of history education. Those national history standards were developed by the National Center for History in the Schools based at the University of California at Los Angeles. By 2017, the future of the UCLA center was uncertain, and there were no plans to update its aging history standards.[48]

Meanwhile, new sets of common state curriculum standards were released for the subjects of language and mathematics in 2010 and science in 2013. At about the same time, the National Council for the Social Studies considered the idea of developing new common state curriculum standards for social studies subjects, including history. After mulling it over, the NCSS decided against issuing new standards and chose instead to issue a "framework" for guiding the development of social studies content standards, with the content itself to be determined by individual states.[49] Nobody, it seems, has the will to develop a new set of common standards for history.

The diminished role of history in education isn't limited to the United States. It's also evident in the European Union's framework of "Key Competencies for Lifelong Learning," meant to guide educational practice in EU member nations. The framework features the traditional core subjects of language, math, and science along with other subjects including civics, digital competence, and entrepreneurship. History is absent from the list of learning's key competencies.[50]

The enfeebled state of contemporary history education may be attributable to a history profession that has little to offer society through schooling. Writing in the mid-1960s, Cambridge historian J. H. Plumb concluded, "Professional historians have failed in their social purpose, which should be to explain to humanity the nature of its experience from the beginning of time." Instead, historians were busy producing "an arid desert of monographs."[51] Historical study, said Plumb, had become "largely an end in itself, a pursuit by professionals, for professionals." Any "generalizations" derived from history that might be useful to the larger society "must, it would seem, be put off until the buried facts, billions of them, are brought back into academic light."[52]

Plumb was writing before the wave of postmodernist theory overtook the academic world, including the field of history, in the latter part of the twentieth century. By questioning the possibility of knowing the truth of anything, postmodernism further undermined any connection between historical study and knowledge useful to society. History educators, aware that students needed more than a constant diet of isolated facts, cast about for instructional fixes that might compensate for history schooling's fundamental lack of relevance.

With financial backing from technology mogul and philanthropist Bill Gates, historian David Christian has been promoting "Big History," which combines human history with natural history to tell a story of the past that stretches from the Big Bang to the present. Other educators have advocated teaching history meant to foster empathy with peoples of other times and places. But the most widespread and consistent attempt to revive history education has been the campaign to teach students so-called historical thinking skills.

HISTORICAL THINKING SKILLS

Historical thinking skills are said to be the kinds of skills employed by professional historians when plying their craft of history writing. With history education in trouble, it's not surprising that history professors might encourage history teachers to come home to mama, so to speak, and emphasize the practices of their profession. Dutiful history teachers accepted the guidance offered by their mentors in academe.

Historical thinking skills stand in contrast to historical content knowledge. With history education crippled by its burden of trivial content, advocates of historical thinking skills want to change the focus to skills.

Sets of historical thinking skills can vary considerably in number and composition, depending on the source. Stanford University's History Education Group identifies four historical reading skills,[53] while the Advanced Placement history program recognizes nine historical thinking skills, and the National Standards for History, with customary

extravagance, specify 36 skills, including the handy abilities to "distinguish between past, present, and future time" and to "read historical
narratives imaginatively."[54]

Sets of historical thinking skills may have features in common. Some
include the venerable historical perspectives of *cause and effect, continuity
and change*, and *comparison of cultures* across time and space. Sets of
thinking skills often call on students to analyze sources, usually primary
source documents, in terms of the author's point of view, purposes, and
possible biases, a practice termed *sourcing* or *source analysis*. The skill
of *corroboration* seeks to identify where sources agree and disagree, and
contextualization is the effort to understand an event within its historical
context: What were attitudes like for people back then; what else was
going on at the same time?

AN EXAMPLE FROM HIGH SCHOOL. Over recent decades, historical
thinking skills have surfaced in a number of history-education agendas,
including the influential Bradley Commission report on history in
the schools published in 1988 and the National Standards for History
released in 1996. But in practice such thinking skills rarely served as
more than high-minded window dressing to accompany the real business of history teaching, which was content coverage.[55] In recent years,
educators have gotten more serious about building curricula around
thinking skills, and perhaps the most ambitious effort of this kind
originated with the History Education Group at Stanford University,
led by Sam Wineburg.

Wineburg's Stanford group developed teaching materials supplied free
of charge to teachers over the Internet. One of the projects is *Reading
Like a Historian* (*RLH*), a complete 75-lesson US history curriculum for
high school students that shuns factual memorization in favor of using
historical thinking skills to "evaluate the trustworthiness of multiple
perspectives on historical issues."[56] The Stanford group also developed
similar lessons for world history.

The *RLH* curriculum neatly sidesteps the problem of covering all
the messy factual content usually found in survey courses by rejecting
coverage as the goal of historical learning. The objective here is to get
students to read and think like historians, and factual learning occurs
as a by-product of evaluating historical case studies. Advocates of this
approach say that students become better readers and actually learn more
historical facts this way than with traditional methods.

Professor Wineburg has also suggested that practice in evaluating
historical sources could help students with evaluating sources found on

the Internet. Wineburg has made it clear that the *RLH* curriculum is not meant to transform high school students into young historians. In a speech before the American Association for State and Local History, he said,

> It's time for me to come clean about the real intention of the *Reading Like a Historian* curriculum. Our materials have nothing to do with preparing students to be historians. If our curriculum has any pretense of career preparation, it is for the vocation of citizen.[57]

AN EXAMPLE FROM COLLEGE. By contrast, Lendol Calder's approach to historical thinking skills is fixed squarely on the history profession. Writing in the *Journal of American History*, Calder suggested that history professors teach their undergraduates the practices of professional historians, much as the professional schools of law and medicine teach their students the practices of lawyers and doctors.

He urged his fellow college instructors to reject the traditional coverage model of instruction typical in introductory history courses and replace it with "a signature pedagogy of instruction." A signature pedagogy, he explains, "is what beginning students in the professions have but history beginners typically do not: ways of being taught that require them to do, think, and value what practitioners in the fields are doing, thinking, and valuing."[58]

Calder described his own efforts to apply a signature pedagogy of instruction to the US history survey course he taught at Augustana College, where he trained students in the use of six historical thinking skills that included sourcing, questioning, and, my favorite, recognizing limits to one's knowledge.[59] What were the results of this approach? Calder said he was convinced that his students were learning more historical knowledge than in his previous textbook-and-lecture-based survey course, and students made on average "modest to occasionally dramatic gains" in the six aspects of historical thinking he taught.[60]

In his journal article Professor Calder doesn't explain why college freshmen—who may not be history majors and are unlikely to pursue careers as historians—should learn the practices of professional historians, like graduate students in schools of law and medicine learn the professional skills they will use during their lifelong careers. It's a curious juxtaposition of curricula, considering that the signature pedagogies of law and medicine are characterized by extensive factual coverage, an approach that Calder rejects as a "wrongheaded way to introduce students to the goodness and power of history."[61]

Of what, exactly, do history's "goodness and power" consist? How, exactly, can knowledge of historical thinking skills summon forth these desirable qualities? The professor doesn't say.

Learning the job skills of historians often seems to be promoted as an intrinsic good, with little explanation as to how students and society might benefit from this type of knowledge. An unquestioning reverence for the history profession is evident in many secondary school classrooms where students are schooled in historical thinking skills. Such students are said to be *doing history*, whereupon they become *apprentice historians*,[62] or better yet, they may "function as practicing historians."[63]

Possibly some educators have gotten a bit carried away by their hopes that historical thinking skills can rescue history teaching. This is how historian Richard J. Evans describes the work of actual historians:

> They must absorb not only the Rankean principles of source criticism and citation but also ancillary skills, such as languages, paleography, statistics, and so on. Moreover, they have to read and digest a large amount of contextual material and master the secondary literature relating to their subject....[They read] hundreds, even thousands of documents in the course of a single research project."[64]

It's not likely that many students are doing history of this sort in secondary school classrooms or in introductory college courses. Cognitive scientist Daniel Willingham of the University of Virginia points out that "no one thinks like a scientist or a historian without a great deal of training."[65]

Even if students in their classrooms were capable of emulating in some meaningful way the work done by professional historians, this leaves unanswered the question of why the history profession is being favored over other professions such as doctor and lawyer (Calder's models of learning) or the professions of auto mechanic and plumber—all professions that arguably affect people's lives more profoundly than do historians and that each create an average of about 165 jobs for every historian job.[66] Yet the job skills of these professions are not taught as core subjects in the nation's schools.

If the value of general education lies in its capacity to teach job skills, then instruction in the job skills of doctors, lawyers, auto mechanics, plumbers, and numerous other professions would logically take precedence over job skills of a relatively few historians. If logic were to prevail, either these various other professions would be added to the curriculum taught to all students in school—which is impossible—or history would be removed from general schooling and taught in career programs, just as medicine, law, auto mechanics, and plumbing are taught. The notion that every American student should attend history classes to learn the job skills of historians is not rational.

Education exists to impart important knowledge of the world—the big wide world, not the limited world of the history profession. History warrants a place in the schools only if it's a fundamental realm of knowledge alongside mathematics, language, and science, which provide essential understandings of how the world works. When history educators emphasize knowledge of the historian's skills over knowledge of history, they negate the very reason that history has been invited into schools in the first place.

CRITICAL THINKING SKILLS

Some educators would extend the range of thinking skills that students should learn in history courses beyond those associated with the history profession to encompass the more general field of *critical thinking skills.* Such skills are often cited as central to the practice of "21st-century schooling," a popular buzz phrase in contemporary education circles.[67] One of these educators is Greg Milo, a former high school history teacher who has this to say about history education in his book *Rebooting Social Studies*: "Who cares what the topic is?...The point is that students are practicing critical thinking skills."[68]

Can you imagine a science teacher declaring, "Who cares if students learn about the forces of motion or the genes that make up our heredity? We needn't bother with all that dreary knowledge stuff because we're teaching critical thinking." Such a declaration from a science teacher would be...unthinkable. The fact that a history teacher can sell books based on the premise that subject-matter knowledge doesn't matter—and that he can be taken seriously by the *Washington Post*[69]—is emblematic of the dysfunctional state of present-day history schooling.

Milo is reacting to the trivial and pointless nature of much history schooling by suggesting that the focus of history instruction should shift from the acquisition of historical knowledge to the acquisition of thinking skills. Let us subject Mr. Milo's assertion to logical scrutiny.

His position amounts to an "if...then" proposition, also termed a conditional statement: "If the subject matter of history education is irrelevant, then history education should focus on thinking skills instead." The premise is valid: The subject matter of history education *is* largely irrelevant. But the conclusion doesn't follow from the premise; thinking skills are not a fix for irrelevant knowledge. The conclusion is a non sequitur and is therefore logically false.

A more logical conditional statement would be this: "If the subject matter of history education is irrelevant, then history education should focus on relevant subject matter instead." Relevant knowledge is the fix for irrelevant knowledge. The next chapter will discuss several kinds of historical knowledge that are relevant for educational purposes.

By dismissing the importance of subject matter knowledge as he does, Milo appears to believe that critical thinking is a free-floating process that exists independently of the subject being thought about—that the subject matter is immaterial. If so, he is mistaken: *Thinking is knowledge dependent.* (See Chapter 6 on cognition.)

The Center for Advancement of Learning and Assessment at Florida State University observes, "Higher order thinking skills...are linked to prior knowledge of subject matter content."[70] A college textbook on critical thinking identifies six steps of critical thinking, the first of which is knowledge.[71] Bloom's Taxonomy, long a staple of teacher training programs, likewise identifies knowledge as the first stage of six thinking processes. In describing the development of Bloom's Taxonomy, Patricia Armstrong of Vanderbilt University's Center for Teaching notes, "The categories after Knowledge were presented as 'skills and abilities,' with the understanding that knowledge was the necessary precondition for putting these skills and abilities into practice."[72]

Daniel Willingham has written a book devoted to the subject of thinking titled *Cognition: The Thinking Animal.* Willingham writes extensively about education and learning, including the subject of critical thinking. He says, "The very processes that teachers care about most critical thinking processes such as reasoning and problem solving—are intimately intertwined with factual knowledge that is stored in long-term memory....Factual knowledge must precede skill."[73]

Perhaps no school subject has been researched more extensively than reading, and Willingham points to a number of studies that show reading skills have less effect on student understanding than does background knowledge of subject matter. He cites one study that asked junior high school students to read a story about half an inning of a baseball game. Some of the students knew a lot about baseball, and others knew little; half of the students were identified as good readers through standard-ized testing, and half were identified as poor readers. Willingham writes, "The dramatic finding...was that the students' knowledge of baseball determined how much they understood of the story. Whether they were 'good readers' or 'bad readers' didn't matter nearly as much as what they knew."[74]

Education is not necessarily an either-or proposition. Those students in the reading study who possessed more knowledge of baseball *and* had good reading skills were likely to be the most proficient at understanding the story. In this age of twenty-first century schooling with its attendant emphasis on "21st century skills,"[75] conscientious educators would be well-advised to store in their long-term memories the vital pieces of information that subject-matter knowledge is a necessary prerequisite to critical thinking, and in many learning situations, subject-matter knowledge may be more decisive to student understanding than skills.

THINKING SKILLS
CAN'T SAVE HISTORY EDUCATION

I am not suggesting that thinking skills—historical, critical, or otherwise—have no place in history education; I am saying they can't be the *reason* for history education. According to Willingham and others, attempts to teach critical thinking as a discipline have not fared well in large part because critical thinking requires content knowledge to think about. Regarding the push to teach critical thinking in schools, Willingham writes:

> After more than 20 years of lamentation, exhortation, and little improvement, maybe it's time to ask a fundamental question: Can critical thinking actually be taught? Decades of cognitive research point to a disappointing answer: not really. People who have sought to teach critical thinking have assumed that it is a skill, like riding a bicycle...and once you learn it, you can apply it in any situation. Research from cognitive science shows that thinking is not that sort of skill. The processes of thinking are intertwined with the content of thought (that is, domain knowledge).[76]

David N. Perkins of the Harvard Graduate School of Education agrees: "You cannot practice thinking skills well without something substantive to think about." Both Perkins and Willingham believe that thinking skills should be "infused"—as Perkins puts it—into "the teaching of content, so that learners simultaneously develop better thinking skills and dispositions and deepen content understanding."[77]

Various educational domains, including history, tend to emphasize some thinking skills over others. The more technical fields may possess more specialized skills, such as modeling and statistics in the discipline of mathematics (although these processes could play a helpful role in identifying historical trends and estimating probabilities of future outcomes). But many critical thinking processes are similar across educational domains as depicted in the figure below, which illustrates that comparable elements of critical thinking may be infused into different school subjects. Of the many general thinking skills put forward by educators, Figure 5 features a sample of 10.

Figure 5. Infusing critical thinking into content areas

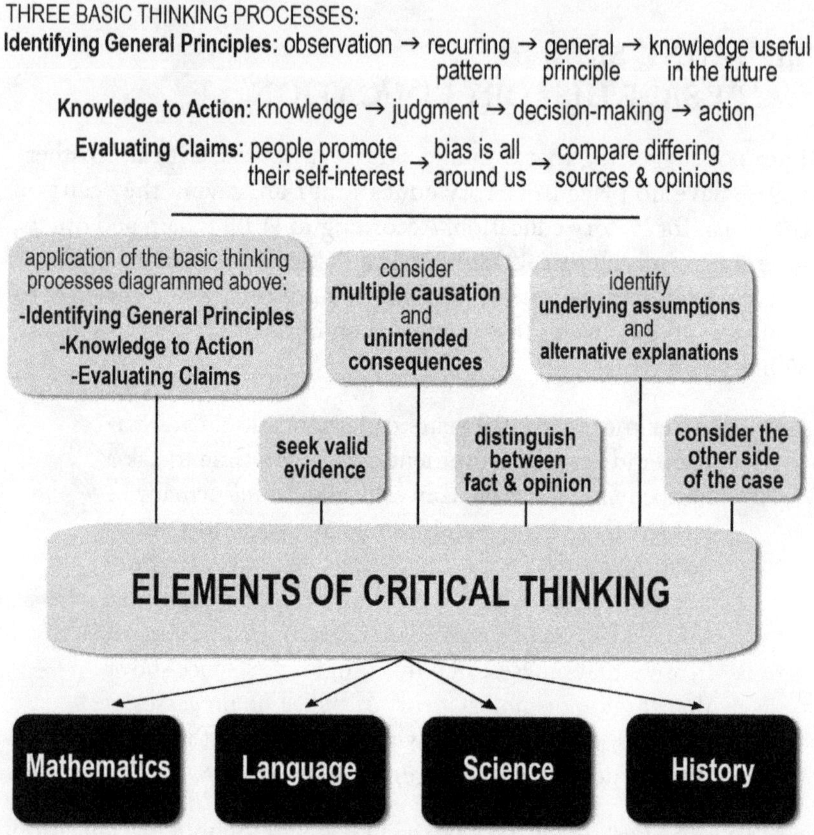

THREE BASIC THINKING PROCESSES:

Identifying General Principles: observation → recurring → general → knowledge useful
                                     pattern   principle   in the future

Knowledge to Action: knowledge → judgment → decision-making → action

Evaluating Claims: people promote → bias is all → compare differing
                 their self-interest   around us   sources & opinions

application of the basic thinking processes diagrammed above:
-Identifying General Principles
-Knowledge to Action
-Evaluating Claims

consider **multiple causation** and **unintended consequences**

identify **underlying assumptions** and **alternative explanations**

seek valid evidence

distinguish between fact & opinion

consider the other side of the case

ELEMENTS OF CRITICAL THINKING

Mathematics   **Language**   **Science**   **History**

History teachers might not be aware that the historical thinking skills they thought to be the special province of history education may have wider applicability because they are based on general principles useful in various fields. The historical thinking skill of causation, for instance, involves recognition of the general principle that major events usually result from multiple causes, some long-term and some more immediate. (The long-term cause of the US Civil War was the issue of slavery; an intermediate cause was the issue of states' rights, and the immediate cause was the shelling of Fort Sumter.) Multiple causation is also an important principle in the sciences, where experimenters must carefully control for various extraneous causes—or variables—that might affect research findings. Multiple causality also plays a big role in areas as varied as the stock market and weather patterns.

The chief thinking skill of science is termed the scientific method, which involves hypothesizing the existence of a general principle and verifying the principle through sustained observation (which may include experimentation). The scientific method is therefore a general principle for identifying general principles, and it can be useful in a wide variety of fields including mathematics, language, and history.

The historical thinking skill of source analysis compares conflicting accounts of events in an effort to determine which source is more trust-worthy, a skill grounded in the general principles that *people promote their self-interest*, so *bias is all around us*, and *comparing multiple sources is a good way to approach the truth*. The critical thinking skills prescribed in the Common Core State Standards for math and language cover much of the same ground.

The Common Core standards declare that mathematically proficient students are "able to compare the effectiveness of two plausible arguments, distinguish correct logic or reasoning from that which is flawed, and—if there is a flaw in an argument—explain what it is."[78] The standards in English language arts assert that competent students have the ability to "evaluate other points of view critically and constructively....They also question an author's or speaker's assumptions and premises and assess the veracity of claims and the soundness of reasoning."[79]

Given the common ground shared by thinking skills in history and other school subjects, I asked Lendol Calder about the special strengths of historical thinking skills. He replied:

> History seems to be better than other disciplines for learning the skill of sourcing and for developing an apti-tude for recognizing and empathizing with difference. True, historians are not the only ones who do either of these things. But the research seems to suggest that in practice historians do more of such things than others, like, say, biologists.[80]

Biologists, yes...but do history courses do more of such things than, say, language arts courses?

Because the thinking skills associated with history—such as source analysis, corroboration, causation, comparison, and the fostering of empathy—tend to be general in nature, the educational system does not need history in order to teach these skills to students; other school subjects can adequately handle the job. The big distinction between history and other school subjects does not lie in the type of thinking skills that history offers but in the type of subject matter that history offers.

Mathematics describes the quantitative realm, language the communicative realm, science the physical realm, and history the realm of human affairs. The educational system needs history in order to teach students about the crucially important realm of human affairs. If history education fails to do so, there is little reason to include history among the subjects taught to students in school; history might as well be relegated to a genre of literature taught occasionally in English classes. Once again, to deny the importance of content knowledge in history education is to negate the reason that history has a role in the schools in the first place.

HISTORY EDUCATION AS MISHMASH. The de-emphasis of historical knowledge in favor of thinking skills has produced unintended consequences that well-meaning reformers could hardly have foreseen. Many secondary schools and colleges no longer require students to take survey courses to satisfy the history or social studies curriculum requirement, which means these schools have abandoned the once-desirable goal of introducing students to an overview of human development through time.

Since any classroom activity can be said to foster some sort of thinking, history courses may now consist of any peripheral or idiosyncratic take on history—"conspiracy theories in history," say—or any random hodge-podge of disconnected topics divorced from any larger structure or meaning. In a laudable effort to limit the memorization of scads of pointless facts, educators may have traded one kind of trivia for another.

As a result, parents can be baffled as to what their children are learning in history class. One concerned parent wrote to me:

> There is no textbook, just a handful of photocopied articles....My daughter does not seem to know anything more about "world history" than when she started, except a little on the Israeli-Palestinian conflict. She thinks the class is a waste of time....
> Is this actually good teaching?

An uncritical embrace of thinking skills as the be-all and end-all of history instruction can result in an incoherent jumble of pseudo-historical learning that leaves students with neither a coherent "sense of history" nor principles of historical knowledge that can be applied in the future. Any intelligible rationale for retaining history as part of the school curriculum becomes further eroded, accelerating the decline of history education.

. . .

History simply can't compete for time in the school day against other school subjects that not only offer thinking skills but also impart important principles of how the world works that can help students and society to function effectively in the future. History education is stuck between a rock and a hard place: Trivial content is crippling it, and thinking skills can't save it. From grade school through graduate school, these are hard times for history education.

DECISION POINT. History educators have a choice to make. Either history is a fundamental realm of knowledge that deserves a place in the schools—or it isn't. If it is a fundamental realm of knowledge, it needs to supply fundamental knowledge of how the world works that can be applied in the future, much as math, language, science, and other school subjects do.

So long as history educators choose not to supply this kind of useful knowledge to the educational enterprise, they would do well to stop complaining about the inevitable consequence of their choice, which is the further decline and possible demise of history in education.

For my part, I am reluctant to accept the second choice because I have seen—many times over—the power of past experience to inform judgment about the future. And so have you. Which is why this book has a Part Two.

NAEP social studies assessments

Not only do American students perform much worse in history than in other core subjects on the National Assessment of Educational Progress, they also perform much worse in history compared to history's fellow social studies subjects.

The most recent NAEP assessments in social studies were conducted in 2018 among eighth graders. Fifteen percent of these students performed at or above the proficient level in American history, compared to 24 percent in civics and 25 percent in geography.

Considering that American history has long been the most prominent social studies subject taught in the nation's schools, one would expect history to come out on top in this comparison. What can explain why history performs so poorly?

The probable answer: Other school subjects, including social studies, are based on imparting an established set of coherent general principles for students to learn and remember, whereas history schooling is comprised of an amorphous collection of sundry one-time events devoid of any unifying structure to render the knowledge intelligible, meaningful, or memorable.

(Figures from the National Center for Education Statistics.)

PART TWO
SEEKING SOLUTIONS

I have written not for immediate applause but for posterity. I shall be content if the future student of these events—or of other similar events which are likely in human nature to occur in later ages—finds my narrative of them useful..

–Thucydides, *History of the Peloponnesian War*, 423 BC

CHAPTER FIVE

Historical knowledge suitable for education

*Isolated events of the past are replaced
by knowledge useful in the future.*

I t's almost as though history education has adopted an unwritten
and unquestioned first commandment: "Thou shalt not learn from
history." Let me illustrate through examples drawn from public
television. In 2017, millions of viewers tuned in to watch two historical
documentary series about wars involving the United States. *The Great
War* was released on the one-hundredth anniversary of the US entry into
World War I. *The Vietnam War* was produced by accomplished video
historians Ken Burns and Lynn Novick. Aside from formal schooling,
such documentaries may represent society's most ambitious efforts to
impart historical learning to a large segment of the populace.

The World War I series ended on a triumphant note with the Allied
victory made possible by America's belated but decisive entry into the
war. In contrast, the Vietnam series was relentlessly sad and depressing,
as befits a protracted war that claimed over three million lives in the
defeat of the world's most powerful nation by the stubborn inhabitants
of a small rural country. Although many viewers no doubt found these
series to be interesting, in the end each amounted to—in the words
of historian Arnold Toynbee—"just one damn thing after another."[81]

Neither historical account identified lessons to be learned from these
tragic events that might help society to function more wisely in the future.
Near the end of the final episode of the Vietnam War series, a veteran
of the North Vietnamese army appears on-screen and says, "The war
is over. Now we need to focus on the living. What is most important is
to find some meaning—some lessons in the war for our lives."

Shortly thereafter, the series narrator intones, "Lessons were learned, and then forgotten."[82] If the producers of this series know what those lessons are, why not tell us so the lessons no longer remain forgotten? But to do so would violate the unspoken first commandment of history education: "Thou shalt not learn from history."

RELEVANCE AND IMPORTANCE

In our society, we may learn *about* history, but we seldom learn *from* history. Probably the best-known adage about history in our culture is Santayana's familiar warning: "Those who cannot remember the past are condemned to repeat it." Why does society routinely fail to learn from the past?

The answer is obvious enough: When history amounts to "just one damn thing after another," it provides no lessons from history—no general principles or recurring dynamics—that can be applied in the future. When history education fails to provide knowledge useful in the future, society is deprived of its only formal, systematic opportunity to learn from the past.

This book is guided by the understanding that *education exists to impart important knowledge of the world that can help students and society to function effectively in the future.* That sentence identifies two essential characteristics of knowledge suitable for educational purposes: It is relevant to the future, and it is important. If the knowledge is important from a historical standpoint, but it's not relevant to the future, it's not suitable for educational purposes. If the knowledge is relevant to the future, but it's unimportant, it's not suitable for educational purposes. Knowledge suitable for educational purposes will be both relevant and important.

Harvard's David Perkins uses the term *lifeworthy* to describe knowledge that is both important and likely to be useful in the future. He encourages educators to ask, "How often is a particular fact, understanding, or skill likely to come up? With what importance? Would it grow in breadth and depth and significance over time—or do we simply forget it?" Perkins points out that "knowledge not used is simply forgotten."[83]

When selecting historical content to be taught in history classes, the content must first be relevant to the future. Knowledge satisfying this requirement can be weighed in terms of historical importance, with more-important knowledge taking precedence over less-important knowledge. Chapter 7 discusses criteria for weighing the relative importance of historical events. This chapter will identify four kinds of historical knowledge that are relevant to the future and therefore satisfy the first requirement of knowledge appropriate for education.

However, we should note, not all history is intended to serve educational purposes, so not all historical knowledge need be relevant to the future. People may enjoy stories from history as they would enjoy any interesting story well told, as a form of literature or entertainment. For the purposes of literature or entertainment, historical knowledge need only be interesting; it doesn't need to be useful in the future.

I've noticed that people often consider a "good" history teacher to be a teacher who can make history interesting to her or his students. Naturally, we want students to find their school courses interesting as an aid to learning, but entertainment is not the purpose of schooling. The first priority of the teacher is to identify relevant and important knowledge to teach, and then the teacher can seek ways to make this knowledge interesting to students so that the knowledge may be retained in memory, where it will be available to inform future thought and action.

No school system would abide science instruction that merely told an interesting story about Isaac Newton sitting under an apple tree. We expect schooling to describe the principle of gravity that Newton discovered while sitting under the apple tree—an important and universal principle of knowledge applicable to the present and future. The bar is set extremely low for history teachers if they are considered successful when they merely entertain.

Imagine a talented history teacher equipped with important knowledge relevant to the future and cognitive strategies that would help students to retain this knowledge and apply it in life. In possession of such assets, perhaps even average history teachers (such as myself) could successfully fulfill the mission of education.

GENERAL RATHER THAN SPECIFIC KNOWLEDGE

School learning that is relevant and important in the future is likely to be general, rather than specific, in nature. The term *general education* refers to the formal education that students receive during their years in school and college other than the specialized learning associated with vocational programs and college majors. Most formal education is general education. As the term implies, general education is suited to supplying general knowledge—and for very good reasons.

Education supplies *internal knowledge* that we carry in our heads, and internal knowledge is limited by the amount of information that our brains can absorb and retain in the amount of time available to learn it. Internal knowledge includes not only facts about history but knowledge of other school subjects as well as the knowledge needed to perform our occupations and pursue personal interests, along with knowledge of computer programs, smart phone apps, the layout of streets and roads, personal memories, song lyrics, selections on restaurant menus, and all of the other myriad pieces of information that fill our heads.

Educational knowledge, however, has a special responsibility that other kinds of knowledge may not share. Because education is meant to prepare students for the future, educational knowledge needs to last longer than a day, a week, a month, or a year. To be effective, educational knowledge must be learned so well that students can retain this knowledge into adulthood, and it must be understood so well that students know when and how to apply the knowledge to new situations arising in the future. Such deep learning requires a significant investment of time and effort.

Because effective education requires deep learning, and because the amount of knowledge we can carry in our heads is limited, education must necessarily focus on imparting the most important knowledge relevant to the future. General knowledge applicable to a range of future situations is clearly more important than learning about specifics of the past that may have no larger meaning beyond themselves and little relevance to the future. Consequently, general education should focus on general knowledge.

Fortunately, we have access to a vast wealth of specific information that may be accessed when desired in the form of *external knowledge* available from sources such as history books, periodicals, the Internet, news reports, and television documentaries.[84]

As a student in school, I was taught nothing about Vietnam, so when I later wanted to understand how I came to be involved in a war on the other side of the world, I had to read history books. History schooling can never be complete, effective, or prescient enough to teach students everything they will need to know about every situation that may arise in the future. No, the only reasonable way to obtain such specific information is to consult external sources when the need arises. This idea that external sources can provide specific knowledge when needed for understanding contemporary concerns is a basic principle of knowledge acquisition that students should learn in school.

In today's world of personal computers and smart phones, it makes little sense to require students to memorize large quantities of specific facts when these facts are readily accessible at their fingertips. In today's world of information overload, it makes far more sense for students to acquire deep learning of important general knowledge that can provide the context needed to recognize which specifics may be relevant to a given situation. As University of Chicago economist Steven Levitt observes, "It used to be that data was the scarce resource, but now it's the talent to understand [the data] that is a really scarce resource."[85]

While external knowledge is extensive—and the internal knowledge we carry in our heads is limited—internal knowledge is extremely important to our thinking because it constitutes how we conceptualize the world. It's the lens through which we perceive all new experience, and it's the armature to which all subsequent learning is attached. Internal knowledge informs our attitudes, judgments, and decision-making on a daily basis. Internal knowledge is another name for knowledge held in long-term memory, which is another name for *learning* itself.

External sources can supply us with specific historical knowledge when needed. It's the job of education to supply the general knowledge that informs our thinking all the time.

· · ·

No school subject, and certainly not history, can teach students everything there is to know about an intellectual discipline. We have to be realistic in our expectations about what can and should be taught in general education courses in school and college. Knowledge suitable for general education will possess three key characteristics: It will be relevant to the future, it will be important, and it will be general in nature.

Four kinds of historical knowledge would appear to satisfy these criteria. The first is enduring *principles of historical knowledge* that can inform future judgment in human affairs. The other three kinds are *events with continuing effect, foundational concepts of history and geography,* and a *big picture of human development through time.* All four provide background knowledge of the world around us—what might be called "situational awareness" of the world as it exists in the 21st Century. We'll begin by looking at the most valuable form of knowledge available from any intellectual discipline: general principles of how the world works.

1. PRINCIPLES OF HISTORICAL KNOWLEDGE

Have you perhaps become proficient at merging into heavy traffic on a freeway or lining up a golf shot? If so, it's probably because your actions are guided by general principles derived from patterns of prior experience. Such general principles are the most valuable kind of knowledge because they are the linchpins upon which effective judgment, decision-making, and action depend, and they have proved valid in the past; they remain valid in the present, and they are likely to remain valid into the future.

I'll illustrate with another example, this one drawn from my own recent experience. I live in a rural area on a private gravel road that serves seven families. A hill on this road had been deteriorating for 20 years as the gravel was gradually pulverized by traffic, and it eventually washed away. The situation became so bad that rain or snowmelt would turn the hill into a slippery mud bog, and vehicles commonly slid down the hill into the intersection with another road, posing a grave danger to people using both roads.

The road had to be fixed, so we collected funds from property owners and hired a contractor to perform the work. My neighbor Bill and I were helping the contractor one day when Bill asked me about the book I'm writing. I told him it's about using knowledge from the past to help people make judgments in the future. He said, "It's like making a prophecy."

I hadn't thought of it that way, so I paused a moment before replying, "You're right; based on our past experience, we know that when it rains, this road will get muddy and people will slide into the intersection."

"Yeah," said Bill, "and sooner or later somebody is gonna get creamed."

"Exactly!" I said. "Based on your past experience, you just made a prophecy that someone could get hurt. Then, based on the possibility of this happening, you and I and our neighbors made a judgment that we should spend money to fix the road." Bill got what my book is about: It's about the commonsense idea that knowledge of the past can inform judgment in the future.

Today our neighborhood has a solid new road surface on the hill, and people no longer face a dangerous situation when the road gets wet. Let's break down my road repair scenario to examine how relevant knowledge from history supplied the basis for taking effective action.

It began with our knowledge of past experience, which is the most reliable indicator of future outcomes. This isn't just my opinion; it's a basic premise of Bayes' theorem of statistical probability, one the most prominent theorems in the field of statistics.[86] Bayes' theorem takes into account two main factors: knowledge of past experience and knowledge of the particular situation at hand.[87]

From several years of past experience, my neighbors and I recognized a recurring pattern: When the road gets wet, it gets slippery, and cars slide into the intersection. From this observed pattern, we derived a general principle: Our road has become dangerous to the people using the road. Based on this general principle, we made a judgment that the road needed to be fixed. Responding to this judgment and informed by our knowledge of the situation at hand, we made a decision to form a limited liability company (LLC) to raise funds for the project and to hire a contractor to do the work. And lastly, we took action to implement our decision.

This logical progression from observation to action might be the essential critical thinking skill, and it seems to come naturally to us humans without being formally taught. It begins with observing a recurring pattern that represents a general principle, which, in turn, informs future judgment, decision-making, and action. People everywhere routinely use similar thought processes to produce informed decisions, and not just when dealing with a life-threatening situation like a dangerous road, but also when engaging in everyday activities like deciding which television show to watch, lining up a golf shot, or merging into traffic.

In all of these cases, general principles derived from prior experience are the linchpins that inform future judgment, decision-making, and action. The general principle possesses the extraordinary power to transport knowledge from the past into the future, where it can help people to make informed judgments helpful in living their lives.

But here's the odd thing: The discipline of history, which is all about past experience, doesn't officially recognize patterns from the past that can inform judgment in the future. This situation is all the more peculiar considering that every other productive human activity that I can think of learns from patterns of prior experience to identify principles useful in the future.

The failure of the history professions to do likewise is revealed in every textbook, curriculum standard, Advanced Placement course, and television documentary that fails to mention a single recurring pattern or general principle of history that can be applied in the future. It's beyond ironic that history education may be the only intellectual discipline that fails to learn from history.

PATTERN RECOGNITION. General principles begin with an observer who recognizes a recurring pattern in the environment. This recurring pattern is consistent enough to be considered a principle that can be usefully applied to similar situations arising in the future.

observed phenomena → pattern recognition → principle formulation → knowledge that can be applied in the future

A single event from the past—an *n* of 1—is not a reliable indicator of future outcomes. A single event might be a random occurrence or an anomaly; it provides scant evidence that something similar will occur in the future.

History educators commonly encourage students to "make connections" in their history classes. Students are typically asked to connect an event from the past to another situation of the past or present.[88] The value of this kind of learning is usually left unspecified or vague; making connections appears to be accepted as another intrinsic good, much like learning historical thinking skills. Assuming that this lesson is meant to be more than busywork, what is the intended point of the exercise—unless it is to gain insight useful in the future? However, an *n* of 2 is not much more reliable than an *n* of 1 for predicting future outcomes. Two similar events might simply be a coincidence.

Events of the past become reliable indicators of possible future outcomes only when they have been repeated multiple times in similar situations. The more often that a pattern has been observed, the more reliable it is likely to be.[89] Prediction in history "is most feasible on large spatial scales and over long times," says Jared Diamond, who explored large-scale human history in books including *Guns, Germs, and Steel* and *Collapse*.[90]

If educators think it desirable for students to make connections between just two similar events, how much more desirable is it for students to study patterns involving multiple events that represent general principles applicable to the future? Yet the making of connections is commonly encouraged in history courses, while recurring patterns and their associated general principles go unrecognized and untaught.

Recognition of recurring patterns is basic to how animals learn. It's how babies begin to acquire speech, how children learn to perform mathematical operations, and how the earliest farmers knew when to plant crops. It's how livestock learn to stay clear of an electric fence and how my dog knows to expect a treat after dinner. Useful learning is grounded in pattern recognition.

When patterns are repeated consistently enough, they become accepted on a subconscious or conscious level as informal or formal principles to guide future thought and action. When the discipline of history fails to recognize recurring patterns and their associated principles, society is unable to learn from history on the most basic level.

Historians seem willing to recognize recurring patterns in limited slices of history, such as a recurring pattern of cultural diffusion in Eurasia during the early middle ages[91] or a recurring pattern in the conduct of trench warfare during World War I. David Christian and other advocates of "Big History" are willing to look at a very large scale of history, extending from the Big Bang to modern times, and to recognize one-time patterns in the past such as the era of hunter-gatherers. The history profession appears less willing to combine the large time scale with recurring patterns to identify enduring principles of historical knowledge applicable to the future. One exception is the Applied History Project at Harvard University, which I discuss below.

FROM PATTERN TO PRINCIPLE. How does thinking progress from pattern recognition to the identification of a general principle? The basic model for this leap in understanding is exemplified in the scientific method. Scientists, mathematicians, linguists, business people, sports coaches, military strategists, and people from various walks of life observe individual phenomena that suggest the existence of a recurring pattern that might represent a general principle. In science, this potential principle is termed a hypothesis, which is tested through further observation.

In science, further observation may include experiments designed to learn whether the hypothesis consistently predicts future outcomes (what my neighbor Bill might call prophecies). Not all disciplines lend themselves to experimentation, however, including scientific fields such as geology and astronomy.[92] In these other fields, the hypothesis can be tested only through sustained observation. If the hypothesis holds up over time, it may be accepted as a general principle of knowledge—termed a *general theory* in science—and this principle can be applied to situations arising in the future.

This cycle of inductive and deductive reasoning—from the particular to the general to the particular—produces useful principles of knowledge in most human activities, including mathematics, language, and science. For instance, some 2,500 years ago, Pythagoras observed a recurring pattern in right triangles (each being a *particular* occurrence). This pattern suggested a *general* principle of mathematics that a builder in the United States will use today to square the foundation of a house (a *particular* event).*

There is no inherent reason why this same cycle of logical reasoning can't be applied in the field of history. The following diagram illustrates how inductive and deductive reasoning may supply useful principles of historical knowledge.

---

* The Pythagorean theorem yields the "3, 4, 5 rule" for measuring 90-degree angles such as those that form the corners of a house. The builder attaches two layout strings at right angles to one corner stake of the structure and marks one string at three feet from the stake and marks the other string at four feet from the stake. The diagonal measurement between the two marks (the hypotenuse) should equal five feet. If not, the builder adjusts his strings to achieve a true 90-degree angle.

Figure 6. The cycle of inductive and deductive reasoning in history

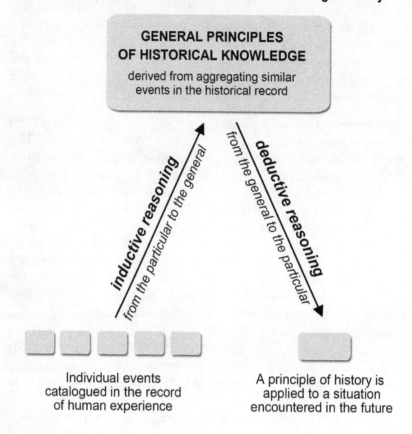

People may harbor an instinctive belief that history education should help us learn from the past, because people routinely learn from past experience in other realms of life. But without pattern recognition and principle formulation, history is unable to provide knowledge useful in the future as other school subjects do.

PRINCIPLES OF HISTORY HAVE A LONG HISTORY. Although principles of history are absent from the official curricula taught to students in schools and colleges, they have been supplying humans with useful wisdom since at least the fifth century BC,[93] when Thucydides in Greece and Sun Tzu in China recognized principles of history that continue to remain relevant some 24 centuries later. In his *History of the Peloponnesian War*, Thucydides identified a number of principles of history including three basic motives for war—fear, honor, and self-interest—and the principle that *those who promote war tend to scorn those who resist war as cowardly or unpatriotic.*[94] In *The Art of War*, Sun Tzu identified principles of history that are required reading among military strategists today.

The founders of the American republic intentionally mined the past for principles that could guide their new nation into the future.[95] The Declaration of Independence is based on the principle that people have a right to exercise self-determination and live free of foreign control. The US Constitution enshrines principles including freedom of speech, due process under law, and separation of powers, principles that have served America well for over two centuries.

Present-day historians at Harvard University have noted a pattern in the past that can inform judgment in the future. The Harvard Applied History Project is warning of the "Thucydides Trap," a principle of history (they term it a *historical analogue*) that may portend conflict between China and the United States: *the tendency of a rising power to go to war with an established power*

> as Athens challenged Sparta in ancient Greece, or as Germany did Britain a century ago. Most such contests have ended badly, often for both nations.[96]

The Harvard group hopes that raising awareness of this recurring dynamic of history may help China and the United States to avoid a devastating future war between the two superpowers.

Could awareness of principles of history—or historical analogues, recurring dynamics, lessons of history by whatever name—have prevented any past American wars? Prior to the US invasions of Vietnam and Iraq, the presidential administrations of Lyndon Johnson and George W. Bush and the American public seemed unaware of two obvious and related principles of history: *Humans resist being controlled by outsiders*, and *many or most military invasions of distant lands fail over the long term.*

If Americans had learned these basic principles of history in school, might two long and costly wars have been averted? There is no guarantee that a different kind of history schooling can produce a different kind of history, but it's reasonable to assume that people will exercise better judgment when they are acquainted with reality than when they are ignorant of it. A great many people may have died due to the lack of useful knowledge that we get from history education.

ARE PRINCIPLES OF HISTORY VALID? Despite the ages-old recognition of the useful knowledge available from principles of history, some historians have questioned their validity. Perhaps the most prominent of these skeptics was the noted German philosopher of history Georg

Wilhelm Friedrich Hegel, who claimed that such principles do not and cannot exist, because each historical event is unique:

> Peoples and governments have never learned anything
> from history, or acted on principles deduced from it.
> Each period is involved in such peculiar circumstances,
> exhibits a condition of things so strictly idiosyncratic,
> that its conduct must be regulated by considerations
> connected with itself, and itself alone.[97]

Yet Hegel is probably best known for proposing a grand principle of history usually described as thesis, antithesis, and synthesis. In Hegel's dialectical system, a historical development such as the French Revolution contains an internal contradiction that will bring forth its opposite (the Reign of Terror), and eventually the tension between the thesis and antithesis will be resolved in a new synthesis (constitutional monarchy), which in turn becomes the new thesis.

Hegel is correct, of course, that historical events vary in their particulars; but they may have underlying principles in common, as Hegel himself implicitly acknowledged by proposing his grand principle of history. Hegel is also correct in observing that peoples and governments never seem to learn from history or principles derived from it, a fault that might be attributed to an educational system that fails to teach such principles. Society at large appears to lament the fact that we continually fail to learn from the past as demonstrated by the popularity of Santayana's maxim: "Those who cannot remember the past are condemned to repeat it."

George Santayana and the many people who have quoted him obviously believed that we can and should learn from the past, as did one of Hegel's prominent contemporaries, the Scottish philosopher and historian David Hume. Hume declared that history's *main purpose* is to identify principles of history:

> Mankind are so much the same, in all times and places,
> that history informs us of nothing new or strange in this
> particular. Its chief use is only to discover the constant
> and universal principles of human nature.[98]

HUMAN NATURE AS A SOURCE OF GENERAL PRINCIPLES. Other thinkers—before Hume and since—have likewise recognized human nature as a source of valuable wisdom applicable to the present and future. Thucydides, in his history, repeatedly pointed to the proclivities of human nature as motivators of human actions.[99] Niccolò Machiavelli was the Renaissance historian and diplomat considered the founder of modern political science. He wrote, "Human events ever resemble those of preceding times [because] they are produced by men who ever have been, and shall ever be, animated by the same passions, and thus they necessarily have the same results."[100]

The contemporary author and Harvard professor Steven Pinker has observed, "The commonality of basic human responses across cultures has profound implications. One is that there is a universal human nature....And our decisions on how to organize our lives can take the facts of human nature into account." How might human nature be taken into account? Pinker says, "We need to discern *patterns in the past*, so we can know what to *generalize* to the predicaments of the present." (emphasis added)[101]

Human nature, it should be noted, is not the same as human behavior. Human nature remains largely consistent through the ages, while human behavior can and does change in response to changing circumstances. The liberal positions of the Enlightenment (e.g., constitutional monarchy) would be seen as conservative positions today. Human nature didn't change; we still have liberals and conservatives, but circumstances changed, and human behavior changed with them.

Human-on-human violence remains the scourge of our species, but according to historical evidence cited by Steven Pinker, homicide has declined sharply in Europe since the middle ages.[102] Human nature didn't change, but if Pinker is right, human behavior changed for the better. If human behavior were incapable of change, there would be little point in trying to learn from history.

While human nature may be the chief source of principles of history, historical principles may also be derived from the nature of reality. The principle that *people resist external control* comes from instinctive human nature, while the principle of *unintended consequences* comes from the nature of reality. Both types of principles represent recurring patterns that are revealed through the historical record, which makes them general principles of historical knowledge.

WISDOM AND GENERAL PRINCIPLES. Wisdom is a highly regarded but elusive form of knowledge thought to accrue to especially perceptive persons often called sages. These are people who have experienced life and drawn from it refined insights useful for approaching new situations.

On the first page of his book *Too Big to Know*, Harvard's David Weinberger describes the DIKW pyramid, an attempt to further define the concept of wisdom. DIKW stands for data, information, knowledge, and wisdom, and according to Weinberger, the concept was popularized in 1988 when Russell Ackoff sketched a four-tier pyramid in his presidential address to the International Society for General Systems Research.

Figure 7. The DIKW pyramid

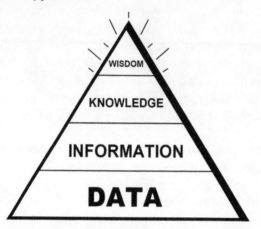

Under this formulation, the structure of knowledge is seen to resemble a pyramid, with large quantities of data collected at the wide base of the pyramid. As data becomes refined and rises through successive levels of the pyramid, it takes on more meaning and value until it achieves the rare status of wisdom, residing at the apex of the pyramid. As Weinberger wryly noted, "There's obviously plenty of data in the world, but not a lot of wisdom."[103]

Does this conception of wisdom sound familiar? It is the highest form of knowledge; it is knowledge gained from past experience that can be usefully applied in future situations. It would appear that wisdom is another name for general principles of knowledge—with one caveat.

When people use the term *wisdom*, they are referring to useful knowledge in the realm of human affairs, not knowledge of other realms such as the physical world of science or the quantitative world of mathematics. When an engineer designs a bridge, the principles she employs are considered technical skills, and when a builder uses the Pythagorean theorem to square the foundation of a house, this principle is termed a mathematical formula. Neither technical skills nor mathematical formulas would be considered wisdom.

History is the fundamental realm of knowledge concerned with human experience, and history has been recording evidence of this experience for well over two millennia. Since wisdom may be defined as general principles that apply in the realm of human affairs, and since history is the field of knowledge dedicated to studying human affairs, it would seem that history is society's greatest potential source of wisdom.

INERTIA FAVORS INACTION. Although principles of history have been supplying useful wisdom for millennia, not everyone—Hegel, for example—has accepted these principles as valid, and inertia favors inaction. History's principles have yet to find their way into the official curricula taught to students in school, with the result that society remains ignorant of the wisdom these principles may have to offer, and society remains condemned, as Santayana put it, to keep repeating mistakes of the past.

Because historians and history educators have yet to reach a consensus on the value of principles of history, this determination rests with the larger society that education is meant to serve. Members of the public are fully capable of looking at the evidence and deciding for themselves if principles of history should be part of an informed person's education.

Is it true that major cultures and civilizations have followed a general pattern of growth, flowering, and decline throughout history, that societies have repeatedly been ravaged by epidemic disease, and that humans tend to position themselves along a political spectrum that ranges from conservative to liberal? Is it true that humans manifest an instinct to exercise power over others and that humans exhibit a countervailing instinct to resist external control? Is there any doubt that humans promote their self-interest and the interests of their group, so we are constantly surrounded by biased information? Is it also true that humans tend to fear, dislike, subjugate, and kill people from groups different than their own? If these things are true, which they are, then principles of historical knowledge exist, and they are valid.

A NOTE ABOUT TERMINOLOGY. In the preceding paragraph, I used the word *true* several times. The words *true* and *truth* can make some people uncomfortable, but in this time of swirling claims about "fake news," truth might be an especially desirable commodity. By *truth*, I mean an accurate representation of reality based on empirical evidence.

Use of the term *truth* may raise red flags among those who subscribe to postmodernist theory, which proposes that absolute truth is unknowable because our notions of truth are based on individual, subjective perceptions of reality rather than complete knowledge of actual reality. I have no quarrel with this view of truth on a theoretical or philosophical level

(although on a logical level, it's difficult to understand how we can accept the truth of postmodernism if we can't accept the truth of anything.)

Other people may be wary of the word *truth* because they have seen instances in which individuals and groups who feel that they possess the absolute truth have been willing to impose their personal "truths" on others (Stalin and Hitler come to mind), a dynamic responsible for much death and destruction visited on humans by other humans throughout history.

When I use the terms *true* or *truth* in this book, I am not referring to absolute truth but to *practical* truth, the kind of truths that make it possible for us to function in the everyday world. When I depress the brake pedal on my car, I must believe in the practical truth represented by the general principle that such an action will slow or stop a vehicle. Otherwise, I would be unwilling to ride in planes, trains, and automobiles.

Do train and automobile braking systems sometimes fail? Yes; I'm afraid the truth of braking is not absolute, but if I were unable to accept the practical truth of braking on a daily basis, I would be unable to travel to the store for groceries, to town to see a movie, or to Ohio to visit my sister. In terms of travel, I would be paralyzed.

Let's not allow the lack of absolute truths in history to paralyze us in the realm of human affairs. The truth that humans tend to resist control by outsiders is not absolute, but as a practical matter, it is a general principle of history that possesses sufficient truth to inform our thinking about the workings of the world and thereby to help us function effectively in the future.

HISTORY'S GENERAL PRINCIPLES ARE TENDENCIES. History's principles can't be considered hard-and-fast laws or rules that always apply in the same way to similar circumstances. Historian Richard J. Evans observes that history is capable of producing "instructive and workable generalizations....But history cannot create laws with predictive power."[104] The Harvard history group determined that the Thucydides Trap applied in 12 of 16 cases over the past 500 years, a 75 percent likelihood of occurrence. Rather than rules, general principles of history are *tendencies* that humans would be wise to respect, like the tendency of cigarettes to cause lung cancer or the tendency of a child to be struck by a car if she dashes into a busy street without looking both ways.

History's general principles are not so different from principles supplied by social science fields such as psychology and sociology that likewise deal with variable human behavior. Not every human is afflicted with depression or subject to mob behavior, yet these principles are widely accepted in academic circles and routinely taught to students in psychology and sociology courses. What, I would like to know, is the distinction between these principles of knowledge and principles of history such as *people resist being controlled by outsiders* and *many or most military invasions fail?*

The biggest distinction I can discern is that history's principles may deal with momentous events that intensely affect entire societies, including events with the potential to involve large-scale death and destruction. It would seem that few intellectual disciplines can offer society more crucial principles of knowledge than history can, yet history education systematically fails to provide such vital knowledge to students and society.

Because enduring principles of history supply *important knowledge of the world that can help students and society to function effectively in the future*, principles of history qualify as our first kind of historical knowledge appropriate for educational purposes. If historians choose not to recognize this kind of knowledge, so be it—that's their business.[†] Then this task falls to history educators, who bear the professional responsibility to impart important knowledge of the world useful in the future. Because that's *their* business.

Historical Evidence for Representative Examples of Principles of Historical Knowledge

a. Major cultures and empires have followed a general pattern of growth, flowering, and decline throughout history.
    Evidence includes two thousand years of Chinese imperial dynasties and every other former empire that has existed on the face of the earth.

b. Humans tend to position themselves along a political spectrum that ranges from conservative to liberal.
    Evidence includes Akhenaten's attempt to replace the polytheistic religion of ancient Egypt with worship of a single god, the contrasting political systems of ancient Athens and Sparta, the French Revolution, the US Civil War, and the present polarized condition of American politics and government.

---

†Historians have other useful work to perform. Their accounts describe varieties of human experience that can help us gain a deeper appreciation of the human condition. Their accounts can supply specific background knowledge when needed to help with understanding contemporary issues. And their stories constitute the historical record from which general principles of historical knowledge may be derived.

c. Humans manifest an instinct to exercise control over others.

Evidence includes the Babylonians, Persians, Athenians, and Romans of ancient times; the Mongol, Aztec, Inca, Spanish, French, Dutch, and British empires of more recent times; the Japanese and German invasions of Asia and Europe that initiated World War II, the Soviets in Afghanistan, and the United States in the Philippines, Iran, Vietnam, and Iraq.

d. Humans exhibit a propensity to fear, dislike, kill, subjugate, and discriminate against people from groups different than their own.

Evidence from history includes tribal warfare, genocides, slavery, India's caste system, South Africa's apartheid system, America's Jim Crow laws, the US internment of Japanese-Americans during World War II, and the examples cited in Item *c.* above.

e. Humans exhibit an instinct to resist external control.

Evidence includes Greeks in the fifth century BC, Cleopatra in 31 BC, Jews in 66 AD, Joan of Arc in 1428, England's Elizabeth I in 1588, American colonists in 1776, Toussaint Louverture in 1791, Native Americans at the Little Big Horn River in 1876, Zulus in Natal in 1906, Mahatma Gandhi in the first half of the twentieth century, and the Vietnamese people for the past thousand years.

f. Many or most military invasions of distant lands fail over the long term.

Evidence includes the Persian invasions of ancient Greece; the Roman Empire; the Crusades; the Mongol conquests; European imperialism in the Americas, Africa, and Asia; Napoleon and Hitler in Europe; the Japanese Empire in China and Southeast Asia; the Soviets in Afghanistan; and the United States in Vietnam. Counteroffensive coalitions formed to throw back an initial aggressor generally appear to be more successful than aggressor-initiated invasions and serve to reinforce the general principle. Examples include the defeats of Napoleon, Hitler, the Japanese Empire, and Saddam Hussein in Kuwait.

(Additional principles of history are identified in the Appendix.)

The question: Are people more likely to understand, retain, and benefit from historical knowledge if individual historical events such as those listed above are learned in meaningless isolation or if these events are learned in the context of principles that describe how the world works—principles that students and society may apply in the future to inform judgment in human affairs?

2. EVENTS WITH CONTINUING EFFECT

ISOLATED EVENTS ARE NOT SUITABLE FOR HISTORY INSTRUCTION. Much traditional history schooling consists of teaching students about one-time events from the past that provide little or no knowledge useful in the future. Because education exists to impart knowledge useful in the future, such isolated events are not appropriate topics for schooling. Even momentous events of history may lack continuing relevance in the contemporary world if they are taught in isolation.

Some people might find it interesting that the Roman Empire conquered a great deal of territory and that Julius Caesar was assassinated on the Ides of March in 44 BC, but these facts by themselves represent inert knowledge because they do little or nothing to help people function in the contemporary world. While such facts may be interesting, as isolated events they don't advance the mission of education by imparting knowledge useful in the present or future.

Even important events that occurred within living memory may do little to provide today's students with useful awareness of the world around them. Today, the country of Vietnam is one of America's Asian trading partners; it manufactures products that Americans purchase and use. This is how Vietnam affects American students in the contemporary world.

How would it assist today's students to function in the world if they were to learn specifics of the American involvement in Vietnam such as the fall of Dien Bien Phu, the Gulf of Tonkin Resolution, the Tet Offensive, and the Paris peace talks? How would this knowledge amount to anything more than "just one damn thing after another"?

But if we were to combine historical knowledge of the Vietnam War with historical knowledge of the Roman Empire and knowledge of various other wars fought throughout history, students might recognize recurring patterns that represent enduring principles of knowledge applicable well into the future, principles such as *people resist being controlled by outsiders*, and *many or most military invasions of distant lands fail over the long term*. Being relevant to the future, this kind of learning is appropriate for educational purposes.

If a history teacher feels it's important for students to know something of the Vietnam War, the subject may be usefully included in instruction as one context for students to learn and understand such enduring principles of history.[105] This kind of teaching advances the mission of education by imparting knowledge useful in the present and future, whereas the teaching of isolated and inert facts from the past does not.

If an individual has a need to acquire more specific knowledge of the Vietnam War (an official of the Veteran's Administration, for instance, or a military strategist, or a student writing a research report), such specialized information is available from external sources such as history books and the Internet. People who want specialized knowledge of a topic will always need to consult specialized sources because general education can never teach everything there is to know about a subject.

Instructional time is limited. It should be spent wisely on important knowledge applicable to a range of future situations rather than wasting it in a futile attempt to teach large quantities of isolated facts from the past, which can only produce superficial, trivial, and easily forgotten learning.

INDIVIDUAL EVENTS SUITABLE FOR HISTORY INSTRUCTION. Some individual events of the past, however, continue to exert considerable influence in the contemporary world. Because such events are not isolated and inert, they can be appropriate topics for educational purposes. As would be expected, events with continuing effect in the contemporary world are likely to be those events that have occurred nearest to us in time, mostly during the last five hundred years or so.

Events with continuing effect include a limited number of truly momentous historical developments such as Columbus's voyage to the New World, European imperialism, the Scientific Revolution, the Enlightenment, industrialization, and world wars. While these developments do not rise to the level of general principles applicable to all times and places, they remain so influential in our time and place that they can provide situational awareness of the world in which we live.

Columbus's voyage led directly to the decimation of Native American populations and the horrors of the Atlantic slave trade, which produced Indian Wars and Indian reservations and the Civil War and racial segregation, and which continue to generate media headlines in the United States regarding matters such as pipelines encroaching on Native lands and the Black Lives Matter movement. European imperialism set the stage for a century of Western intervention in the Middle East that has drawn the United States into a series of long and costly wars in that unsettled region of the world.

Events with continuing effect can also include more recent developments that might fall under the category of current events. Such developments would include the resurgence of Asia, nuclear proliferation, the Arab-Israeli conflict, terrorism, globalism, climate change, biotechnology, and so on. Students need a working understanding of such developments to operate effectively in the contemporary world, and schools have an ethical obligation to provide it. History education is the obvious venue for supplying this knowledge, as these events are the contemporary products of historical development through time.

It might not always be easy for educators to decide if a historical event is entirely isolated in the past, or if it maintains relevance in today's world, but so long as teachers are committed to the idea of imparting knowledge with continuing relevance in the world, historical study can steadily move away from the curse of trivia and advance in a productive direction.

Knowledge of events with continuing effect provides situational awareness of the world in which we operate today and the world in which today's students will likely continue to operate in the foreseeable future. Knowledge of these events therefore qualifies as a second kind of relevant historical knowledge suitable for educational purposes.

3. FOUNDATIONAL CONCEPTS OF HISTORY AND GEOGRAPHY

Foundational concepts of history and geography are major historical and geographical concepts that provide necessary background knowledge for understanding historical developments of the past, present, and future and for providing situational awareness of the world around us. While history describes human experience across the dimension of time, geography describes human experience across the dimension of space, and both dimensions are in constant interaction with each other. History, being the story of human experience, is incomplete without taking into account both dimensions, time and space.

The following three examples illustrate the inseparable relationship between history and geography.

–History's earliest civilizations grew along river valleys that provided abundant water and fertile soils for growing crops and a means for transporting crops to market.

–Great classical civilizations of ancient times were brought down by nomads who developed cavalry skills by herding livestock on the grasslands of central Eurasia.

–We can't fully comprehend the continuing conflicts in the Middle East without understanding the cultural factors of religion and ethnicity associated with that piece of geography.

Foundational concepts of history would include topics such as primary sources, agriculture, religion, civilization, government, ancient times, the Iron Age, imperialism, socialism, capitalism, and proxy wars. Essential background concepts of geography would include hemispheres, continents, oceans, climate zones, regions, nations, distribution of religions, and so on. Because such concepts are essential for understanding past, present, and future historical developments and features of the contemporary world, and because these concepts are likely to remain relevant into the foreseeable future, they constitute a third kind of historical knowledge appropriate for educational purposes.

4. A BIG PICTURE

A fourth type of historical knowledge suitable for educational purposes is a big picture of human development through time. Such a big picture may be represented through two complementary formats: as a written chronological narrative and as a pictorial timeline that depicts important developments in national or world history.

The big picture can perform several useful functions in history education. As a written historical narrative, the big picture can serve as the essential instructional tool that brings together in one place all four kinds of historical knowledge described here: general principles of history, events with continuing effect, foundational concepts of history and geography, and the big picture itself.

The big picture itself provides the raw material for recognizing recurring patterns and enduring principles of history, and it provides the multiple historical contexts that students need in order to understand and internalize these principles. Thus, the big picture is both the *source* and the *teacher* of general principles of historical knowledge.

By placing specific events and concerns of the present in the wider context of extended human experience, the big picture provides situational awareness that can help to limit costly errors in judgment.

And the big picture can help to fulfill the human psychological needs to bring constituent elements together to form a satisfying picture of the whole and the urge to know who we are and where we came from.

THE BIG PICTURE PROVIDES MULTIPLE CONTEXTS. Writing in 1776, Thomas Paine provided an example of how a big picture of history can supply the multiple contexts needed in order to identify a principle of history that informs judgment about the future. In that fateful year, American colonists issued their audacious Declaration of Independence from the British crown, and Paine issued his 77-page pamphlet that supplied the rationale for the American declaration. Paine's pamphlet, titled *Common Sense,* was so influential in its time that John Adams remarked to Thomas Jefferson, "History is to ascribe the American Revolution to Thomas Paine."[106]

As British subjects, American colonists had knowledge of British history and government practices, and in *Common Sense,* Paine drew on a big picture of British history in his effort to discredit one of the main arguments in favor of monarchy, the claim that hereditary monarchy preserves a nation from unrest and civil war.

"The whole history of England disowns the fact," wrote Paine. "Thirty kings and two minors have reigned in that distracted kingdom since the conquest, in which time there have been (including the [Glorious] Revolution) no less than eight civil wars and nineteen rebellions."[107] Here Paine draws on a big picture of history to identify the multiple contexts that form a pattern—a pattern that represents a general principle of history: *Hereditary monarchy is no insurance against civil war and insurrection.* Then Paine applies this principle to the particular case of American independence to inform the judgment of American colonists.

As it did for Paine, a big picture of history can provide students with the multiple examples of similar events needed to recognize recurring patterns in history, patterns that represent principles of knowledge that can be applied in the future. Only by encountering manifestations of such principles in multiple contexts in the historical record can students come to truly understand and internalize the underlying principles common to different situations.

THE BIG PICTURE CAN IMPROVE JUDGMENT. Seeing a big picture of human development through time allows us to place individual events and present concerns in a wider context, thereby reducing the possibility of committing errors in judgment.

If you wanted to build a house, you would begin by visualizing a big picture of the house: the size of the building, the number of stories, its architectural style. Only after this big picture is firmly in mind would you consider all the various elements that go into a house: the placement of windows and doors, room dimensions, traffic patterns, and the like.

It would be foolish to make decisions about these various elements without considering them in the context of the big picture. In the same way, we are more likely to make poor judgments about contemporary issues if we can't place them in the context of the big picture of human experience.

THE BIG PICTURE CAN HELP TO SATISFY HUMAN PSYCHOLOGICAL NEEDS. Evidence from years of history schooling suggests that society expects historical learning to provide an overview of human development through time. This desire is expressed in the chronological overviews of history supplied by textbooks, content standards, and curricula like Advanced Placement history courses, which have long dictated the content and structure of history schooling.

Groups of history-education experts have endorsed this idea that students should be taught a chronologically based historical overview. The respected Bradley Commission on History in the Schools said that historical study "should cultivate the perspective arising from a chronological view of the past down to the present day."[108] The National Standards for History say, "Chronology provides the mental scaffolding for organizing historical thought....Without a clear sense of historical time—time past, present, and future—students are bound to see events as one great tangled mess."[109] (A remarkable statement coming from the folks whose voluminous history standards generated their own mental mess.)

History education's longstanding inclination to base instruction on a comprehensive overview of human experience may spring from a deep-seated psychological need to draw related elements together to form a satisfying picture of the whole. Psychology has a name for the human impulse to integrate knowledge into a meaningful representation; what I am calling a big picture, and the Bradley Commission called perspective, and the National Standards for History called mental scaffolding, psychologists term a *gestalt*, which is defined as a configuration or pattern of phenomena integrated to constitute a unified whole.

Michael Gazzaniga of the University of California is a pioneer in the field of cognitive neuroscience. His research found a physiological basis in the brain for the human urge to integrate knowledge to form a coherent representation. Gazzaniga identified what he called an "interpreter" function in the left hemisphere of the brain that assembles actions and feelings into "a story" that makes our behaviors "feel coherent and unified."[110]

Few stories can be more central to our understanding of ourselves than the story of human experience, a story that can help to satisfy the human need to understand who we are and where we came from. It's only natural that we humans would want to acquire a meaningful understanding of our own experience, and it's only logical that history schooling would be the place to provide it.

THERE IS A PROBLEM. For the reasons cited above, the big picture of human development through time provides historical knowledge with continuing relevance in the world, which qualifies the big picture as our fourth kind of historical knowledge suitable for educational purposes. There is a problem, however. The big pictures currently supplied to students in history textbooks and survey courses don't provide students with a coherent understanding of human experience because they include more factual information than human brains can absorb and integrate into a meaningful understanding of the whole. These overviews are too comprehensive to be comprehensible, so history remains "one great tangled mess" in students' minds.

For the big picture to perform its several useful functions, it needs to be both concise enough to be comprehensible and extensive enough to provide the multiple contexts that students need in order to learn, understand, and internalize important historical knowledge, so that this knowledge may be usefully applied in the future. (My attempt to devise such a big picture narrative of world history is described in Chapter 10.)

ESSENTIAL INSTRUCTIONAL TOOLS

Three essential teaching tools can help students grasp the four useful kinds of historical knowledge described here. One such tool is maps, large-scaple maps that provide students with a big-picture overview of the physical environment and cultural features associated with those locations, including nations, religions, and major historical developments.

For world history courses, these maps would include a map of the world and a map of the Eastern Hemisphere—the second map being necessary due to the large size and complexity of this region of the world. For US history courses, the essential map is a map of the United States including border regions. These large-scale maps can be supplemented with additional maps of smaller regions as appropriate, but instruction should always return to the large-scale map to place locations in broad spatial perspective.

A second indispensable tool is a chronological narrative that provides a comprehensible overview of history, and the third tool is a large-scale timeline that depicts history's major developments on a national or global scale. These two tools—the graphical timeline and the written chronological narrative—can work together to provide students with a big picture of human development through time. Examples of large-scale timelines for use in US history and world history courses are depicted below.

Figure 8. Example of a large-scale US history timeline

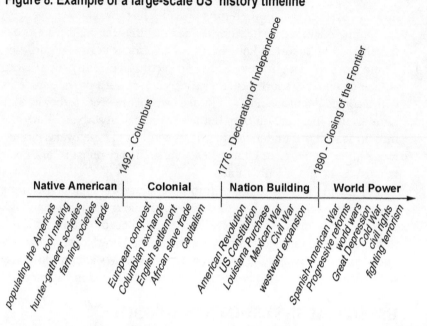

Figure 9. Example of a large-scale world history timeline

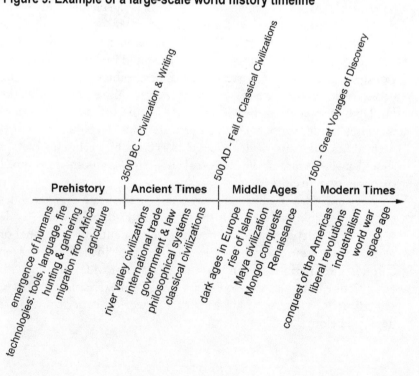

SUMMARY OF HISTORICAL KNOWLEDGE FOR EDUCATIONAL PURPOSES

UNSUITABLE HISTORICAL KNOWLEDGE. The following three kinds of historical knowledge provide little or no knowledge useful in the future, which makes them unsuitable for educational purposes.

–Unfocused and superficial coverage of large quantities of one-time events from the past that are disconnected from any larger meaning that could be applied in the future (otherwise known as inert knowledge or trivia).

–Instruction in isolated historical events, even major ones, that fail to help students function in the contemporary world and bear no larger meaning useful in the future.

–The indiscriminate teaching of specific events from the past in the vague hope that they may somehow illuminate specific but unknown events that may arise in the future. In the absence of a crystal ball to see into the future, most of this teaching will be wasted. The only rational method for acquiring historical background knowledge about specific events of the future is to consult historical accounts pertinent to those events when the events occur.

SUITABLE HISTORICAL KNOWLEDGE. Knowledge appropriate for general education possesses three characteristics: It is relevant to the future, it is important, and it is general in nature. Being general in nature, it applies to a range of situations that may arise in the future, which makes this knowledge far more useful than isolated facts that only apply to individual events of the past. The chart on the following page summarizes four kinds of historical knowledge that satisfy these criteria, which makes this knowledge suitable for educational purposes.

Figure 10. Kinds of historical knowledge suitable for education

KNOWLEDGE	DESCRIPTION
Principles of history	Timeless and universal principles of historical knowledge describe how the world works and are applicable to the future.
Events with continuing effect	Historical developments that exert significant, continuing impact in the contemporary world are likely to continue to affect students' lives into the future.
Foundational concepts	Foundational concepts of history and geography are necessary for understanding historical events of the past, present, and future, and they provide situational awareness of the world around us.
A big picture	A big picture of human development through time can tie together the three kinds of historical knowledge described above. It is the source of principles of history, provides multiple contexts for students to learn the principles, can inform judgment by placing events in historical perspective, and can satisfy human psychological needs to know who we are and where we came from.

The preceding chart is the first of four key charts in this book; it lists four kinds of historical knowledge appropriate for educational purposes, or *what* to teach. The next chapter, Chapter 6, will identify four essential cognitive learning strategies, or *how* to teach. Chapter 7 will combine these elements with three others to identify five basic principles of history education. Chapter 7 also includes a chart that identifies criteria for weighing the importance of historical events.

If readers don't remember anything else about this book, I hope that they will remember the existence of these four charts, which are readily accessible at the front of the book. These charts identify commonsense fundamentals that are as basic to history schooling as throwing and catching are to baseball. Baseball players who don't learn to catch and throw will never be successful baseball players. How successful can history teachers hope to be if they don't practice the fundamentals of history education?

The whole of science is nothing more
than a refinement of everyday thinking.

–Albert Einstein, *Physics and Reality*, 1936

CHAPTER SIX

Cognition and the grand assumption

Cognitive science reveals learning strategies compatible with how human minds work.

In the film *Field of Dreams*, Kevin Costner portrays an Iowa farmer who hears a voice saying, "If you build it, they will come."[111] The farmer builds a baseball diamond in the middle of a cornfield, and legendary baseball players show up to play ball. It was a charming fantasy that can never come true in real life. Educators engage in a similar kind of charming fantasy: "If you teach it, they will learn."

Government in the United States spends over a trillion dollars annually on education based on the grand assumption that if schools teach it, students will learn—an assumption that is called into question by findings from cognitive science. *Cognition* is the term applied to the mind's process of acquiring and using knowledge, and cognition is critical to schooling because learning will be ineffective if it's delivered in a manner that is incompatible with the way human minds work.

Cognitive science research, if done well, can provide objective findings about the workings of the mind and the effectiveness of schooling. But not all scientific research is done well; individual research projects may be flawed or false.[112] Scientific research becomes trustworthy when it holds up under extended scrutiny—when it survives the test of time. For over a century, cognitive scientists have been assembling research about the workings of the mind, some of which has withstood the test of time and has become widely accepted as valid within the field of cognitive psychology—although this knowledge has been slow to enter the mainstream of educational practice.

Before we examine research about the effectiveness of school learning and how history education might be improved, it will be helpful to have a basic understanding of how human minds learn.[113]

HOW LEARNING WORKS

WORKING MEMORY. Learning is essentially a two-stage process: The brain encounters new information and stores it for later use. The encounter with new data takes place in what scientists call *working memory*, where information processing is highly dynamic but capacity is extremely limited. As we go about our daily lives, our minds are constantly being bombarded by data streaming in from the senses, much of which is processed subconsciously and automatically by the brain. Other inputs rise to the level of consciousness, as when a student is trying to understand new information presented by a teacher.

Whether new information is processed consciously or subconsciously, the brain must decide quickly whether to store the new information or let it fall away—quickly because the brain must be ready to make the same decision regarding ever newer information about to arrive in the next few seconds. During the fleeting period of time when information has the brain's attention, it's said to be held in working memory, where it remains for only moments unless we mentally repeat it, as with a phone number we're about to call. Researchers have found that working memory holds about as many words as can be spoken in two or three seconds—roughly six or seven words, the number of items in a phone number or street address—and the mind can visualize no more than about four items simultaneously in working memory.[114]

Figure 11. The learning process

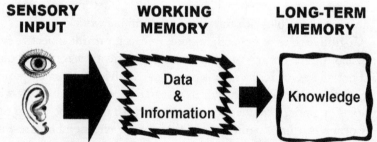

LONG-TERM MEMORY. When the mind chooses to retain new information, the brain sends it from working memory into *long-term memory* storage. According to the Princeton psychologist Daniel Kahneman, only a minority of inputs that we encounter in life ever make their way into long-term memory. He has calculated that people experience about 600 million of these encounters during a lifetime or about 600,000 a month, which works out to an average of about 20 for every waking minute, and "Most of them don't leave a trace," says Kahneman. "Most of them are completely ignored by the remembering self."[115]

For information to get past the gatekeeper of working memory and enter into long-term memory storage, the information must be meaningful to the learner in some way; maybe it's emotional, like the vision of an airliner striking the World Trade Center, or it reminds us of an old friend, or it connects to previously learned knowledge, or it promises to be useful in the future. Once inputs find their way into long-term memory, they may last a lifetime or fade within minutes; it all depends on the strength of the initial memory input and how well the memory is reinforced over time. The image of an airliner striking one of the Twin Towers is strong enough to be retained in memory with little reinforcement over time, but less intense memories require reinforcement to prevent decay from the passage of time or from lack of use.

Memories can also degrade due to *interference* from similar information encountered at a later time. Here's an example. Shortly after my flight took off from the airport in Mexico City a few years ago, I pulled the safety card from the seat pocket in front of me and saw that we were flying aboard a Boeing jet, which caused me think of the airplane manufacturer that is Boeing's chief rival. I had flown on their aircraft a number of times, and I knew that this was the European consortium that built the Concorde supersonic airliner, and it was involved in a controversy over a contract to supply tanker planes to the US Air Force. I knew all this about the company, but to my surprise, I couldn't remember the company's name.

Two weeks later, I awoke in a hotel room with the word "bus" on my mind, which I recognized as part of the company's name; but even with this big hint, I still couldn't come up with the name, so I went online and looked it up. Immediately, the cause of my memory lapse was clear. In recent years, my wife and I had flown several times with a Mexican discount airline called VivaAerobus, and I had seen their colorful planes parked on the tarmac in Mexico City. *Aerobus* completely blocked access to my memory of the similar name, *Airbus*. Knowledge acquired at a later time had *interfered* with remembering similar knowledge acquired earlier.[116]

THINKING. Learning is the process of receiving and storing new information, and it is the prerequisite to thinking. Thinking occurs when we retrieve knowledge from long-term memory and bring it back into working memory to assist with an immediate task such as solving a problem, understanding new information, or ordering from a restaurant menu. Working memory is the active workspace of the mind where new inputs meet prior knowledge to generate understanding. As noted in Chapter 4, thinking is knowledge dependent: Thinking requires relevant knowledge to think about. But our thinking can become constrained when we can't access previously stored knowledge due to decay or interference.

Figure 12. The learning-thinking process:
Only strong memories survive

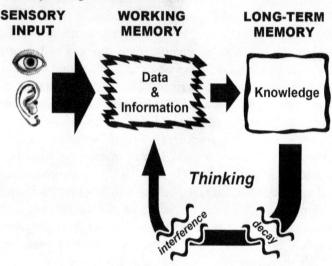

The reality of cognition is a hard reality: It can be hard to get knowledge into memory, and it can be hard to keep it there. Rather than cope with this hard reality, history education tends to do the easy thing, although the easy thing is not cognitively effective. We don't trouble ourselves much with matters like long-term memory retention, memory decay, and interference. Seldom do we focus on helping students retain their knowledge over the long haul, and seldom do we teach students how to apply their knowledge to new situations that may arise in the future.

Traditional history education simply asks students to memorize a quantity of inert facts long enough to pass the next big exam, be it a unit exam, a final exam, a state standardized assessment, or an Advanced Placement test.[117] If this is the only kind of learning that is likely to be tested, it's the only kind of learning that history educators need worry about. This simplistic approach to instruction is so ingrained in our educational culture that many history teachers may be unaware that any other approach to learning is possible or necessary.

HOW SUCCESSFUL IS SCHOOL LEARNING?

LEARNING DEPENDS ON MEMORY. In a report on cognitive practices useful in schooling, the Institute of Education Sciences (IES) of the US Department of Education recognized the essential role that memory plays in learning: "It [is] our central organizing principle that learning depends on memory."[118]

In 1885, German psychologist Hermann Ebbinghaus published his pioneering studies on memory. He found that memories of nonsense syllables declined rapidly and disappeared within minutes unless they were periodically reinforced, or spaced over time. More than a century of research since Ebbinghaus has confirmed that *spaced learning* is more effective than massed learning, which is learning that occurs all at once. *Distributed practice* is the name given to the instructional approach meant to achieve spaced learning in the classroom.

Harry Bahrick of Ohio Wesleyan University may be the world's foremost researcher in the field of long-term retention of school learning.[119] In his landmark 50-year study of Spanish-language acquisition, Bahrick found that knowledge retention dropped off rapidly following instruction, and students retained *almost nothing* of what they learned three to six years after taking one Spanish course—three years for memory recall and six years for memory recognition (the kind of memory usually tested by multiple-choice tests). However, if students took three Spanish courses, retention of the tested material leveled off at around 29 percent and stayed there for 25 years before falling off again. Five Spanish courses yielded a stable 25-year retention rate of 63 percent.[120]

Other researchers who have studied long-term retention of knowledge acquired in secondary school and college classrooms have consistently replicated Bahrick's general findings, and his seminal studies are cited prominently in their papers.[121] All found that school knowledge largely disappears within a few years unless it's diligently reinforced.

This research makes it clear that it is possible to achieve long-term retention of school knowledge, but it's not easy, and it requires reinforcement of learning over an extended period of time, probably years.[122]

Such a long-term approach to learning is not how most knowledge is presently taught outside the elementary grades or much later in schooling, with the extended instruction associated with college majors and skilled vocations. Based on his findings, Bahrick concluded, "Much of the information acquired in classrooms is lost soon after final examinations are taken."[123]

TRANSFER OF LEARNING. Remembering learned knowledge is one thing; being able to apply it is another. In an extensive study of cognitive science research and its implications for schooling, the National Research Council (NRC) identified the transfer of learning from school to life beyond school as "the ultimate purpose of school-based learning."[124] Successful learning transfer requires knowledge to pass into all three phases needed to achieve *real learning*: Learned knowledge is remembered, and remembered knowledge is applicable to future situations.

The life cycle of real learning

Temporarily memorizing facts for an upcoming exam leaves learning stuck in phase one, which is only *pretend learning*. Successful learning transfer requires that knowledge be remembered over the long term so that it can be used to inform life after schooling. But even if a student should manage to remember school learning into adulthood, transfer of learning still won't be achieved unless the student can *apply* this knowledge to new situations arising in the future.

Cognitive science research has long established that learning transfer is difficult to achieve. Humans, it seems, aren't very good at applying knowledge learned in one setting to a similar situation in a different setting; we can be thrown off when the surface details don't match.[125] The journal *Educational Psychologist* devoted an entire issue to transfer of learning, and the lead article observed that a large body of research "finds systematic failures in people's ability to apply their relevant knowledge in new situations," and some researchers have concluded that meaningful transfer of school learning "seldom if ever occurs."[126]

Yet successful learning transfer does routinely occur in certain school settings, and it's a boon to humankind. You are reading what I am writing, and we learned these skills in elementary school years ago.

Teachers of language and math in the primary grades are forced to adopt instructional practices that achieve effective learning transfer, because their work is measured not only by the next big exam but by the successful functioning of students in later grades of school, and there is no hiding whether or not Johnny and Maria can read and add their sums by the time they reach middle school. If they can't, elementary teachers didn't do their jobs. No equivalent real-world test applies to the general education courses taught in secondary school and college.

In the absence of significant learning disabilities, our children do successfully learn to read, write, and do their sums in elementary school, and these students can still apply this knowledge as elderly adults. What is the secret sauce of elementary teachers? How do they consistently achieve successful long-term learning transfer?

It needn't remain a secret: Cognitive science has found that learning transfer relies on a cognitive triad consisting of *general principles* learned in *multiple contexts* over an *extended period of time*. A fourth component follows from the first three: The curriculum needs to refrain from covering excessive, superficial content that interferes with student acquisition of deep, effective, long-term useful learning.

COGNITIVE LEARNING STRATEGIES

As described above, extensive scientific research about memory retention and learning transfer reveals an uncomfortable reality regarding the bulk of schooling as presently taught: "Much of the information acquired in classrooms is lost soon after final examinations are taken," and people experience "systematic failures in [their] ability to apply their relevant knowledge in new situations." Thus, school learning is not likely to be remembered for long, and if remembered, it's not likely to be applied. The grand assumption—if we teach it, they will learn—appears to be a grand illusion.

Nonetheless, scientific research and everyday experience from elementary school tell us much of what we need to know about how to achieve real learning. The success of learning transfer in the primary grades and Bahrick's findings about the benefits of multiple years of instruction later in schooling are beacons that can light the way *if* our educational system is willing to face the hard realities of imparting real learning.

Next, we will take a look at four cognitive learning strategies that can help to achieve long-term transfer of learning. These four strategies are summarized in the following table.

Figure 13. Cognitive learning strategies for education

STRATEGY	DESCRIPTION
Emphasize key knowledge	Relevant and important principles and concepts are essential to the transfer of learning from school to life beyond school.
Teach knowledge in multiple contexts	When students learn knowledge in multiple contexts, they see how it applies in different situations, which increases the likelihood that students can apply their learning to new situations arising in the future.
Teach knowledge over time	For knowledge to be retained into adulthood, knowledge should be reinforced over an extended period of time through spaced learning (distributed practice).
Avoid excessive content	Effective transfer of school learning requires deep study of a limited number of important principles and concepts, and deep learning is not possible in an overstuffed curriculum.

1. EMPHASIZE KEY PRINCIPLES AND CONCEPTS. Our first cognitive learning strategy involves teaching the key principles and concepts of a school subject. General principles are the highest form of knowledge available from any intellectual discipline, because they provide knowledge of how the world works that has proved valid in the past, continues to be valid in the present, and is likely to remain valid into the foreseeable future anywhere that humans are present.

General principles are derived from recurring patterns, and they are the linchpins that can transfer knowledge of the past across the boundary of time into the future, where they may serve to inform judgment, decision-making, and action. General principles of knowledge constitute the foundation of learning in school subjects other than history, just as they are the foundation of knowledge in virtually every productive human activity from medicine to fly-fishing to small-engine repair.

Cognitive science indicates that principles of knowledge are more than a highly useful kind of knowledge; they are also instrumental to the learning process. The National Research Council's study of learning and schooling observed that one of the conditions most likely to produce successful transfer of learning is "when instruction includes specific attention to underlying principles." The NRC study asserted, "Effective comprehension and thinking require a coherent understanding of the organizing principles in any subject matter."[127]

The NRC appears to be telling us that history education without principles of historical knowledge is not likely to be cognitively effective. So now we have encountered a second compelling reason why principles of history should play a central role in history education: Not only are they the most valuable kind of knowledge, they are essential to the learning process. Principles of knowledge are key to both *what* students need to learn and *how* students can learn it.

In another report that focused on high school education, the NRC noted that important concepts, as well as principles, are worthy of concentrated instruction: "[Curricula] should focus on central organizing concepts and principles...that can be studied in depth during the time allotted."[128] The previous chapter identified four kinds of historical principles and concepts that are suitable for educational purposes: general principles of historical knowledge, events with continuing effect, foundational concepts of history and geography, and a big picture of human development through time.

2. TEACH KNOWLEDGE IN MULTIPLE CONTEXTS. Our second cognitive learning strategy calls for students to learn important knowledge in multiple contexts. Cognitive science research has determined that students can best learn principles of knowledge by two means: by learning the principles as clearly identified abstract concepts and by encountering the principles in multiple concrete contexts. When students encounter a principle operating in various settings, they have opportunities to recognize and internalize the underlying principle common to the different situations, thus improving the chances that students will know when and how to apply the principle to various future situations.

It makes sense; if you want students to apply principles in multiple contexts, then teach students the principles in multiple contexts. This is how students learn to read, write, and do math in the primary grades. And it's how we teach subjects like clarinet and basketball (multiple musical scores, multiple opponents), where the success or failure of learning is readily apparent. When schooling needs to achieve demonstrable results, it teaches knowledge in multiple contexts—because it works. A report on cognitive practices in education from the Institute of Education Sciences concurs:

> When a subject is taught in multiple contexts...and includes examples that demonstrate wide application of what is being taught, people are more likely to abstract

the relevant features of concepts and to develop a flexible
representation of knowledge....The transfer literature
suggests that the most effective transfer may come from
a balance of specific examples and general principles,
not from either one alone.[129]

3. TEACH KNOWLEDGE OVER AN EXTENDED PERIOD OF TIME.

Knowledge can't be used if it isn't remembered. As the Institute of
Education Sciences says, "Learning depends on memory." Cognitive
science research from Ebbinghaus to Bahrick and beyond, and cred-
ible sources including the IES and the National Research Council,[130]
have confirmed that long-term retention of knowledge requires spaced
learning, or distributed practice, over an extended period of time. The
IES report states:

> Spacing effects appear to be large in magnitude....
> It would appear that whenever it is desired that the
> learner retain information for many years, it is advis-
> able to utilize spacing of at least several months—and
> spacing even greater than that would seem more likely
> to improve retention over the longer term.[131]

The *testing effect*, sometimes called *retrieval practice*, is another
well-established cognitive strategy that could play a role in distributed
practice. Extensive research has shown that using practice quizzes or
tests to re-expose students to key information improves remembering
far better than simply reviewing the material.[132] It appears that bringing
information to mind from memory helps to make it stick. The testing
effect seems to work well with a wide variety of materials from word
lists to pictorial information, and it appears to be effective across all ages
from elementary school through college.[133]

In current educational practice, the testing effect is typically used
to prepare students for the next exam, but because it extends practice
beyond the initial learning phase, the testing effect could serve as a
useful tool for promoting extended distributed practice.

Practice can't end with the initial learning phase, because knowledge
tends to fade over time due to non-use and interference. Knowledge
learned in school isn't likely to be retained throughout adulthood unless
distributed practice extends beyond school into the rest of life, which is
why David Perkins emphasizes the teaching of "lifeworthy" knowledge in
school—knowledge that is most likely to be encountered in life and used

in the future. As he notes, "Knowledge not used is simply forgotten." We remember how to read and add numbers throughout our lives because we practice this knowledge throughout our lives.

The figure below depicts several stages involved in the progression from the identification of useful knowledge to be taught in school to the application of this knowledge in life.

Figure 14. Steps leading to the application of school knowledge

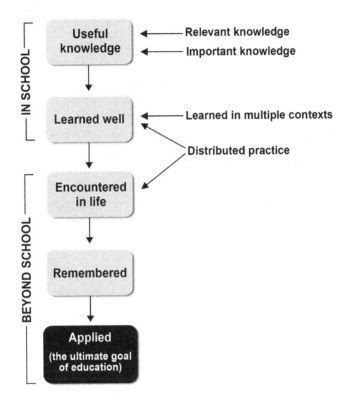

There is no separating the knowledge to be taught from the manner of teaching it. Using knowledge in the future depends on effective cognitive practices. Effective cognitive practices depend on useful knowledge to be learned.

4. **AVOID EXCESSIVE CONTENT.** Our fourth basic cognitive learning strategy calls for teachers to avoid covering excessive content. Even if pointless and trivial content knowledge were to be completely eliminated from history schooling—even if instruction were limited to just the four kinds of useful historical knowledge described in this book—instruction

might still include more information than could be taught effectively in the amount of time available to teach it.

The fourth cognitive learning strategy, *avoid excessive content*, is meant to remind educators to keep their eyes fixed on the ultimate goal of education: real learning useful in the future. Deep and focused instruction is the price that must be paid if learning is to be transferred to life beyond school, and deep learning isn't possible in a curriculum that tries to cover too many topics.

In his summary of research useful to schooling, cognitive psychologist Frank Dempster writes, "If there is one indispensable key to effective learning, it is distributed practice. But in an overstuffed curriculum, there is little opportunity for distributed practice."[134] The National Research Council's study of learning and schooling agrees: "Time on task is a major indicator for learning....Superficial coverage of all topics in a subject must be replaced with in-depth coverage of fewer topics that allows key concepts in that discipline to be understood."[135]

In short, cognitive science research makes it clear that superficial coverage of lots of isolated facts in history courses won't get the job done. We are wasting everyone's time and money unless students are taught and retaught important principles and concepts in multiple contexts over an extended period of time.

In history, a great volume is unrolled for our instruction, drawing the materials of future wisdom from the past errors and infirmities of mankind.

–Edmund Burke, *Reflections on the French Revolution*, 1790

CHAPTER SEVEN

Basic principles of history education

*Five commonsense principles address
the five basic problems of history education.*

It's often said that every problem presents an opportunity, and this may be true in the field of history education. In Chapter 2, we encountered five basic problems that undermine history education: It lacks a coherent *purpose* to guide instruction, and it lacks principles of knowledge *relevant* to the future. The *importance* and *scale-to-detail* problems work together to produce superficial and trivial learning, and the *cognition* problem results from instruction that is incompatible with the way human minds learn.

If educators wished to address these five basic problems of history education, each problem could be turned around to represent a positive principle for improving historical learning. Chapter 5 tackled the *irrelevance* problem by showing that history, like other school subjects, possesses enduring principles of knowledge, plus three additional kinds of knowledge relevant to the future. Chapter 6 addressed the *cognition* problem by identifying four cognitive learning strategies meant to facilitate the transfer of useful learning from school to adult life.

This chapter addresses the remaining three basic problems of history education. It seeks to identify the rightful *purpose* of history education and to identify reasonable measures for countering the *importance* and *scale-to-detail* problems. Taken together, these commonsense solutions represent five positive principles designed to achieve effective history instruction as summarized in the following table.

Figure 15. Five basic principles of history education

PRINCIPLE	DESCRIPTION
Purpose	A mission of fostering judgment in human affairs gives history education a coherent and useful purpose to guide instruction.
Relevance	Historical knowledge is suitable for educational purposes when it imparts principles and concepts relevant to the future.
Importance	Superficial and trivial learning can be limited by emphasizing more-important knowledge over less-important knowledge.
Scale-to-detail	Superficial and trivial learning can be limited by appropriately matching the level of factual detail in a history course to the scale of the course.
Cognition	The transfer of school learning to life beyond school is most likely to succeed when relevant and important knowledge is learned in multiple contexts over an extended period of time.

THE *PURPOSE* PRINCIPLE

The first ingredient for teaching a school subject is a good reason to teach it. It's commonly said that history is taught in schools and colleges so that students can "learn about the past," with little or no explanation as to how such learning will benefit students and society.[136] Learning about the past appears to be another of those unspecified intrinsic goods that characterize history education, much like learning historical thinking skills or making connections. Such vague and empty rationales are not helpful. History education requires a clear and coherent purpose to guide instruction toward productive use and away from the trivia that always threatens to overtake history instruction.

What, then, is the rightful purpose of historical learning? I'll leave that question to a number of smart people who have reached essentially the same conclusion down through the ages from ancient times to the present day: *The purpose of historical learning is to inform future judgment in human affairs.*

Writing in Greece of the fifth century BC, the pioneering historian Thucydides identified his role as providing knowledge of the past as an aid to understanding the future."[137]

During the Renaissance, Machiavelli wrote, "Whoever wishes to foresee the future must consult the past; for human events ever resemble those of preceding times."[138] Thomas Jefferson, the primary author of America's Declaration of Independence, described how historical learning would benefit the citizens of his new nation:

> History, by apprising them of the past, will enable them to judge of the future. It will avail them of the experience of other times and other nations; it will qualify them as judges of the actions and designs of men.[139]

Woodrow Wilson, president during World War I, is quoted as saying that history's highest aim is to endow society with "the invaluable mental power we call judgment."[140] The Bradley Commission on History in the Schools said, "The study of the past is essential to informed judgment and democratic citizenship."[141] Jacques Barzun, a founder of the field of cultural history, described "the highest value of history [as] judgment in worldly affairs."[142] The contemporary historian of education Diane Ravitch says that history "helps to inform us so that we might make better decisions in the future."[143]

Are these people correct? Is the rightful purpose of historical learning to foster future judgment in human affairs? Let's apply a bit of logic to the question to see where it leads. As you know, the guiding premise of this book is this: *Education exists to impart important knowledge of the world that can help students and society to function effectively in the future.* Assuming this premise is valid, history education likewise exists to impart knowledge that can help students and society to function effectively in the future.

What does it mean to "function effectively in the future"? Effective future functioning is based on sound judgment, which informs effective decision-making and action. Thus, the chain of logic goes like this: (a) history education exists to impart knowledge that can help students and society to function effectively in the future, (b) effective functioning in the future depends on informed judgment, and (c) history is the realm of knowledge concerned with human affairs. Therefore, the logical first purpose of history education is to foster (a) future (b) judgment in (c) human affairs.

Society itself appears to agree that history's mission is to inform judgment in human affairs, for society has granted to history the unique and exalted position of Grand Judge of Human Actions. A truly momentous event is said to be "historic." Nobody wants to be judged "on the wrong side of history." No greater compliment can be paid to an individual or to an idea than to say he, she, or it "will go down in history." And the true value of a leader or an undertaking will be "judged by history." Society, it seems, has assigned to history the responsibility for making the ultimate judgments of human actions available on this mortal plane.

Society is onto something. Of the fundamental realms of knowledge, none is better suited than history to inform judgment in human affairs. History maintains an extensive record of cases of both good and bad judgment, and it traces the circumstances that prompted these decisions, as well as their outcomes. By contrast, mathematics and language function as skills, and science is concerned with the physical world. No other realm of knowledge shines a spotlight as history does on the judgments that humans make for good or ill.

Unlike the present-centered disciplines of language, math, and science, history takes the long view. It places today's concerns in the context of extended human experience. A single event might appear unique and inexplicable when viewed in isolation—as the Vietnam War first appeared to me as a young soldier—but a series of such historical events viewed over time may reveal patterns that can inform judgment. The long vantage of history revealed my disturbing war to be nothing more than business as usual among our violence-prone species.

And finally, people are simply incapable of exercising sound judgment without consulting past experience. This may seem a bold statement, but it's merely common sense, and it's backed by Bayes' theorem of statistical probability, which holds that prior experience is the primary indicator of future outcomes. Questions of probability are central to making sound judgments because it's unwise to undertake actions that are likely to fail.

So, yes, those smart people through the ages appear to be correct: The rightful purpose of historical learning is to inform future judgment in human affairs—a most worthwhile undertaking. As I noted earlier, any society that has developed the capacity to destroy most life on earth needs all the good judgment it can get, and—for the reasons cited above—there is no better place to seek it than in the long record of human experience.

THE *IMPORTANCE* PRINCIPLE

It's easy to say that curriculum designers should weigh the relative importance of historical topics and eliminate the less-important ones, but as a practical matter, how might this be accomplished? A Victorian gentleman named John Emerich Edward Dalberg-Acton offered some advice. Better known as Lord Acton, he was the English historian who notably remarked, "Power tends to corrupt, and absolute power corrupts absolutely." (A general principle of history?)

In his *Lectures on Modern History*, Acton proposed that the history of nations be told "according to the time and the degree in which they contribute to the common fortunes of mankind."[144] Acton's criteria of time and degree may be extrapolated to yield three reasonable measures of historical importance: the amount of people and land area affected by a historical event, the extent of change it prompted, and the duration of the event's consequences.

We can take Lord Acton's formulation out for a test drive to see how it applies to actual historical events. Earlier I proposed a hypothetical exam question that was meant to illustrate the difference between a question that asked for trivial name recall and a question that asked about an important historical concept, European imperialism. In my hypothetical question, I cited two historical events from the Age of Imperialism: the Opium War in China and Mahatma Gandhi's independence movement in India. I chose these examples because I considered them more suitable for inclusion in a large-scale world history survey course than the less well-known Mahdi Rebellion that was featured in the Virginia standardized assessment. We can apply Lord Acton's criteria to gauge the relative importance of these three historical events.

EVENT ONE: THE OPIUM WAR IN CHINA. Britain's victory in the Opium War of 1839–42 imposed the British opium trade on China against its will. At the time, China was a perennial superpower and the wealthiest nation on earth. Due to China's humiliating defeat in the Opium War and the indignities that followed, China fell from the status of first-rate world power to the position of a subjugated state under the thumb of Western colonial interests. The war initiated a period of turmoil in China that would bring an end to imperial dynasties dating back two thousand years and culminate in the communist Chinese government that today rules one-fifth of the world's population. The Opium War and its aftermath help to explain why China might still harbor feelings of distrust and resentment toward Western powers.

Applying Lord Acton's criteria, how does the Opium War measure up as an important historical event? Were many people affected by this event? Yes. Did it result in big changes? Yes. What was the duration of its consequences? Nearly two centuries and counting.

EVENT TWO: GANDHI'S INDEPENDENCE MOVEMENT IN INDIA. Gandhi's independence movement ended nearly two centuries of foreign control of India, once regarded as the "jewel in the crown" of the British Empire. Upon gaining independence in 1947, India was divided into the modern nations of India and Pakistan (at the time, present-day Bangladesh was part of Pakistan). Britain's loss of India opened the floodgates for independence movements that brought an end to European colonialism worldwide in a period of just 15 years following World War II. India became the world's largest democracy, and Gandhi provided a model of nonviolent civil disobedience later adopted by civil rights leaders elsewhere in the world, including Martin Luther King Jr. in the United States.

Were many people affected by this event? Yes. Did it result in big changes? Yes. What was the duration of its consequences? About a century and counting.

EVENT THREE: THE MAHDI REBELLION. The Mahdi Rebellion took place in the late 19th century in the Sudan in northeast Africa. It was a three-way conflict involving Great Britain, its client state Egypt, and Arab-Muslim forces seeking independence from both. After 17 years of sporadic conflict, Britain quashed the rebellion and maintained colonial rule over the Sudan that lasted until the mid-20th century.

Were many people affected by this event? Few in comparison to the billions affected by the events in China and India. Did it result in big changes? No, colonial rule was reestablished and maintained well into the next century. What was the duration of its consequences? Seventeen years.

Based on the application of Lord Acton's objective criteria, the Mahdi Rebellion was clearly less important to world history than China's Opium War or India's independence movement, two events that helped to shape the contemporary world and help us understand why the world's two most populous nations behave as they do today. These two events represent the kind of important historical knowledge that permits an informed person to engage in the ongoing dialogue of our culture, which is especially true now that both China and India have resumed their historical roles as major players on the world stage. The Opium War and India's independence movement have continuing relevance in the contemporary world, which qualifies them as useful historical knowledge suitable for educational purposes.

In addition to the criteria suggested by Lord Acton's dictum, another obvious measure of importance is proximity—the nearness of an event to the learner in time, space, or culture. The Mahdi Rebellion in the Sudan is more likely to be significant to a Muslim student in Africa than to a Christian student in Iowa, just as the American Indian Wars of the same period are more likely to be significant to the American student than to the African student.

The proximity factor is one reason why nations invariably teach their students national histories, sometimes to the exclusion of global history. Similarly, the temporal proximity of the Arab Spring uprisings to our own time—and their continuing impact in the world—makes them more relevant to us than the more distant Mahdi Rebellion of the 19th century. Events warrant extra weight in a history curriculum if they help students understand salient features of the contemporary world, especially if the consequences of those events are likely to persist into the foreseeable future.

To summarize, four criteria are useful for determining the importance of historical events, as outlined in the following chart.

Figure 16. Four criteria for weighing historical importance

CRITERIA	DESCRIPTION
Amount	The number of people and amount of land affected by a historical event.
Change	The extent of change prompted by the event.
Duration	The duration of the event's consequences.
Proximity	The proximity of the event to the learner in time, space, or culture.

Emphasizing more-important knowledge over less-important knowledge offers several benefits. It's a reasonable means for controlling the ballooning content of history courses. It's more likely to produce a common basis of historical knowledge that facilitates dialogue and understanding between people.[145] It's more likely to identify knowledge with lasting impact and continuing relevance, thereby helping students to understand the world in which they live.

Identifying the most important historical knowledge could assist with the task of devising a big picture of human development through time that is concise enough to be comprehended by the human mind. And stressing more-important knowledge over less-important knowledge can serve to limit superficial, pretend learning that steals time away from real learning. Perhaps now might be a good time to begin applying rational criteria to the selection of content for history courses.

THE SCALE-TO-DETAIL PRINCIPLE

A large-scale history survey course is like a telescope zoomed all the way out to reveal the largest features of the landscape. If instruction includes so many topics that little time is available per topic, then the telescope is set to the wrong level of magnification, one that reveals too much detail—not the forest, say, but individual trees within the forest. The telescope needs to be dialed back to a lower resolution that reveals fewer topics and leaves more time to explore the remaining topics in sufficient depth to achieve useful understandings of how they illuminate the workings of the world.

Limiting superficial detail can help students comprehend the bigger picture of history that survey courses are suited to reveal. As the historian David Christian writes:

> Some questions require the telephoto lens; others require the wide-angle lens. And as one shifts from smaller to larger scales, the loss of detail is, in any case, balanced by the fact that larger objects come into view, objects so large that they cannot be seen whole from close up.[146]

If your telescope is set to a level of magnification that permits you to see nothing larger than a rock in the middle of a crater on the surface of the moon, you may never see the crater, much less realize that you're looking at a celestial body orbiting Earth.

In a large-scale history survey course, the telescope needs to focus on large and important topics like Enlightenment philosophy, not on superficial details like the names of various men who thought about Enlightenment philosophy. Knowing about the philosophy and its consequences helps students understand how the world works, while knowing a man's name does not. In the same vein, it's fine if a student can recall the names of Columbus's ships, but historical learning should focus on the effects of the Columbian Exchange, for it was this unprecedented global exchange of people, ideas, crops, animals, and diseases that changed the world in profound ways—not ship names.

The other four basic principles of history education specified in this chapter can assist educators with dialing back the telescope to a level of detail appropriate to the scale of the course. A coherent purpose can provide a focus that prevents the curriculum from wandering off in unproductive directions. The relevance principle specifies four kinds of historical knowledge suitable for educational purposes; other kinds of knowledge would be prime candidates for removal from the curriculum. The importance principle's four criteria for weighing the importance of historical events can identify less-important content to be cut. And the cognition principle, with its emphasis on deep learning, supplies the compelling rationale for limiting excessive content that interferes with the transfer of school learning to life beyond school.

. . .

Over the last three chapters, we have examined five commonsense principles of effective history education. As illustrated in the figure below, these five principles can function like a series of filters to screen trivia from the history curriculum, leaving behind useful historical learning.

Figure 17. The five basic principles can filter historical learning

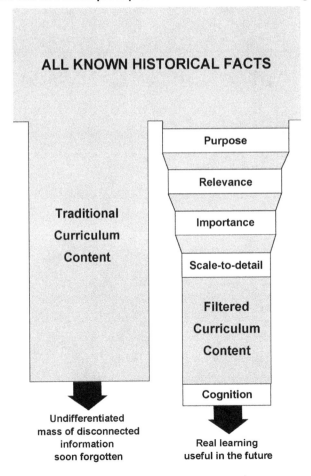

"It seems very pretty," she said when she had finished it.
"But it's RATHER hard to understand!"

–Alice, in *Through the Looking-Glass,* by Lewis Carroll, 1871

CHAPTER EIGHT

How useful is history schooling?

The Advanced Placement history program serves to represent history schooling in America.

Now that we have identified five principles designed to achieve useful and effective history education, we are in a position to use these criteria to address the most fundamental question that may be asked of American history education as currently practiced: How useful is it?

To gain a realistic answer to this question, we will need to apply the five criteria to real-world history curricula. The Advanced Placement history program has been adopted by so many school districts across the country that it has become the closest thing America has to a nationwide history curriculum. So the AP history program will serve as our representative of history education as now practiced in the United States.

The Advanced Placement program is operated by the College Board, a private test-selling company that also markets the SAT college admission exams. The AP division designs courses for a number of high school subjects including US, world, and European history. Participation in AP's US History course is roughly twice the size of its World History course, which is roughly twice the size of the older European History course.[147] Although AP courses are offered through high schools and taught by high school teachers, they are advertised as being equivalent to introductory-level college coursework.

The Advanced Placement program measures student performance with a single examination administered near the end of the school year. If a student performs well on the exam, colleges may choose to grant the student academic credit or advanced standing. The College Board company generates revenues by selling exams to accompany its AP courses.

AP got its start in the mid-1950s as a way to give bright students from elite high schools a way to skip introductory college courses. The AP program grew dramatically in the early 2000s during the climate of school reform that accompanied the No Child Left Behind legislation, as more and more schools turned to the Advanced Placement program to provide a ready-made solution to demands for higher standards and more rigorous coursework.

At the same time, students and their parents came to believe that students needed to accumulate AP course credits to give them a leg up in the competition for college admissions and financial aid.[148] And for years, AP participation rates (not student success rates) were the only factor *Newsweek* magazine considered when compiling its annual list of "Best American High Schools." Due to this convergence of circumstances, the AP program more than doubled in size from 1999 to 2010.[149] Although the AP program promotes itself as the "gold standard in American education,"[150] it's difficult to know if AP now functions more as an academic program or as a vehicle to catch the eye of college admissions officers.

EXAMINING OUTPUTS

In the world of business, it's relatively easy to measure the effectiveness of an enterprise by counting the number of products sold or the number of services delivered and the amount of profit they generate. Such outputs do not apply in the field of education, where outputs are concealed in the brains of young people, and the outputs only matter if they can be usefully manifested at a later time. Nonetheless, the College Board company markets its Advanced Placement courses to parents, school districts, and the federal government on the strength of beneficial outputs described in a body of research about the AP program compiled over a number of years, much of it sponsored by the College Board or conducted by researchers associated with the College Board company.[151]

Such research has consistently found positive correlations between enrollment in high school AP courses and subsequent success in college. But as anyone who has ever taken a basic statistics course knows, correlation does not prove causation. Correlations between AP enrollment and college success do not establish that taking AP courses in high school caused the later success in college. Academically able students are likely to enroll in AP courses and perform well, and these same students would likely perform well in college whether they had taken any AP courses or not.

The high school where I taught was too small to offer any dedicated AP or honors courses. All students attended the same core classes, but we had a solid group of teachers, and our academically able students typically performed well when they elected to take a full academic load at a nearby four-year college during their senior year of high school. It was a matter of able students in, able students out.

The tendency to casually conflate correlation with causation was evident in a 2015 study published in the *Journal of Educational Research* in which the authors noted, "Despite our complex statistical methods, we were still unable to say that participation in the AP program caused students to have higher ACT [college placement test] scores." But on the very next page of the study, the authors concluded, "Our MMW-S analysis provides the best quasi-experimental evidence available that students' ACT scores increase *as a result of* participation in the AP program."(emphasis added)[152] I haven't the foggiest notion of what an MMW-S analysis is, but I am quite confident that the second statement contradicted the first and assumed causation where the research found none.

A number of independent researchers from respected institutions have questioned the efficacy of the Advanced Placement program. A report from the National Research Council (NRC) found fundamental aspects of AP math and science courses to be "incompatible with a curriculum designed to foster deep conceptual understanding."[153] A study issued by the Center for Studies in Higher Education at the University of California, Berkeley, concluded, "the number of AP and honors courses taken in high school bears little or no relationship to student's later performance in college."[154]

Philip M. Sadler is director of the Science Education Department at Harvard University, and he is head of science education at the Harvard-Smithsonian Center for Astrophysics, which means that Sadler doesn't work for the College Board company, that college education is his business, and that he's probably pretty smart. Sadler was chief editor of a book that examined research about the Advanced Placement program, and this is how he summarized the book's findings:

> Many advocates of the AP program make sweeping claims about its broad impact on students: that they graduate college earlier, that they switch college majors less often, and that they are better prepared for college.

But at that gross scale, we find little evidence to support these claims and much evidence that contradicts it. Involvement in AP courses does not appear to bestow these global benefits on participating students beyond the habits and motivations that students already have on enrolling in advanced high school courses.[155]

EXAMINING INPUTS

As research on the outputs of Advanced Placement courses is inconclusive, the usefulness of AP courses remains an open question. Instead of looking at outputs, it might be more fruitful to look at inputs to determine if AP courses are *designed* to provide useful historical knowledge. If not, useful outputs are unlikely to occur. Having identified several basic principles of useful history education in the last three chapters, we can apply these criteria to the design of AP history courses. As a reminder, the five basic principles and their attendant criteria are summarized in the following chart.

Figure 18. Basic principles of history education with their criteria

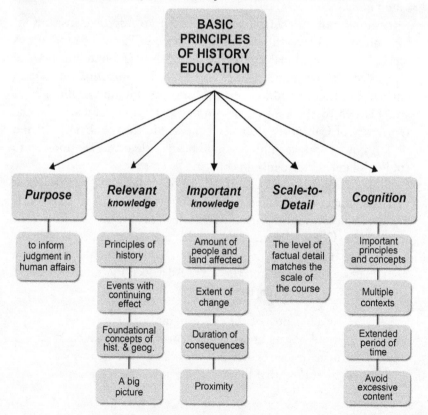

Advanced Placement courses are continually undergoing cycles of revision, which makes AP courses something of a moving target. This chapter's examination of the AP history program will focus on a five-year snapshot in time that extended from about 2009 to 2014, when AP history courses underwent a major overhaul. The AP World History course pioneered the new format, which was subsequently adopted in its essentials by the US and European history courses. (At last report, AP had dropped coverage of ancient times and most of the middle ages from its world history course, but was considering the possibility of adding a separate ancient history course.)

None of these AP courses identified a *useful* purpose for history education. The following phrase from the official US History curriculum guide is as close as they come: "Students should learn to analyze and interpret historical facts and evidence in order to achieve understanding of major developments in US History." Curriculum guides for the other two AP history courses offered the same rationale for historical study, except that the terms *World History* or *European History* were substituted for *US History*.[156] Left unsaid is why it's beneficial to learn about historical developments of the past or to what useful purpose such knowledge may be applied.

To their credit, each of the AP history courses did try to supply students with a broad, chronology-based overview of history, but AP's instructional blueprint has traditionally emphasized so much factual coverage that instruction was necessarily reduced to the superficial. As the *New York Times* reported, AP history courses have "been criticized for overwhelming students with facts to memorize and then rushing through important topics."[157] This is how a high school junior from Chicago explained his decision to opt out of the AP exam in US history:

> The problem with the AP program is that we don't have time to really learn US history because we're preparing for the exam. We race through the textbook, cramming in the facts....A few weeks ago, we were rushing through the 1960s with lightning speed. The Vietnam War is a fog. Somehow the New Frontier turned into the Great Society, which I always confuse with the New Freedom, the New Nationalism and the New Federalism.[158]

Kevin Levin, a history author and high school history teacher in Virginia, wrote on his blog that he advises his more motivated students to avoid AP classes: "If they have any interest in history I tell them to take my regular survey course."[159] College Board officials were getting an earful from other AP teachers who complained about the "tyranny of content coverage" at annual AP exam readings and in online discussion forums.

College Board officials responded to the criticism by repeatedly declaring their intention to reduce AP's emphasis on factual memorization in favor of higher-order thinking skills. In 2009, the College Board announced it was planning changes to several courses, including AP World History, meant to "foster students' capacity to think and reason in a deeper way." In the proposed new world history course, students would "reach beyond memorization" and "apply historical thinking skills" by focusing on "key concepts."[160]

ADVANCED PLACEMENT WORLD HISTORY

When the revised world history curriculum was implemented in 2011, it broke new ground. Whereas in the past, AP teachers had been given a general listing of required subjects, the revised curriculum explicitly identified the content that students were required to learn, a change ostensibly designed to ease pressure on teachers to cover every fact of world history and to silence critics who complained of excessive content coverage. Under this new approach, the fundamental focus of history instruction would shift from coverage of historical facts to coverage of broad historical processes that affected multiple countries or cultures. Specific facts of world history would be called upon to illustrate these larger processes.

The centerpiece of the new world history curriculum was a 66-page "Concept Outline" that specified the course's historical content. The Concept Outline took the form of a three-tier hierarchy comprising Key Concepts, Supporting Concepts, and Supporting Evidence. The top level of the hierarchy consisted of 19 Key Concepts arranged in chronological order that identified very large-scale historical processes. Written in a style that featured multisyllable words and academic-sounding prose, the Key Concepts could be vague and redundant, like these three:

2.3 –Emergence of transregional networks of communication and exchange

3.1 –Expansion and intensification of communication and exchange networks

4.1 –Globalizing networks of communication and exchange[161]

With little loss of information and a helpful gain in clarity, these three concepts could have been reduced to a simple, declarative sentence such as: *Trade and communication networks increased in complexity.* Simplicity and clarity of expression did not appear to be priorities in the new World History curriculum.

The next level down in the content hierarchy consisted of 67 Supporting Concepts arranged under the 19 Key Concepts. This is Supporting Concept 3.3 III from the period 600 to 1450 AD, roughly the middle ages:

> Despite significant continuities in social structures and in methods of production, there were also some important changes in labor management and in the effect of religious conversion on gender relations and family life.[162]

This Supporting Concept encompasses five diverse topics, and if you include the concept of continuity and change to which the entry alludes, that's six. This concept is therefore not a concept at all but a collection of historical developments, and the same was true of many of the Supporting Concepts in the AP course guide. In the world outside AP history class, a concept is a singular mental construct that expresses a coherent idea, such as imperialism or proxy wars; it's not a collection of unrelated topics tossed together in one long sentence. In his book *Applying Cognitive Science to Education*, Frederick Reif of Carnegie Mellon University and UC Berkeley said this:

> The specification of a concept must thus be sufficiently precise that its meaning is unambiguous (so that different persons can communicate with each other by attributing the same meaning to the concept).... Acquiring knowledge with poorly specified concepts is quite dangerous—somewhat similar to building a house on a shaky foundation.[163]

AP's fundamental confusion about the meaning of an educational concept so fundamental as *concept* is indicative of AP's surprising lack of awareness regarding the most elemental aspects of effective instruction.

The third and final level of the Concept Outline consisted of 212 items of Supporting Evidence, which identified additional historical processes along with specific factual information that students were required to know. This factual information fell into two categories: "required examples" and "illustrative examples." Both were required, but illustrative examples might be selected from a list of suggestions, or teachers were free to supply an example of their own choosing not on the list. In the AP curriculum, any of these interchangeable, illustrative examples would serve as well as another to illuminate a given historical process or collection of processes.

A teacher might choose ancient Athens as the example to illustrate the following set of three processes: "Cities served as centers of trade, public performance of religious rituals, and political administration for states and empires." But the teacher was free to select instead any of eight other examples listed in the curriculum guide or any other city of the teacher's choosing. In this way, factual memorization could be reduced because the student need only learn about one ancient city, not 3 or 10. And AP couldn't be faulted for fostering cultural bias by privileging Athens over a non-Western culture such as Teotihuacan or Pataliputra.

This approach, however, ignores the *importance* principle of history instruction, the commonsense notion that a history curriculum should emphasize more-important knowledge over less-important knowledge. By declining to specify which early city or cities students should study, the AP curriculum implied that all were equally important to world history, which is demonstrably not the case.

Teotihuacan, for example, was home to a powerful culture in central Mexico at about the time of the Roman Empire. Teotihuacan's influence extended to other pre-Columbian cultures of Mesoamerica, but the city was abandoned in the first millennium AD, and it had no textual writing system to sustain its legacy. Any residual influence that Teotihuacan might still have exerted some seven or eight centuries later faded with the arrival of Spanish conquistadors.

The classical culture of Athens, on the other hand, is considered the wellspring of Western civilization, and Athens remains a world capital. Classical Athens continues to exert its cultural influence the world over: We still read the same epic poetry that ancient Athenians read; we revere their art, study their philosophy, and base our government on rule by the people. Ancient Athens provides a number of contexts for students to learn about enduring principles of history such as *humans exhibit a propensity to impose their will on others, humans resist external control,* and *democracy can be a difficult system of government to sustain.*

While it makes perfect sense for a Mexican student to study Teotihuacan as part of his national history and heritage, that student can't be considered historically literate if he knows nothing about ancient Athens. Likewise, it's perfectly fine if a teacher in the US wishes to introduce her students to the mysteries of Teotihuacan, but it's absurd to suggest that an American student study Teotihuacan *in lieu of* ancient Athens.

In its choice of historical examples, the AP World History curriculum highlighted the impact of Bollywood and James Bond but overlooked Napoleon and Hitler (I'm not kidding). The curriculum was concerned about the effect of religious conversion on gender relations in the middle ages but unconcerned about the advent of the Space Age (not kidding again). Such blatant disregard for the relative importance of historical events defies logic.

SIX MINUTES AND THIRTY-SEVEN SECONDS. The new AP World History curriculum was meant to address one of the College Board's stated goals: to "reach beyond memorization." From the immense universe of facts that might be taught in a world history survey course, the AP course guide specified just 212 items of factual evidence that students needed to learn. AP students were required to know only two Enlightenment thinkers, for instance, instead of the half dozen or so specified in the Virginia history standards. But what the AP curriculum gave up in required facts, it made up for in required processes.

I spent a couple of hours one evening adding up all the required topics—the discrete items—identified within the 19 Key Concepts, 67 Supporting Concepts, and 212 sets of Supporting Evidence specified in the AP course guide.[164] As we saw above, AP's concept of *concept* could include multiple diverse topics. It wasn't easy to come up with an accurate count due to overlaps and redundancies among the various levels in the Concept Outline, but I tried not to count any topic twice. In all, I tallied 785 required topics, of which 235 were factual examples, and the remaining 550 were historical processes. If the new AP World History course was intended to reduce memorization by limiting factual content, the addition of so many required processes would seem to have defeated the purpose.

Given a typical American school year, an AP World History instructor would, by my calculation, need to teach an average of six new topics per class period to cover all required course content, spending an average of about 6 minutes and 37 seconds on each topic.[165] This figure encompasses all class time related to teaching and learning about the topic during the entire academic year including class discussions, writing activities, projects, reviews, quizzes, and tests.

In fact, this figure substantially overstates the amount the time actually available per topic because I didn't subtract for time the teacher must devote to other required AP tasks such as teaching historical thinking skills and historical themes and preparing students to write essay responses to AP exam questions. But for purpose of this analysis, I'll use the exaggerated figure of 6 minutes and 37 seconds per topic.

People who have attended school know that a student might need somewhat more than 6 minutes and 37 seconds to adequately grasp major historical concepts and events such as imperialism, capitalism, or the Cold War, which means that learning about these big topics would take instructional time away from the more limited and esoteric subjects such as the "effect of religious conversion on gender relations" in the middle ages. Consider for a moment this one multifaceted, multicultural process; how much time would it realistically take for a teacher to teach—and for students to gain a useful understanding of—the effect of religious conversion on gender relations in the middle ages? Could it be done in, say, 1 minute and 15 seconds?

The AP World History curriculum, with its 785 required topics, appeared to call for a great deal of "teaching by mentioning," which is the most superficial kind of instruction, the kind of instruction that reduces historical topics to meaningless tidbits of trivia. In calculating AP's 6 minutes and 37 seconds of instructional time per topic, I am applying real-world numbers to the *scale-to-detail* principle of history instruction.

If too little time is available per topic, the telescope needs to be dialed out to a larger resolution that reveals fewer details and leaves more time for each topic. Might it make sense to forgo instruction about Bollywood and the effects of religious conversion on gender relations in the middle ages in the interest of granting students, say, 20 full minutes to understand the capitalist economic system?

ADDITIONAL CONCEPTUAL FRAMEWORKS. In addition to the required course content identified in the Concept Outline, the AP World History course specified several additional conceptual frameworks. AP mandated that each student be supplied with a college-level history textbook; AP history teachers routinely assign their students the entire textbook to read. The textbook provided students with a second and even more detailed compendium of historical content to learn in addition to the content prescribed in the Concept Outline.

The AP curriculum also specified nine historical thinking skills for students to learn. (The role of historical thinking skills is discussed in Chapter 4.) Here is how the curriculum guide described the thinking skill of contextualization:

> [It] involves the ability to connect historical developments to specific circumstances of time and place, and to broader regional, national, or global processes.

This is how students could *demonstrate* the skill of contextualization:

> students should be able to evaluate ways in which historical phenomena or processes relate to broader regional, national, or global processes.

And this is how students could *develop proficiency* in that same skill:

> by recognizing ways in which historical phenomena or processes connect to broader regional, national or global processes. Students might then progress to explaining ways in which historical phenomena or processes relate to broader regional, national, or global processes.[166]

Apparently, in the peculiar reality of AP world, it's not considered bizarre to state and restate the same vapid verbiage four times in a row.

Students were also required to learn 22 historical themes like technology, religion, trade, arts, and empires subsumed under five general headings such as "development and interaction of cultures." The odd thing about themes is that other Advanced Placement courses don't use them. Students in disciplines other than history don't waste their time studying categories of knowledge when they can study the knowledge itself in the form of principles that can be used to accomplish useful tasks in the world.

The AP course guide for biology, for instance, stated that the course's content and concepts were "organized around a few underlying principles called big ideas."[167] These principles were written in the present tense, which meant they had ongoing and universal applicability. AP Biology's general principles explained, among other things, how DNA synthesizes protein and how species evolve through natural selection, while the 550 one-time, bygone processes specified in the World History course didn't explain how anything does anything in the present or future. Because the current paradigm of history education doesn't provide students with principles of how the world works, the AP program supplied students with 22 categories of knowledge to learn instead.

The final conceptual framework specified in the AP World History curriculum was a periodization scheme. *Periodization* is the term used by history types to describe the periods into which we slice up history. The practice of dividing the long span of history into smaller, more manageable chunks with unifying characteristics is intended to make history easier to digest than confronting one, long, unbroken mass of time. Seldom, however, do two different textbooks or instructional programs use the same periodization scheme.

The AP curriculum divided world history into six time periods dating from approximately 8,000 BC to the present. For purposes that will soon become clear, I've arranged the six time periods in alphabetical order:

a. Accelerating global change and realignment
b. Global interactions
c. Industrialization and global integration
d. Organization and reorganization of human societies
e. Regional and transregional interactions
f. Technological and environmental transformations[168]

Do you find it clear from reading this list which periods of history these labels refer to? Let's try a little quiz. Please mentally assign the following two historical events to their proper time periods in the AP periodization scheme above.

–civilization arises in Egypt
–the greenhouse effect

Finished? If you assigned Egyptian civilization to item d, "Organization and reorganization of human societies," sorry, you got it wrong. If you assigned the greenhouse effect to item f, "Technological and environmental transformations," you missed that one. If you missed them both, my condolences; you're clearly not AP material. (The correct answers are f. and a.)

Here's another brief quiz. Assign the *rise of Egyptian civilization* and the *greenhouse effect* to their proper time periods in the periodization scheme that I used in my world history courses (also arranged alphabetically).

ancient times
middle ages
modern times
prehistory

If you thought Egyptian civilization arose during ancient times, and the greenhouse effect is a feature of modern times, congratulations; you just earned an A+ in my curriculum. Obviously, the point of this exercise is to demonstrate that it is easier to understand simple, clear, and familiar terms than to understand unfamiliar, pretentious, and ambiguous ones.

The purpose of a periodization scheme is to orient one in time. If I tell you that an event occurred in prehistory or in the middle ages, you are likely able to place that event in its general historical context. Your mind may summon images representative of these time periods such as a cave dwelling or a knight in armor. But if I tell you that an event occurred during the period of "accelerating global change and realignment," you have heard a highfalutin' but essentially meaningless phrase that may apply to virtually any era of history. This label is too vague to identify a specific historical period and too devoid of meaning to evoke any mental associations that might serve to orient one in time.

Of these two periodization schemes, AP's and mine, which is more likely to be useful to students operating in the real world that exists outside AP history class? Which is unlikely to ever surface again in the entire lifetime of any student who doesn't become an AP history teacher?

Now that you have completed two quizzes dealing with the usefulness of historical content knowledge, I would like to ask you to engage in a test of cognition. Please take a few seconds to look over my periodization scheme arranged in proper chronological sequence, and try to remember the time periods in order. (It might help to think of your friend Pamm.) Then close your eyes and see if you can name the four eras in order.

Prehistory	Ancient Times	Middle Ages	Modern Times

Piece of cake, right? The four terms in this periodization scheme are widely known in our culture, can be found in a dictionary, can be visualized in working memory, and can be stored in long-term memory, where they will be reinforced repeatedly over the course of a person's lifetime.

Now, here is the AP World History periodization scheme also arranged in correct sequence. Same drill as last time: Look it over for a few seconds, try to memorize it, and then recall it from memory. (It might help to think of your ol' buddy Torgia.)

Technological and environmental transformations	Organization and reorganization of human societies	Regional and transregional interactions	Global interactions	Industrialization and global integration	Accelerating global change and realignments

Finished? How did it go this time? Not so easy, is it? That's because all this vague and unwieldy verbiage is incapable of generating a coherent memory in the human brain.

This AP World History periodization scheme provides a concrete example of the two standard breakdowns in learning that prevent school knowledge from completing the life cycle of real learning: Learned knowledge isn't remembered, and remembered knowledge can't be applied in the future.

Even if a savant with photographic recall were to commit to memory the AP periodization scheme, it could never be applied in the world outside AP class. It will never appear in books, magazines, television, movies, video games, or on the Internet; it will never come up in conversations with friends, family, or coworkers. This AP World History periodization scheme provides an excellent example of entirely wasted learning.

TAKE-AWAYS FROM AP WORLD HISTORY. What does the AP World History curriculum tell us about the usefulness of history education as currently practiced in the United States? As is clear from the periodization scheme described above, the curriculum was little concerned with imparting knowledge that could be transferred from school to life beyond school.

The curriculum identified no useful purpose to guide history instruction. It ignored the commonsense principle that schooling should emphasize more-important knowledge over less-important knowledge. It violated the *scale-to-detail* principle of history instruction by allowing substantially less than 6 minutes and 37 seconds of classroom time on average for students to learn each of the course's 785 required topics.

The large number of required topics and the brief amount of time available to learn each one violated the *cognition* principle that calls for deep learning of a limited number of important principles and concepts. And finally, the AP curriculum violated the *relevance* principle of history education, which calls for imparting knowledge with continuing impact in the world. Most of the AP course dealt with one-time events from the past that had no relevance to the present or future.

In short, the AP curriculum ignored or violated all five basic principles of history education needed to produce useful learning transferable to life after school.

The AP World History course's obliviousness to basic principles needed to produce effective learning might help to explain why the curriculum was prone to vague and pretentious language, meaningless terminology, scatterbrained nonconcepts, and bizarre redundancies. Simplicity of expression requires clarity of thought. But if the AP history program could manage to dazzle the public with its fancy footwork, perhaps nobody would notice that it had no idea where it was going.

ADVANCED PLACEMENT
UNITED STATES HISTORY

If the revamped AP World History course failed to appreciably reduce the amount of course content that students needed to memorize for the AP exam, the College Board company had an opportunity to try again with its proposed revision to the AP United States History course. That didn't happen. The factual requirements of the US History curriculum far outdistanced those of the World History course.

The US History curriculum adopted a Concept Outline similar to the one developed as the centerpiece of the World History course. But US history is a course of a different color. Any attempt to identify specific content in a US history curriculum is fraught with political peril, as was abundantly demonstrated by the ideologically driven "History Wars" of the 1990s, which saw conservatives roundly attack the new national history standards developed at UCLA.[169]

Where the AP World History course specified 235 factual examples to illustrate its 550 historical processes, the US History course left behind no fingerprints in the form of specific examples to rile up touchy politicians and talk-show hosts. The new curriculum identified no required illustrative examples at all, telling teachers to come up with their own. Further, the US History course guide—unlike the World History guide—failed to specify which historical processes should be illustrated with examples or how many examples there should be.

Although it was vague on this point, the course guide could have been read to imply that all processes should be illustrated with examples,[170] which is a practical necessity if students are to actually understand the processes; it's exceedingly difficult to grasp a disembodied, free-floating process in the absence of concrete examples to make the process intelligible. As one experienced AP history teacher told me, "You can't have any sort of real conversation with your students about that particular concept—that Roman numeral and letter—without providing an example."[171]

Where the World History Concept Outline specified a total of some 785 required topics, the US History version listed 1,274 items by my count, and nearly twice that many if each process was to be accompanied by just one illustrative example. Based on 1,274 topics and a typical academic year, students would have on average about 4 minutes and 5 seconds to learn each topic, minus the time devoted to other conceptual frameworks such as themes and thinking skills.[172] If each topic needed to be illustrated with one example, that would leave an average of about

2 minutes and 10 seconds to cover each required content item, less the time devoted to other required AP instructional functions.[173]

I'm aware that these numbers seem absurd, and I wouldn't be surprised if readers doubted my calculations, but the 297 entries in the US History Concept Outline were posted on the Internet for all to see, and many entries contained multiple topics like this one did:

> A burgeoning private sector, continued federal spending, the baby boom, and technological developments helped spur economic growth, middle-class suburbanization, social mobility, a rapid expansion of higher education, and the rise of the "Sun Belt" as a political and economic force.[174]

This entry specifies 10 individual topics, and if students were expected to relate each of the four historical forces to each of the six consequences, then the number of topics jumps to 24. So it's easy to come up with a number like 1,274 required topics, if not many more.[175]

Meanwhile, the AP US History curriculum guide asserted, "It is vital that teachers explore the key concepts of each period in depth."[176] Rather than respond to this incredible statement with the sarcasm it deserves, I'll let the National Research Council do the talking. In a study of AP courses and courses offered by the International Baccalaureate program, a similar high school product, the NRC noted:

> While the written materials produced by the College Board and the International Baccalaureate Organisation acknowledge the importance of depth and focus, the daunting scope of the curriculum guides and the associated assessments in some subject areas sends a very different message.[177]

AP HISTORY FROM THE INSIDE

This overview of the Advanced Placement history program would be incomplete without hearing from AP history teachers, and probably no teachers have more comprehensive insights into the Advanced Placement program than those with one foot in the classroom and one foot in the AP course-design process. I spoke with four teachers who were serving on AP curriculum-development committees, two for US History and two for World History. Two were women, two were men, and they averaged 23 years of history-teaching experience.[178]

This was an impressive group of educators who included two recipients of national teaching awards. I spoke with them after the new AP World History curriculum had been in place for about a year and just before the new US History curriculum was about to be released.

Interestingly, none of the four teachers I interviewed thought that the new curricula would change their own teaching very much. They shared a consensus view that good, experienced teachers such as themselves were already teaching the right way, so they need make only minor adjustments to their classroom instruction to accommodate the new curricula. As one put it, "The better the teacher they are now, the less of a sea change it will appear."

Some of these teachers expressed concern for beginning teachers and teachers new to the Advanced Placement system who might struggle with the revamped AP curricula. Said one, "It's always just the new teachers... that we're really focusing on. The people who have been teaching it didn't have to change anything other than maybe reconsider how much time they're spending [on each historical time period]."

Although the new curricula switched the fundamental focus of instruction from specific historical facts to multicultural processes, and the College Board heralded its new approach as a significant departure from past practices, expert AP teachers were telling me that the new curricula wouldn't change instruction very much. This was my first indication of a disconnect between the official AP curricula and actual teaching practice.

Another indication came when I questioned one of the teachers about a specific entry in the Concept Outline. I wanted to know if teachers were expected to teach each of the many hundreds of discrete items specified in the course guide, and as an example I cited a typical multiple-part entry that discussed a historical process that occurred in several geographic locations. I asked if teachers were obliged to teach how this process affected all the specified locations. Here is a snippet of that conversation:

AP TEACHER: "Well, yes and no. Obliged sounds a little bit too strong for me; teachers have to make choices....Pointing to this one part of the course description and asking me 'Are teachers obliged to teach all of this'—they don't have to teach any of this."

ME: "Oh, okay; I thought it was required content."

AP TEACHER: "Well, it is required. Required just means that it could be on the exam. That's what it means to be required."

Here was an accomplished AP teacher—a teacher who had helped to develop the AP history curriculum and who was a trainer of AP teachers—telling me quite openly that AP teachers needn't teach all the required content specified in the official curriculum, and, in fact, "they don't have to teach any of this." Explaining further, this teacher said, "Teachers have to dare to omit." Another teacher expressed a similar sentiment in a different way: "I have to somehow go through that entire curriculum framework and say, 'Well, I have to cover all of this,' but I know that something has to be underemphasized."

These comments reflected the reality of a curriculum that is too big to teach in the time available to teach it, a mismatch between *scale* and *detail*. Said one teacher, "It's daunting for the students; it's daunting for the teachers."

The gap between AP's extensive curriculum requirements and the capacity of teachers to meet these requirements placed teachers in a difficult position. Each of the AP teachers with whom I spoke used words like *fear*, *scared*, and *high anxiety* to describe the stress teachers are under to meet the demands of the AP curriculum. Said one, "There is tension in the document—there is tension in the community."

Anxiety about the AP exam is warranted. Only about half of AP World and US History students obtain a score of three or higher on a five-point scale, which AP considers a passing grade. Many observers believe that a minimum score of four is a more realistic requirement for demonstrating proficiency on college-level work.[179] According to *Politico*, fully one-third of colleges that award AP credit require their students to earn exam scores of four or five.[180] If these more stringent criteria were imposed on all students, the overall AP history failure rate would jump to 73 percent and 91 percent, respectively.[181]

Meanwhile, AP teachers are "all under pressure to score well," said one of my interviewees. Another observed that savvy teachers are more concerned about the test than the official curriculum: "Teachers don't care about that....They want to see the test...once teachers see the new test, I don't think they're going to be as fearful as they were before they saw it."

If I were to sum up what I learned from this group of talented AP teachers and experienced curriculum designers, it would be this: The AP history curricula contain too many content requirements and conceptual frameworks to be taught by even expert teachers, and this creates stress among teachers and students. Teachers have to choose what to teach and what to cut, and their best sources of guidance are relevant teaching experience and the AP exam. Due to high turnover among AP teachers, many do not have relevant experience, so they are left to teach to the test.

The AP teachers I interviewed readily acknowledged the complexity of the AP history program, with its extensive content requirements and multiple moving parts. But these teachers—some more reluctantly than others—seemed resigned to such complexity as an inevitable aspect of AP culture. "It is complex," said one teacher, "but that's going to be my job I guess...how to make it user friendly. You know, the automobile works pretty well, and it gets us from here to there, so I guess we have to figure it out—how to get all those parts to work together."

It's a telling analogy. We make use of an automobile by turning a key; we don't need to assemble all the moving parts. The value of an automobile lies in its capacity to reduce complexity to a level of simplicity that is useful in living our lives.

WHY IS AP HISTORY SO COMPLEX?

It must involve making money. No other explanation seems plausible.

The College Board company is in the business of selling exams; it sells SAT college-admission exams and exams to accompany its Advanced Placement high school courses. With its official-sounding name and nonprofit status, the College Board cloaks its test-selling business in the guise of a public service agency devoted to "educational opportunity and achievement." Perhaps such noble sentiments play a role in the College Board's activities, but there is no question that the College Board is about selling exams and making money.

The College Board company is apparently not above greasing the political wheels to make even more money. In an article titled "Not-for-profit College Board Getting Rich as Fees Hit Students," *Bloomberg* news reported that the College Board spent $726,000 in 2010 to lobby lawmakers.[182] That kind of political grease can yield impressive results like a 2014 grant from the Department of Education to spend $28.4 million on AP tests for low-income students.[183]

The Advanced Placement program's business model appears to be based on quantity and complexity, a model that may be expressed by the following equation: Quantity and Complexity = Rigor = Elite Status = Sales = $. In order to persuade customers to purchase AP exams, the College Board must distinguish its course offerings from standard history courses offered by high schools at no additional cost to the consumer. This is where AP's "gold standard" motto comes in; it's a marketing slogan that says in effect, "We offer an elite product, so it's worth the extra money."

The elite proposition is based on the claim that AP courses are more rigorous than standard high school offerings. The rigor claim is based on covering more material in AP courses—which makes them "harder" than regular courses—and then testing students over this harder content in a high-stakes testing environment.[184] The rigor claim is substantiated by the high failure rate of students on these tests. In most other educational settings, AP's high failure rate would be seen as evidence of incompetence, but in the looking-glass world of AP, it's proof of rigor.[185]

In the world of AP history, rigor is achieved by covering a large quantity of factual content topped with multiple conceptual frameworks, which produces superficial instruction that leaves substantially less than 4.1 to 6.6 minutes of classroom time on average for students to learn and absorb each required topic. AP's claim to rigor makes sense only if rigor is defined as superficial instruction accompanied by high failure rates.

The Advanced Placement program has some harsh critics. The education historian Tim Lacy wrote that AP "has become a potentially tragic morality tale about corporate-style revenue grabbing and the subversion of AP's non-profit ethos."[186] Ted O'Neill, former dean of admissions at the University of Chicago, said, "The College Board is more interested in marketing and selling things than in its primary responsibility, promoting equity and educational opportunity."[187]

John Tierney taught AP American government courses at a private school after retiring from a career as a professor at Boston College. He calls Advanced Placement "a scam"—a great fraud perpetrated on American high school students. Writing for *The Atlantic*, Tierney said that AP courses are "not remotely equivalent to the college-level courses they are said to approximate....The courses cover too much material and do so too quickly and superficially....The AP classroom is where intellectual curiosity goes to die."[188]

JUDGING THE USEFULNESS OF AP HISTORY

The AP United States History course and the AP World History course followed similar approaches to instruction, teaching large quantities of inert facts possessing little or no relevance to the present and future, and teaching these facts in a manner that is incompatible with how human minds learn. The AP history program's curriculum guides exhibited no discernible indication that any thought whatsoever was given to how historical knowledge acquired in its courses might be applied to life in the future.

By contrast, the five basic principles of history education featured in this book are specifically designed to produce learning useful in the future. The figure below is a visual metaphor that likens the five basic principles of history education to five basic components needed to keep an airplane in the air and flying toward a desired destination

Figure 19. A visual metaphor for the five basic principles of history education

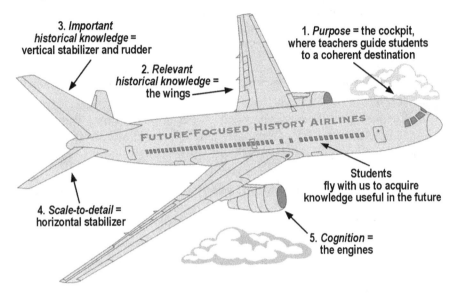

The following visual metaphor represents a different kind of history curriculum, one that ignores or violates the five basic principles of history education.

Figure 20. A visual metaphor for history instruction lacking the five basic principles

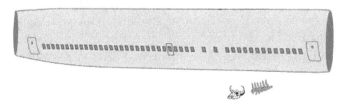

This airplane isn't going anywhere because it lacks five basic components needed to make it fly, a situation similar to a history curriculum that lacks five basic components needed to make it fly. Nobody would design an

airplane like this, so why do we continue to design history courses like this? My point is simple: If an airplane or a curriculum is not designed to fulfill a useful purpose, it will not fulfill a useful purpose. In the case of history instruction, it will not fulfill the fundamental purpose of education to impart knowledge useful in the future.

In my view, the Advanced Placement history program could hardly be more effectively designed to produce useless learning. Nonetheless, the AP history program thrives, so the College Board must be doing something right. The success of any endeavor depends on the purpose it is designed to accomplish. AP history instruction has at least three purposes:

Purpose One: To generate revenues for the College Board company. Result: resounding success.

Purpose Two: To enhance college applications. Many colleges and universities consider AP course credit as one factor in making admission and financial-aid decisions, while the more selective and prestigious institutions may not.[189] Result: a partial success.

Purpose Three: To fulfill the purpose of education by imparting knowledge useful in the future. If AP history is judged on the basis of how well it addresses the five basic principles of history education identified in this book, it can only be judged a dismal failure.

If the Advanced Placement history program truly is the gold standard of history education in America, it's easy to see why American history education is in such deep trouble.

. . .

Nothing here should be construed to reflect poorly on AP teachers. My only son was one, and I respect both his intentions and his abilities. AP teachers are the everyday heroes in this story; they are the people who work day in and day out to bring a sense of history to their students while working under unrealistic conditions imposed by others. They are the ones who never stop encouraging students to succeed on those all-important AP exams despite what are often overwhelming odds against them. And unlike the lavishly compensated executives at the College Board company,[190] they are lucky to earn an average wage.

If a nation expects to be ignorant and free...
it expects what never was and never will be.

–Thomas Jefferson, letter to Charles Yancy, 1816

CHAPTER NINE

Threats to judgment: ignorance and bias

Can history educators and the larger society face uncomfortable realities?

B ased on the evidence presented in the last chapter, the Advanced Placement history program is not designed to impart knowledge useful in the future—which is the fundamental purpose of education. If AP history is representative of mainstream history education in the United States, American history schooling in general is likewise not designed to fulfill the first purpose of education. History educators may choose to ignore this awkward reality, imagine that all is well, and go about their business, or they may choose to seek ways to impart historical knowledge that can help students and society to function effectively in the future.

The five basic principles of history education identified in this book offer a way forward. These commonsense measures are specifically designed to produce learning useful in the future. Other observers may favor different approaches, but unless history instruction is redesigned to impart knowledge useful in the future, nothing much can change for the better.

The beginning point of the five principles is a coherent purpose to guide history instruction, a purpose that addresses an unmet need in present-day schooling, the need to foster informed judgment in human affairs. No educational undertaking could have a more worthwhile mission. This chapter will consider how history education might deal with two major threats to judgment, ignorance and bias.

Countering ignorance and bias will take history teachers to places where they don't normally go, to places like emotion, intuition, patriotism, ethics, and possibly a gathering around the water cooler. We'll begin by looking at ignorance, a condition that may be reduced by acquiring realistic knowledge of how the world works as revealed in the historical record—but only if society wants to acquire such knowledge and only if society can manage to retain this knowledge in collective memory.

THE CYCLE OF HISTORICAL IGNORANCE

Jacques Barzun was a founder of the field of cultural history, and following a distinguished career as an author and educator at Columbia University, he died in 2012 at the age of 104. Barzun spent much of his long professional life thinking, writing, and talking about education, and he had a somewhat unconventional take on the concept of schooling. For him, schooling wasn't so much a process of adding information to young minds as a process of subtraction. He said, "The prime object of the school...is the removal of ignorance."[191]

The difference between imparting information and removing ignorance has significant implications for teaching. If a teacher has in mind the objective of removing ignorance, the teacher is relieved of the burden of trying to teach everything there is to know about a subject. Instead, the teacher can direct her or his energies toward the more limited and useful agenda of removing a student's ignorance about important matters in the world.

The teacher no longer asks, "Have I covered everything in the textbook?" The teacher asks instead, "Have I used my allotted time effectively to remove as much ignorance as possible from these students' minds about important workings of the world?"

When it comes to the task of ignorance removal, history education operates at a distinct disadvantage compared to other school subjects that supply universal principles of how the world works. Because history doesn't systematically codify its knowledge into principles that can be passed on from generation to generation, historical ignorance can persist indefinitely.

THE VIETNAM-IRAQ EXAMPLE. Americans have recently acquired a heightened awareness of the true nature of war, owing to the country's unsatisfactory experiences following the invasions of Afghanistan and Iraq. Americans have learned that invasions don't always turn out as expected and that they can hurt the interests of the invader due to the great human and economic costs involved. Today, commentators say that Americans are weary of war and in no mood to favor new invasions in places such as Iran or North Korea. This is a recurring pattern in history; it has happened twice in just my lifetime.

Americans gained a similar realistic understanding of warfare after years of bloodshed and frustration in Vietnam, and when it was finally over, I assumed that America had learned an enduring lesson from history. But with the passage of a few decades, memories faded. Fired up by emotions of outrage and revenge following the 9/11 terrorist attacks, America was ready to invade again—not once, but twice.

In Vietnam, America paid a high price for the simple but vital piece of knowledge that invasions can fail; but largely because education fails to carry forward such basic knowledge to future generations, this knowledge was soon lost. When a similar situation arose again involving Iraq, the relevant knowledge was forgotten or neglected,[192] and America repeated the same kind of mistake it had made earlier in Vietnam by attempting to impose its will on the people of a distant land—the same kind of mistake made by countless other nations and leaders throughout history. As Santayana said, "Those who cannot remember the past are condemned to repeat it."

WHEN ARE HISTORICAL ANALOGIES VALID? Care must be exercised, however, when attempting to apply lessons from the past to situations of the present and future. History is full of all manner of events, and a past event of one sort or another can always be found to serve as a "lesson" to justify any proposed course of action—an approach often employed by politicians, among others. In the run-up to the Iraq War, for instance, President George W. Bush compared Iraq's leader, Saddam Hussein, to Nazi Germany's Adolf Hitler and said that America must oppose Saddam to avoid appeasement of the kind that preceded World War II.[193]

Appeasement is the term applied to the efforts of England and France following World War I to avoid another terrible war by giving in to Hitler's demands—until Hitler's armies invaded Poland in 1939, which prompted England and France to declare war on Germany, marking the beginning of World War II in Europe.

While President Bush thought it advantageous to claim a correspondence between Saddam Hussein and Hitler, he denied similarity between the unsuccessful American war in Vietnam and his newer war in Iraq.[194] How is the public to judge when historical analogies such as these are valid and when they are not?

It's very difficult to judge, when society is uninformed about basic principles of how the world works in the realm of human affairs. If a politician were to declare that "Two plus two equals seven," and if we were ignorant of the principle of addition, we would have no basis for judging the validity of this claim. Similarly, the public's ignorance of basic principles of history deprives it of the knowledge needed to judge the validity of historical claims made by politicians and other opinion-makers.

If, however, Americans had learned in school the important and basic principles of history that *people resist being controlled by outsiders*, and that *many or most military invasions of distant lands fail over the long term*, Americans would have been in a position to recognize that these two principles applied to the invasions of both Vietnam and Iraq. Because our schooling system left Americans ignorant of basic principles of how the world works, the public was in no position to recognize the fundamental similarities between the two situations.

The appeasement of Hitler prior to World War II was a one-time historical development, and historians have disagreed about its implications. Many historians now view Britain's Munich Agreement with Hitler as a rational response to the existing situation, one that bought England time to build up its armaments before going to war against the Nazis.[195]

Any individual historical event—an *n* of 1—is not a dependable indicator of future outcomes. It's only when similar dynamics have been repeated with some frequency over time that historical knowledge can reliably serve to inform future judgment—and even then, such knowledge can serve only to inform; it cannot prescribe a specific course of action in a particular case. Informed judgment requires more than one or two previous examples of a dynamic in history; judgment also involves factors such as the persistence of the dynamic in history, knowledge of the particular case at hand, and a fair weighing of differing opinions.

Future-focused history education could provide the public with assistance in judging the validity of historical claims in at least two ways. It could teach students basic principles of how the world works that would provide a foundation for judging such claims, and it could teach students to require more than one example of a historical analogy to justify a proposed course of action.

A NOTE ABOUT TERMINOLOGY. People typically use the term *lessons of history* to describe knowledge gained from past experience that can be applied in the future. However, this term might not be the best designation for knowledge derived from multiple past occurrences, because a *lesson of history* may refer to a single historical event. (The term *historical analogue*, favored by the Harvard Applied History Project, can involve a similar ambiguity.) And a *lesson from history* may imply prescription rather than useful intelligence.

The terms *general principles, recurring dynamics, recurring patterns*, or *tendencies* of history might be more appropriate for describing generalizations derived from historical experience, because these terms denote knowledge gained from multiple similar occurrences rather than from a single event. Although a term such as *recurring dynamics* of history may be more palatable to some historians, I settled on use of the term *general principles* in this book for several reasons.

General principles useful in the future constitute the fundamental knowledge taught in school subjects other than history, and *general principle* is a generic term used in a wide variety of fields to label their enduring elements of core knowledge. It is history's lack of general principles that sets history apart from other disciplines.

The term *general principles* is related to the word *generalization*, which is how people such as Richard J. Evans, Steven Pinker, and J. H. Plumb—as quoted in this book—describe knowledge from the past that can be applied in the future. Also quoted in this book are G. W. F. Hegel and David Hume, who used the term *principles* of history in a similar way. Combine *generalization* with *principles*, and you get *general principles*, which is the term chosen by Jared Diamond (as quoted in this book) to describe this variety of historical knowledge.

And the terms *general principles* or *underlying principles* have been used by cognitive scientists, also quoted in this book, to identify the kind of learning that is most likely to produce successful transfer of school learning to life beyond school. All in all, *general principles* seemed to be the most apt term to describe knowledge derived from recurring patterns or tendencies in history—knowledge of how the world works that can be applied in the future, making it possible for students and society to learn from history.*

FROM IGNORANCE TO NEGLIGENCE. In Chapter 5, I noted that history's general principles are tendencies rather than laws or rules that always apply in the same way to similar circumstances. History deals with variable human behavior, which involves far more potential causal factors than, say, a chemical reaction. Just because history's general principles

---

* Educators have long wrestled with the question of what to call the most important knowledge available from a school discipline. The *Understanding by Design* curriculum model uses the term *big ideas*, while Harvard's David Perkins prefers the term *big understandings*.

describe tendencies rather than rules is no reason to ignore them any more than we would ignore important tendencies in other areas of life.

History's general principles are similar to the tendency of cigarettes to cause lung cancer and the tendency of a child to be struck by a car if she dashes into a busy street without looking both ways, and the tendency identified by sociology for people to engage in mob behavior and the tendency identified by psychology for a segment of the populace to suffer from mental disorders. Is society better off knowing about such tendencies—even though they are not invariable laws—or would society be better off remaining ignorant of them? How many people would suffer and die due to such ignorance? Surely, rational people would choose to know about these tendencies rather than to remain ignorant of them.

Yet, in the realm of history, society remains largely ignorant of powerful tendencies such as *people resist being controlled by outsiders, many or most military invasions of distant lands fail over the long term, war often breaks out between an established power and a rising power,* and *even superpowers experience limits to their power.* Is society better off knowing about such crucial tendencies in history, or better off remaining ignorant of them? How many people have suffered and died due to such ignorance? Surely, rational people would prefer to know rather than to remain ignorant.

But in the field of history education, ignorance prevails because the history professions do not officially recognize such tendencies and pass them on to future generations through education. With apologies to my admirable and dedicated educational colleagues, I must ask a hard question: How does the failure of history education to inform society about such critically important tendencies amount to anything less than an abdication of professional and moral responsibility that verges on criminal negligence?

A REPOSITORY OF VITAL KNOWLEDGE. There is only one place in society where knowledge of such tendencies may be retained and systematically passed on to future generations, and that place is history schooling. History education should be the place where society holds fast to important knowledge of how the world works in the realm of human affairs—gripping this knowledge like a life preserver on stormy seas—and transmits this knowledge to the young so they might avoid repeating unnecessary tragedies in the future.

But that's not what contemporary history schooling does; history education is preoccupied with relating one-off events of the past with little or no significance to the present or future. Unless history education identifies and imparts important principles of historical knowledge, today's realistic understanding of warfare will soon be lost again, and the cycle of historical ignorance can repeat indefinitely.

The cycle of historical ignorance isn't limited to matters of warfare; it can afflict other important areas of societal functioning, such as economic stability. During the 1800s, the US experienced a series of economic depressions before the Great Depression struck in 1929. Following the Great Depression, governments in the United States and other countries implemented financial controls meant to limit the likelihood of similar financial meltdowns in the future, and these measures helped to prevent another depression during the remainder of the 20th century.

By the early 21st century, however, Americans had forgotten that economies are inherently unstable and tend to careen out of control if not carefully monitored. It was uncontrolled stock market speculation that triggered the US stock market crash of 1929 that brought on the Great Depression. Seventy-nine years later, it was uncontrolled specula-tion in complex mortgage-backed securities that blew up the US housing market, triggering the Great Recession of 2008, the worst economic downturn since the Great Depression.

Treasury Secretary Timothy Geithner was the American official responsible for preventing the Great Recession from turning into another Great Depression. He attributed the financial crisis largely to a failure of memory: "There was no memory of crisis, no memory of financial panic," he said. "The system outgrew the safeguards of the Great Depression."[196]

Neel Kashkari, now president of the Federal Reserve Bank of Minneapolis, was placed in charge of saving American banks considered too big to fail because their demise could topple the entire American economy and possibly the world economy along with it. When asked if something like this could happen again, Kashkari replied,

> Sure it could. These things repeat themselves. The problem is, if we don't take action now while we still remember how devastating the crisis was, we're going to forget, and 20 or 50 years from now, it's going to happen again....Let's learn the lesson.[197]

The hard-won lessons of history—the recurring patterns and general principles—can serve to remove ignorance about important workings of the world, but only if society is capable of remembering them. History education has to serve as society's repository for essential principles of history, such as *economies are inherently unstable* and *people resist being controlled by outsiders.* If students and society can't get this kind of exceedingly basic and exceedingly important knowledge from history schooling, what good is it?

DO WE WANT TO REMOVE IGNORANCE? Principles of historical knowledge can help to remove ignorance by providing students and society with realistic understandings of how the world works. But perhaps not everyone is interested in limiting ignorance. Some social critics have argued that government leaders and powerful elites including corporate interests might prefer to keep the public in the dark about matters such as the causes of foreign wars, the influence of money in politics, and income inequality because it's easier to manipulate an ignorant populace than an informed one.

Noam Chomsky, the noted linguist and leftist critic, points to what he calls a small group of elites in society "who analyze, execute, make decisions, and run things in the political, economic, and ideological systems." These educated elites see the rest of society—to use the words of Walter Lippmann—as a "bewildered herd" in need of guidance. According to Chomsky, some of these elites regard the nation's schools as institutions responsible for indoctrinating the young, for keeping the bewildered herd "in line, out of trouble, and remaining always, at most, spectators of action and distracted from the real issues that matter."[198]

During my lifetime, the nation's ruling elites, including corporate leaders and presidents of both parties, have misled or mistreated the public so often that it has become difficult to trust what they say. Recent examples from the private sector include Enron, Goldman Sachs, Volkswagen, Wells Fargo, and Turing Pharmaceuticals, which infamously hiked the price of a 62-year-old drug by more than 4,000 percent.[199]

Examples from presidential administrations include the US policy of secretly overthrowing democratically elected governments during the Cold War that began under the Eisenhower administration,[200] the Kennedy administration's false warnings about a US "missile gap" with the Soviets, the Johnson administration's Gulf of Tonkin Resolution, the Nixon administration's Watergate conspiracy, the Reagan administration's Iran-Contra affair, President Clinton's declaration, "I did not have sex with that woman," and the second Bush administration's assurances that Iraq's Saddam Hussein possessed weapons of mass destruction.

These untruths turned out badly for many of the people who advanced them, for untold thousands of innocents in foreign lands, and arguably for our country as a whole. But such self-serving falsehoods were nothing more nor less than the nation's founders anticipated when they established the American form of government; they believed that rule by the people would be an improvement over rule by a small group of elites. As Thomas Jefferson said, "Every government degenerates when trusted to the rulers of the people alone." The people must be "the ultimate guardians of their own liberty."[201]

KEEPING OURSELVES IN THE DARK. If certain elites would like to keep the public in the dark about important matters affecting our country, they may be aided and abetted by members of the public who choose to keep themselves in the dark. It's been said that ignorance is bliss, and perhaps this is true for some of us who would prefer to remain ignorant of uncomfortable realities because it can be more blissful than facing the truth. Patriotic Americans, for example, who believe that America is exceptional among the world's nations might be inclined to overlook blemishes on our nation's record because these faults could undermine the exceptionalist viewpoint.

The reality is that America has been exceptionally wonderful at times, as when our forebears developed a constitutional form of government that became a model for the modern world; when America championed the ideals of freedom of expression and due process under law; when our nation welcomed the persecuted and dispossessed of other nations to create a successful multicultural society; when Americans pioneered equal rights for women, minority groups, and the disabled; when innovative and energetic Americans developed technologies that improved living conditions and saved countless lives throughout the world; when Americans enriched world culture with lively contributions to the arts and letters; and when Americans traveled to stricken countries around the globe to combat devastation from earthquakes, tsunamis, and famine and to fight deadly plagues including AIDS and Ebola. These are exceptional contributions of which Americans may be justly proud.

It is also true that America has been exceptionally bad at times, as when it maintained slavery well into the 19th century and legal apartheid for much of the 20th; inflicted genocide on Native Americans and drove the survivors from their lands; interned American citizens of Japanese ancestry in prison camps during World War II; overthrew more sovereign governments in the past century and incarcerated more of its population in prisons than any other nation; experienced more homicides per capita, more deaths of mothers in childbirth, and more of its children living in poverty than any other industrialized nation; and when America became number one in the developed world in terms of economic inequality and lack of social mobility. These instances of American exceptionalism are no cause for pride.

The question is this: Is our society better served by holding a realistic view of the United States and its role in the world, or is society better off choosing to see only what it wants to see? Democracy is based on the assumption that the people as a whole will exercise better judgment than will a small group of elites. But this assumption is based on the premise that the people have access to a realistic rendering of reality, which is primarily dependent on two institutions of democracy that don't flinch from portraying reality: a free and honest press and a free and honest education.

THE INSIDIOUSNESS OF BIAS

Even if we would prefer a valid understanding of reality over ignorance, bias can interfere with this pursuit. Bias may be conscious or subconscious. If I declare that I am a liberal or a conservative, I am consciously identifying my bias in the realm of politics. Subconscious biases, however, do not enter into our conscious thinking, so we might not be aware that they also exist and influence our thinking. A good liberal might believe that he is free of racist attitudes, but remnants of such attitudes may linger on a subconscious level.

We humans like to think of ourselves as rational actors whose attitudes, judgments, and decisions are based on evidence, but subconscious bias, by its very nature, is unknown to the holder of the bias; it presents itself in the form of intuition or emotions that lie below the surface of conscious thought. Although such subconscious feelings can strongly influence our attitudes and actions, they may be at odds with objective reality, which sets up the classic conflict between reason and emotion.

Economists have long subscribed to the *rational-agent model* of decision-making, a fundamental premise of economic theory that presumes people will make rational choices that optimize their financial interests. In recent years, the rational agent model has come under scrutiny by cognitive scientists.

When Daniel Kahneman met Amos Tversky at the Hebrew University of Jerusalem in 1969, they didn't know about the rational-agent model because they were psychologists, not economists. The two quickly became friends, and they set out to understand how people *actually* make decisions. Both ended up in the United States, Kahneman at Princeton and Tversky at Stanford. Their years of research revealed that human judgment is subject to systematic cognitive errors that interfere with rational decision-making.

Tversky died at the age of 59, but the work he did with Kahneman became so useful in explaining economic decision-making that Kahneman became the first psychologist to be awarded a Nobel Prize in economics. Their work supplied much of the impetus for a spate of books in recent years meant to inform the public about cognitive biases.[202]

Kahneman, Tversky, and other cognitive scientists have identified a number of cognitive biases that can interfere with effective judgment and decision-making. Among them, the subconscious mind can jump to conclusions based on little data or the wrong data; it is unduly influenced by that which is familiar or close at hand; it over-weights small samples and low probabilities; it favors loss avoidance over potential gains; it's overconfident about its conclusions, and if it doesn't know the answer to a problem, it may substitute the answer to a different problem.

Among the systematic errors in judgment that Kahneman and Tversky identified was one they termed the *planning fallacy* to describe plans and forecasts that are unrealistically close to best-case scenarios. "In its grip," says Kahneman, people "make decisions based on delusional optimism rather than on a rational weighing of gains, losses, and probabilities."[203]

Apparently, US Secretary of Defense Donald Rumsfeld was firmly in its grip four months prior to the American invasion of Iraq when he predicted the duration of the impending war. Although the three most notable American wars of Rumsfeld's lifetime—World War II, Korea, and Vietnam—averaged 6.3 years in length,[204] Rumsfeld optimistically predicted the Iraq War would last "Five days or five weeks or five months, but it certainly isn't going to last any longer than that."[205] As it turned out, US troops fought in Iraq for more than eight years, and American military forces were later called back to deal with the ISIS (Islamic State) insurgency unleashed by the American invasion.

As a secretary of defense under two presidential administrations, Rumsfeld surely knew how long recent American wars had lasted, but he chose to place his faith in a better-than-best-case scenario instead of a sober analysis of probability based on relevant historical experience.[206] Even Donald Rumsfeld—a man who portrayed himself as the hardest of hardheaded realists—appears to have based the most consequential decision of his lifetime on delusional optimism.

How could Rumsfeld have been so supremely confident and so utterly wrong? Rumsfeld's boss provided a possible clue at a presidential news conference one week earlier. When a reporter asked George W. Bush how he knew the right thing to do in Iraq, Bush responded, "I've just got to know how I feel."[207] In this unscripted moment, the president of the United States attributed the invasion of a foreign country to his personal feelings.

If Bush and Rumsfeld based their decision to invade Iraq on emotion rather than reason, so did a large segment of the American people who were gripped by emotions of fear, outrage, and revenge following the 9/11 terrorist attacks on the United States. The Bush administration successfully drew on these emotions to persuade the American public to accept the invasion of a foreign country that had done nothing to threaten or harm the United States or its allies, an invasion that was not sanctioned by the United Nations or by NATO, America's own military alliance.

Cognitive researchers have conducted a number of experiments that demonstrate the large role that emotion can play in judgment and decision-making. Daniel Kahneman has noted that "emotion now looms much larger in our understanding of intuitive judgments and choices than it did in the past....Judgments and decisions [may be] guided directly by feelings of liking and disliking, with little deliberation or reasoning."[208]

Psychologist Paul Slovic of the University of Oregon has identified what he calls the *affect heuristic*. *Affect* is the psychological term for an emotional response, and a *heuristic* is a mental shortcut or rule of thumb that can be applied when responding to a situation. In layman's terms, the *affect heuristic* describes judgment based on emotion. Slovic and his colleagues conducted experiments that studied the level of risk that people ascribed to societal activities such as the use of pesticides and nuclear power:

> If their feelings toward an activity are favorable, they tend to judge the risks as low and the benefits as high; if their feelings toward the activity are unfavorable, they tend to make the opposite judgment....These experiments indicate that *affect influences judgment directly* and is not simply a response to a prior analytic evaluation. (emphasis added)[209]

Daniel Kahneman cites the affect heuristic as an instance of *substitution*, in which emotion substitutes for conscious thinking: "The answer to an easy question (How do I feel about it?) serves as an answer to a much harder question (What do I think about it?)."[210]

Kahneman came to view the human mind as engaged in two distinct but complementary thought processes; one that is mostly subconscious, intuitive, automatic, and fast—what might be called instinct or gut feelings. This is where our subconscious biases live. The other thought process is conscious, effortful, and slower—what we call rational thought. People tend to be most aware of their conscious thinking, so they might believe that it's the only thinking they do, while in reality most of our thinking is done by the subconscious/automatic system.

The automatic system readily knows that two times two equals four, but if we should wish to multiply 178 times 326, the conscious system is called in to perform an effortful calculation. The subconscious/automatic system does most of our routine thinking for us; it continuously monitors perceptual data streaming in to our senses from the surrounding environment, and it takes appropriate action based on standard operating procedures derived from patterns of prior experience, and it usually gets things right.

It's an effective division of labor between the two systems that has served humanity well. Scientists believe that the automatic system is the older of the two; it's the kind of instinctive thinking we share with other animals. The conscious, effortful thinking system appears to be a newer addition that overlays the older, instinctual system. The conscious system has given humans the capacity, unlike other animals, to create symphonies and weapons of mass destruction, but our instinctual responses to these developments may lie buried in the brain's more primitive, subconscious system.

The subconscious/automatic system is best suited to dealing with routine operations encountered often before; it is less competent in dealing with the unfamiliar. It is with unfamiliar situations—and especially *important* unfamiliar situations—that conscious, rational reasoning is most needed to supplement subconscious thinking. The conscious system can supply factual analysis to counter subconscious biases.

Research suggests that combining the two thinking processes produces the best outcomes. Questions relating to important matters in society, such as waging war and maintaining economic stability, warrant careful application of conscious, evidence-based thinking processes. Simply knowing how one feels might not be enough.

Humans, unlike other animals, can call on the faculty of reason to place a check on their subconscious emotions in the interest of achieving better outcomes. This is not a novel idea; two and a half millennia ago, the ancient Athenians believed that reason was the true source of knowledge and that reason, not emotion, should rule our lives. Unfortunately, they were no better at controlling their emotions than we are. Due in part to emotions of pride and arrogance (which we label with the Greek word *hubris*), Athens suffered military defeat at the hands of Sparta and went into decline.

Nearly a century ago, Sigmund Freud, the founder of psychoanalysis and a relentless investigator of human nature, observed,

> Since men are so little accessible to reasonable argu-
> ments and are so entirely governed by their instinctual
> wishes....The voice of the intellect is a soft one, but it
> does not rest until it has gained a hearing. Finally, after
> a countless succession of rebuffs, it succeeds. This is
> one of the few points on which one may be optimistic
> about the future of mankind, but it is in itself a point
> of no small importance.[211]

MANAGING BIAS. Findings from psychologists and other cognitive scientists have worked their way into the world of business, where effective decision-making is a matter of utmost concern. Writing in the *Harvard Business Review*, two London management consultants and a professor of management at Dartmouth College described their study of 83 flawed leadership decisions.

Campbell, Whitehead, and Finkelstein attributed these errors in judgment primarily to two subconscious components hard-wired into the human brain: pattern recognition based on prior experience and emotions associated with these patterns: "Like pattern recognition, emotional tagging helps us reach sensible decisions most of the time," write the authors. "But it, too, can mislead us."[212]

Research has shown that giving people more information about a topic doesn't necessarily improve their judgment about the topic; it might only serve to reinforce existing beliefs and biases. Daniel Kahneman notes that thinking with the conscious system requires effort, and our brains are lazy, so they are inclined to accept what the subconscious system gives them. He describes the conscious system as more of "an apolo-gist" for the feelings of the intuitive system rather than a critic of those emotions. Psychologists use the term *motivated reasoning* to describe those situations in which "we spontaneously generate arguments for conclusions we want to support."[213] Or, as Kahneman puts it, when the "emotional tail wags the rational dog."[214]

The only defense against the ill effects of subconscious bias is conscious awareness that such bias exists, plus awareness that bias can interfere with sound judgment and decision-making, and the more difficult awareness that bias can affect our own thinking as well as the thinking of others.

Recognizing the existence of unhelpful biases can at least give us a fighting chance to reckon with them, but even Daniel Kahneman—who has spent a career studying cognitive bias in judgment and decision-making—admits that he finds it difficult to overcome his own biases: "My intuitive thinking is just as prone to overconfidence, extreme predictions, and the planning fallacy as it was before I made a study of these issues."[215] Ultimately, Kahneman places his faith in the wisdom of the water cooler, the kind of useful understandings that can arise from the give-and-take of discussions around the office water cooler.

Because it can be so difficult for us to recognize biases in our own thinking, the informed observations of others can help to root them out. This appears to be the consensus view. The management experts writing in the *Harvard Business Review* put it this way: "Given the way the brain works, we cannot rely on leaders to spot or safeguard against their own errors in judgement." The authors recommend "introducing further debate and challenge. This safeguard can ensure that biases are confronted explicitly."[216]

Here, then, are three general principles for managing bias:

–Begin by recognizing that we all possess biases that may interfere with sound judgment and decision-making.

–Seek multiple viewpoints including those that differ from our own. They can help us recognize and confront our own biases, and they might point up salient aspects of the situation that we have overlooked, thus improving our judgment and limiting future embarrassment or failure.

–Make an effort to forecast probable outcomes. Bayes' theorem would have us base these forecasts first on historical experience and second on circumstances of the present situation. And we need to be ready to update forecasts as circumstances change. Forecasting sets people to thinking rationally about likely results rather than relying wholly on subconscious assumptions. But it's necessary to recognize the uncertainty in our forecasts; seldom do we have complete knowledge.

When it comes to making judgments about matters of public importance, many people are gathered around the water cooler, and in a democratic society all are invited to participate in the discussion. Democracy may be a messy form of government, but it would appear to offer the best hope for arriving at sound judgments that serve the best interests of society as a whole—that is, if democracy possesses a citizenry equipped with a realistic understanding of how the world works coupled with awareness of how bias may impair judgment. Such a citizenry would be positioned to prevent its leaders from wandering too far astray.

And where might the citizenry systematically acquire such a valuable combination of knowledge? Only in school, and only in history class.

PRACTICING JUDGMENT

If history education were to adopt as its mission the fostering of judgment in human affairs, history teachers would want to give their students practice in making sound judgments. Teachers might involve students in *judgment-synthesis activities* along the lines of the source-analysis activities featured in Stanford University's *Reading Like a Historian* program. Judgment activities, however, would extend the process by considering additional factors involved in arriving at sound judgments. The judgment-synthesis activity I am about to describe represents a preliminary attempt to contemplate how such a school lesson might be structured.

This judgment-synthesis activity would take students through a process designed to counter the two major threats to judgment: ignorance and bias. It would begin by introducing students to a case study in which parties have expressed opposing positions. At the conclusion of the exercise, students would make judgments regarding these differing positions. The case study could be a situation from history or, preferably, a contemporary issue.

Students would begin the judgment-synthesis activity by studying historical accounts and other source materials relating to the specific topic under study. Students would then analyze these materials through use of a source-analysis process such as the one outlined in the Stanford program, which features four historical thinking skills:

Sourcing. Identify the source's *perspective* based on who the author is, his or her background, biases, and motivations.

Close Reading. Identify the author's *position*, including supporting evidence, persuasive language, and omissions.

Contextualization. What were the salient conditions, attitudes, and pressures present in society at the time that might have prompted the situation and influenced a source's position?

Corroboration. Do other sources support or disagree with the sources' positions?

The process of reviewing and analyzing sources relating to the issue is meant to provide students with a solid understanding of the particular situation under study, which is one of two kinds of knowledge specified by Bayes' theorem for estimating future outcomes. The other factor is past experience, which places the present case in the context of previous outcomes.

Relevant past experience may be found in the historical record—specifically, in the four kinds of knowledge identified in Chapter 5 as relevant to the future: enduring principles of historical knowledge, events with continuing effect, foundational concepts of history and geography, and a big picture of human development through time. General principles of history derived from similar situations of the past might be most helpful for informing judgment about the current situation.

Students would be asked to combine this knowledge of past human experience with their knowledge of the case at hand to identify who stands to gain and who stands to lose under the competing arguments and to make predictions about probable outcomes. Combining knowledge of past experience with knowledge of the case at hand provides students with a *factual basis* for making informed judgments, but such knowledge is not sufficient for arriving at a sound judgment.

Also needed are an *ethical basis* upon which to ground judgments and a *way to cope with bias*. Arriving at sound judgments would require students to synthesize knowledge from all four components, an ability that could improve with practice, especially if practice were distributed over several years of schooling.

These are the four key components of the judgment-synthesis activity:
–knowledge of the case at hand
–knowledge of relevant historical experience
–an ethical basis
–a method to cope with bias
We've considered the first two components. Let's now look at the last two.

AN ETHICAL BASIS. In seeking a suitable ethical basis, students needn't become bogged down in the specifics of various philosophical or religious systems if they choose to adopt the simple and familiar utilitarian formulation: *The greatest good for the greatest number of people that doesn't unfairly harm the minority*. This is the ethical formulation upon which enlightened, modern democracies including the United States are based.

Such an ethical formulation might be considered the prime ethic upon which additional ethical positions may be based. When considering the question of whether or not a nation should go to war, students might develop an ethical basis for determining when war is justified. In my history classes, we discussed this question after studying a number of wars in history. I asked my students to complete an opinion survey that presented a range of choices about when war is appropriate. The survey looked like this:

1. Never.
2. When our country is attacked.
3. When our ally is attacked.
4. When a country other than our ally is attacked.
5. When the US believes a country is committing an atrocity against its own people such as genocide or ethnic cleansing.
6. When an international organization such as the United Nations or NATO agrees that a country is committing an atrocity against its own people such as genocide or ethnic cleansing.
7. When a country has done nothing to threaten or harm the US or our ally, but the US wants to place a different government in control of that country.
8. When a country has made no threat against the US or its allies, but the US says it might become a threat in the future.

I tallied anonymous responses from my students and presented the results to the class. The most common choices were 2, 3, and 6. Very few students chose option 8, which was interesting because many students in class supported the Iraq War, which was raging at the time, and the US invasion of Iraq was predicated on choice number 8. When I pointed out the discrepancy between student responses on the survey and their attitudes toward the Iraq War, neither seemed to change very much. Perhaps these discussions prompted students to think more about the matter on their own, as cognitive dissonance can sometimes do.

RECOGNIZING ONE'S OWN BIASES. Now that students in our judgment-synthesis activity have acquired a good grasp of the situation at hand, have placed the situation in the context of extended historical experience, and have developed an ethical basis for judging it, they are nearly ready to formulate a tentative judgment about the competing claims in the case study. Because we know that bias can impair judgment, we need to give students an opportunity to cope with bias by asking them to explore their own biases and the biases of their classmates before making a judgment.

Survey questionnaires are available that measure a respondent's relative position on the liberal to conservative spectrum, a scale that might include designations (arranged from political left to political right) such as strong liberal, moderate liberal, neutral, moderate conservative, and strong conservative. Any student uncomfortable with revealing his or her political attitude should not be required to do so—responses may be collected anonymously—but in my classroom many young people were eager to state where they stood politically (which was usually where their parents stood).

At this point, students would be asked to formulate preliminary judgments about the competing arguments in the case—judgments free of personal bias, grounded in an ethical basis, and backed by evidence from historical experience and from the case at hand.

THE WATER COOLER DISCUSSION. Now it's time for students to share their tentative judgments with other members of the class. The purpose of this discussion is to make students smarter by challenging their evidence, biases, and conclusions—to ensure that nothing important is overlooked in a student's synthesis. This purpose should be made explicitly clear to students beforehand.

The teacher might begin the discussion by asking students to consider if they are locked into their positions or if they are open to persuasion by a good argument.

A student might preface the explanation of his or her judgment with a statement such as "My political attitude falls in the strong conservative (or moderate liberal) range." Class discussion would continue until all major positions had been explored, criticized, and defended. Ideally, this water cooler discussion would cause some students to modify their viewpoints. If such occurrences were made known to the class, they could serve as helpful models of open-mindedness.

FINAL JUDGMENT. Students are now ready to make their final judgments. All of the judgments could be compiled to determine the majority view of the class, a microcosm of democracy in which the majority view prevails. If judgment activities such as this were repeated several times over the course of a student's schooling, they would not only provide practice in making sound judgments; they could also provide multiple contexts for students to learn and internalize important principles of historical knowledge useful later in life.

BRIDGING THE GAP. A judgment-synthesis activity such as this could bring together the two camps of educators who now disagree about the basic purpose of history instruction: those who say that history should be taught as a discipline based on the practices of professional historians and those who say that history should be taught as a way to promote good citizenship.

Students who practiced formulating sound judgments in history class would learn to analyze conflicting arguments by applying historical thinking skills such as sourcing, contextualization, and corroboration. And students who learned to combine this analysis with knowledge of relevant historical experience, an ethical basis, and awareness of bias would be in a position to exercise informed judgment as citizens of a democratic society.

History teaches all things, even the future.

–Alphonse de Lamartine, *History of the French Revolution of 1848*, 1849

CHAPTER TEN

Taking the vision to school

*How future-focused history teaching might be
implemented in the American system of schooling.*

"**I** never understand World War II. Can you explain it to me?"
That admission and request came from the woman occupying
the front seat of the canoe we were paddling on the fifth day of a
river trip in the red rock canyon country of southeastern Utah. She is a
clinical psychologist and health-care administrator, an educated person of
more than sufficient intelligence to grasp the basic dynamics of the most
important war of our age—the greatest war of any age—but like many
people, she knew only bits and pieces of the story of World War II. She
had not learned the story in a coherent way that was meaningful to her.

As I proceeded to relate the story of World War II, other boats in
our little flotilla pulled near to hear it. I began with the wars of aggression launched by Japan in Asia and Germany in Europe, wars fueled
by nationalistic pride, racism, and the perennial human impulse of the
stronger to take what the weaker has—all recurring patterns in history,
all based in human nature, and all standard causes of war.

The story continued with the attack on Pearl Harbor that connected
the fighting in Asia to the fighting in Europe and brought the United
States into a global conflict. I discussed the Battle of Britain, the Allied
bombing of Germany and Japan, the Russian victory at Stalingrad,
the invasion of Normandy, and I concluded with the nuclear blasts at
Hiroshima and Nagasaki, events that ultimately reduced the invader
nations to rubble and illustrated another recurring pattern of history:

Many or most aggressor-initiated invasions eventually fail—a standard consequence of war.

My listeners asked questions, and with help from my son the history major, we answered them. The whole process lasted about 20 minutes. When we had finished, another paddler asked us to explain the Vietnam War. What does this brief episode of a summer afternoon on an ancient river tell us about historical learning and the American system of history schooling?

I believe it says that people have a yearning to understand the important historical events and forces that shape their lives, and that history education as presently constituted fails to provide it. Instead of hearing a story full of meaning about the world's greatest human conflicts and achievements—a story that illustrates enduring realities of the human condition—students hear disconnected fragments that add up to little or nothing.

. . .

We are nearing the end of our journey together through the landscape of history education, a journey that began by identifying five basic problems afflicting history education and proceeded to look for solutions. This book has been building toward a vision of history education which proposes that historical learning can take on meaning and value by imparting knowledge of the past relevant to the future. It's a straightforward and sensible idea that dates back millennia.

In proposing this vision of history education, I make no claim to special expertise or insight; I am simply an interested person who immersed himself in a subject and thought very hard about it. While my passion about the subject has led me to take some strong positions, it has never been my intent to say, "This is how it is," but only to say, "This is how I see it."

I am under no illusion that I have discovered the final truths of effective history education, but I hope this book can contribute to a frank conversation about the best ways to achieve it. Some readers will see things differently than I do, and I hope they will be able to look beyond their specific objections to recognize any grains of truth that might be lurking in these pages. Perhaps an improved version of this book might result from thoughtful feedback that I receive from readers at studentsfriend.com/book.html.

The vision of future-focused history schooling offered here is grounded in ages-old wisdom, common sense, empirical evidence, cognitive science, and my best efforts to apply logic to observable reality. These inputs have yielded five basic principles of history education that encompass a coherent and useful purpose for history schooling, four kinds of useful historical knowledge, four criteria for weighing the importance of historical events, and four essential cognitive learning strategies.

It's the mission of this final chapter to consider how such a vision of future-focused history education might be implemented in the American system of education. As this model of history schooling does not to my knowledge presently exist in current practice, it amounts to a hopeful suggestion that could only be validated and refined through the trial-and-error of classroom practice.

HISTORICAL LEARNING BEGINS EARLY

Cognitive scientist Daniel Willingham observes, "Some educational thinkers have suggested that a limited number of ideas should be taught in great depth, beginning in the early grades and carrying through the curriculum for years....From the cognitive perspective, that makes sense."[217] Future-focused history education is an attempt to conduct the business of history schooling in a manner that makes sense.

TELLING STORIES. Perhaps it's because humans began telling each other stories around the campfire in prehistoric times that the human brain seems especially attuned to learning from stories.[218] I have relied on several stories in this book to help get my meanings across. Stories collected by historians over millennia form the great record of human experience, and these stories are the starting point of historical learning.*

In the vision of future-focused history education proposed here, students begin to learn stories from history in the early grades of elementary school, stories that are developmentally appropriate to the age of the learner and—no matter how simple—are intellectually honest. As Jerome Bruner has said, "We begin with the hypothesis that any subject can be taught effectively in some intellectually honest form to any child

---

* The Story Corps project is a wonderful source of stories told by ordinary Americans. Unlike the nightly news reports, these stories usually reflect the more positive aspects of human nature. See https://storycorps.org.

at any stage of development."[219] The stories are carefully crafted to be, first, clearly understood and, second, meaningful; otherwise there is little chance the stories and the principles they represent will find a place in the student's long-term memory.

Whenever possible, the stories are tied to enduring principles of history that are valid both on the playground and on the world stage. For example, students might discuss the reality that people sometimes want to help and cooperate with others, while at other times people may want to take what someone else has. These are perennial human behaviors that even young children have experienced firsthand.

ASKING QUESTIONS. At Thanksgiving time, students might hear the story of how Native Americans helped early white settlers, and how later settlers drove Indians from their lands. I can imagine elementary students engaged in a lively discussion of the question "Does might make right?" Years later in a student's schooling, the same question can be revisited when discussing the Roman Empire, the age of European imperialism, and the American invasion of Vietnam. Grant Wiggins, co-developer of the *Understanding by Design* curriculum model, suggests orienting curricula around such essential questions "to put students in the habit of thoughtful inquiry."[220]

Additional questions that might be suitable for the future-focused history classroom could include these: Which is the more powerful force in history: reason or emotion? Are we smarter today than ancient people were, or do we just have better technology? When is war appropriate? Can ideas be more powerful than armies? Why do economies undergo cycles of boom and bust? What circumstances can contribute to the success of a revolution? Who has the best argument: liberals or conservatives? Is geography destiny? Is democracy fragile like an egg or strong like a rock? How did local fighters in America, Vietnam, and Afghanistan manage to defeat superpower armies? Which will win out in the end: the cruel, beast-like side of human nature or the side of reason? What things remain constant in history, and what things change? What does it mean to have an open mind? Which general principles of history might be relevant to this situation?

These open-ended questions have few definite right or wrong answers. When students in my classes encountered such questions, they were expected to take a stand and express an opinion, although I advised students that their opinions mattered little unless they were backed by historical evidence. These questions were meant to foster deeper understandings of important concepts of history and geography and to give students practice in recognizing what constitutes good evidence to support a solid argument. My students weren't graded on the positions they took but on the strength of the arguments they made. Always at the ready on my desk whenever I graded papers was a rubber stamp bearing the demand: "EVIDENCE?"

Such questioning can encourage critical thinking of the kind that Plato attributed to the instruction of his teacher, Socrates. David Perkins offers this brief summary of Socratic questioning:

> Questions in a broadly Socratic style can call for clarification: "Can you say a little more about what you mean?" "Can you give me an example?" "How would you compare and contrast these two ideas?" Socratic questions can seek evidence: "What makes you say that?" "What is your evidence?" Socratic questions can reach for other perspectives: "How might someone on the other side of the case look at that?" "What would a person from this or that nation or ethnic group or profession think about that?" Socratic questions can challenge generalizations: "Can you think of a counterexample?" "What do you think of this case, which doesn't seem to fit?"[221]

IDENTIFYING GENERAL PRINCIPLES OF HISTORY. After students in the future-focused classroom have developed familiarity with the concept of general principles of history, they are encouraged to identify potential principles on their own, based on recurring patterns they have observed in the historical record. Every principle of history proposed by student or teacher is subjected to scrutiny: Do civilizations follow a pattern of growth, flowering, and decline? Do humans exhibit a tendency to kill, subjugate, and discriminate against people from groups different than their own? Do most foreign invasions fail? Are economies inherently unstable? What is your evidence?

Students bear in mind that historical principles need only be tendencies that are likely to occur in the future—not invariable laws or rules. Students evaluate proposed general principles based on three criteria: Do multiple similar events constitute a recurring pattern? Does the pattern represent a valid principle of history? How likely is this principle to come up during the lives of students? Students might assign ratings to the last two criteria to determine the class's assessment of the validity and usefulness of proposed historical principles. The class can maintain an ongoing record of principles that students deem most *lifeworthy*, to use Perkins's term.

DEEP LEARNING. Teachers universally hope that students will be motivated to remember historical knowledge, at least in part because students will encounter the information later on exams. In the future-oriented history classroom, teachers emphasize a limited number of important historical principles and concepts to be remembered for exams, and this knowledge is reinforced and deepened over time through distributed practice. This learning is worth the concerted effort required to embed it deeply in a student's memory, for it is the most valuable kind of historical knowledge: wisdom that can inform future judgment in human affairs.

Deep learning of important knowledge is facilitated through judicious use of various resources and learning activities that can include written texts such as a concise narrative of national or world history, primary sources, secondary sources, literature, and poetry; through visual materials that may include timelines, maps, videos, photographs, objects, and websites; and through activities such as writing assignments, investigations, projects, simulations, and presentations.

Because no one can grasp the record of human experience in its entirety, future-focused history education attempts to appropriately match the amount of detail covered by the history course to the scale of the course, and it weighs the relative importance of historical events to ensure that the curriculum is not overwhelmed with excessive content that will interfere with learning important principles and concepts. The essential topics that remain are compiled into a big picture of human development through time that is capable of being grasped by the student's mind at the student's level of intellectual development.

LARGE-SCALE TIMELINES

The big picture is represented both visually and in narrative form. In visual form, it takes the shape of a large-scale timeline that depicts important eras of world or national history. In a world history course, the basic timeline might look something like the periodization scheme we encountered in Chapter 8:

Prehistory	Ancient Times	Middle Ages	Modern Times →

When this timeline is introduced to students in elementary school, they might learn a story about one characteristic historical development from each era, perhaps like this:

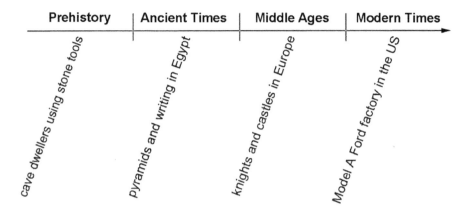

These four eras with their associated historical developments give students a solid, big-picture overview of how technology and lifeways have developed and changed over the course of human history. If both the societal and technological aspects of these topics are discussed, these lessons can serve as both early science and history lessons. This scenario presumes that a modest amount of time is carved from the school year to teach primary students something more than the math and language skills tested by standardized assessments.

To make the most of the spacing effect, learning about the four eras and their associated historical developments is distributed over most of the school year, with each new encounter providing a fresh opportunity to reinforce student memories of the time structure, its attendant eras, and their characteristic events. Learning is seen as circular as well as linear, with each new cycle of distributed practice deepening student understandings and strengthening their resilience in long-term memory. Imagine a coil spring in which each circular revolution advances historical understanding toward the ultimate goal of informing judgment and decision-making in adult life.

The following year, the teacher reviews the world history timeline with her students and asks, "Where is our country's history on this timeline?" Instruction then zooms in to the modern period to consider a few characteristic developments in US history. Then, the next year, the teacher zooms the telescope back out to view the world history timeline again, and students dig deeper into its structure by considering watershed developments that serve as dividing lines between the four eras, something like this:

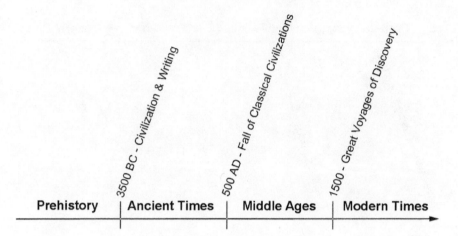

At this point, our students possess a basic foundation of historical knowledge: They know four eras of history, they understand characteristic historical developments associated with each era, and they recognize major historical developments that marked transitions from one era to the next. Without recourse to extensive memorization, students by fourth grade now possess a more sophisticated picture of history than do many adults. This foundation of knowledge is the structure upon which all subsequent knowledge will be attached during later years of schooling.

The importance of establishing early on a clear organizational foundation for learning is emphasized by Frederick Reif in his book on cognitive science and education:

> As much attention must be paid to the organization of knowledge as to its content. When trying to convey a body of knowledge, teachers should attempt to develop explicitly, and then gradually expand, a well-organized knowledge structure that students can actively use.[222]

The next year, students return to US history and consider watershed developments that serve as dividing lines between the four eras in American history. As the students' understanding of historical time grows deeper and their reasoning abilities grow stronger, they explore additional principles of history such as multiple causation, unintended consequences, and perhaps the three motivations for war identified by Thucydides.

Such general principles are applicable to both US and world history, and each course of study reinforces understandings acquired in the other. As students move into the higher grades and more formal history courses, their scope of knowledge expands to include major historical events that formed the developmental patterns of US and world history. At this point, a US history timeline might look like the timeline we saw in Chapter 5.

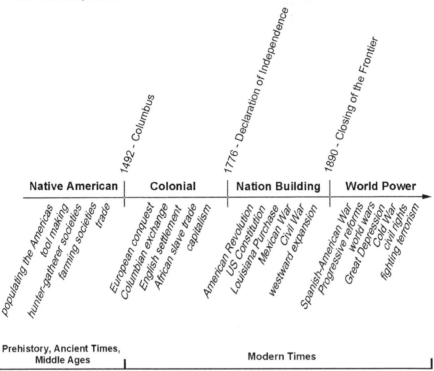

The Native American segment of this US history timeline is concurrent with the first three eras of the world history timeline: prehistory, ancient times, and middle ages. The last segment of the world history timeline, the modern era, is concurrent with the last three segments of the US history timeline: colonial, nation building, and world power.[†]

As students move through high school and into college, they may consider current trends that will affect their future lives after graduation, trends that might point to ways in which human behavior is evolving to

---

[†] The dividing line between the last two segments of the US history timeline is the 1890 US Census, which declared the American frontier closed. This was also the year that the last Native American hopes for independence from the white man were shattered by the 7th Cavalry's massacre of Sioux men, women, and children at Wounded Knee, South Dakota.

meet changing circumstances. Students engage in increasingly sophisticated judgment-synthesis activities, which not only provide practice
in making informed judgments but also provide additional contexts for
learning and internalizing important principles of history. The timeline
keeps pace by adding additional branches to the same trunk that students
first encountered in the second grade.

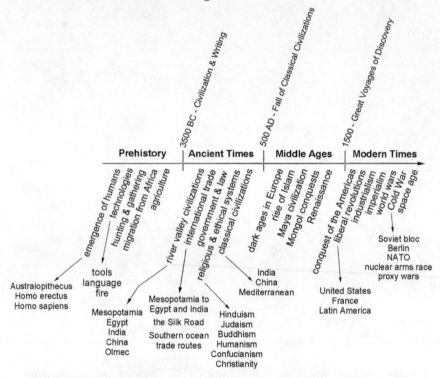

The timeline could be made to expand indefinitely to encompass
ever-greater levels of detail and complexity, but such is not the goal of
future-focused history education. The goal is to use multiple contexts
to deepen the student's understanding of important underlying principles and concepts of history that can help to inform future judgment
in human affairs. In order to achieve this goal, the amount of factual
content is consciously restricted to prevent coverage of excessive content
from interfering with deep learning of the most important knowledge.

A CONCISE HISTORICAL NARRATIVE

The large-scale timelines depicted above provide big-picture overviews
that make it possible for students to grasp the overall shape of national

or world history. These birds' eye views are fleshed out with written chronological narratives of national or world history that serve several instructional functions. Unlike thousand-page textbooks that supply the historical narrative in traditional history classrooms, the future-focused historical narrative is concise enough to be comprehended by the human mind.

When I began teaching, I set out to devise such a chronological narrative for use in my world history courses. In the classroom, my *Concise Outline of World History, Parts 1 and 2* came to be called the *Student's Friend* for short. As a standard 6" x 9" book, the *Student's Friend* runs to 121 pages. Unlike some concise histories that concentrate on impersonal historical processes, the *Student's Friend* includes men and women who helped to shape history and who reveal timeless aspects of human nature.

If I were to design a history course now, I would structure the course around important principles of historical knowledge, but my primary instructional tool would remain the concise historical narrative.

ELIMINATES GAPS AND DISCONTINUITIES. The *Student's Friend* formed the backbone of my curriculum, serving as a road map with a starting point, a destination, and checkpoints along the way; it kept my history course *on course*. Because I knew exactly which page we needed to complete by the end of each week, my students experienced something rare in history classes: They finished the text at the same time they finished the semester. As a public school student in the 1950s and 1960s, I grew up in the shadow of World War II and the atom bomb, but my history courses never got that far, so my classmates and I never had an opportunity to learn about these historical developments that profoundly affected the lives we would live.

When, as a student teacher, I was forced to rely on a textbook to cover course content, I had to skip sections and entire chapters because there wasn't enough time to adequately teach all the information contained in the book, which left big gaps in my historical coverage. The *Student's Friend* was designed to include no more information than students could realistically cover during a standard high school course. Within this constraint, the *Student's Friend* identifies a coherent body of knowledge targeting the most important events, people, and concepts of history and geography. Because the picking and choosing was carefully done and logically sequenced, continuity is maintained and gaps eliminated.

BALANCES BREADTH AND DEPTH. The *Student's Friend* offered another benefit. It left time in the curriculum for other learning activities meant to be meaningful and engaging to my students. By replacing the traditional textbook with the *Student's Friend*, I was able to strike a balance between coverage of factual content and exploration of selected topics in greater depth through activities such as research papers, multimedia presentations, projects, source-analysis activities, and simulations, a practice sometimes called "post-holing."

In my view, the historical narrative performs a unifying function, like a fence that gives shape to the landscape and provides the connecting fabric between events, while postholes are occasions to dig more deeply into the human dimensions of history—to explore the motivations that prompted or stifled change and to understand how events of the past affected people's lives then and now.

PROVIDES RELEVANT KNOWLEDGE. In the future-focused history classroom, a concise historical narrative such as the *Student's Friend* can serve as the essential instructional tool that brings together in one place the four kinds of historical knowledge identified in Chapter 5 as suitable for educational purposes, because they provide knowledge relevant to the present and future. As a reminder, these four kinds of knowledge are general principles of history, events with continuing effect, foundational concepts of history and geography, and the big picture itself.

The big picture supplies the raw material for recognizing recurring patterns in history, and it supplies the multiple contexts that students need in order to understand and internalize general principles derived from these patterns. In the *Student's Friend*, I tried to identify the most important events in world history. In the future-focused classroom, it would be the job of students and their teachers to determine which events form patterns that represent general principles, and which of these general principles are most relevant to the future.

The big picture also supplies a historical overview that can serve to inform judgment by placing current and future concerns in the broad context of human experience. And the concise narrative can help to fulfill the human psychological needs to bring constituent elements together to form a satisfying picture of the whole and to provide a sense of who we are and where we came from.

SUPPORTS COGNITIVE LEARNING PROCESSES. By focusing on the most important historical knowledge, a concise historical narrative supports cognitive learning strategies, which call for emphasizing important principles and concepts and avoiding excessive content coverage.

Cognitive science research has indicated that the mind organizes information into meaningful "chunks" of related information, while long-term memories are stored under mental categories similar to the file folders in a file cabinet. Each page of the *Student's Friend* is organized into four sections, and each section is labeled with a topic heading that represents a related set of facts and ideas. Thus, the information in the *Student's Friend* is organized into meaningful chunks, making it easier for this knowledge to enter long-term memory and become available to inform student thinking in the future.

CONCISENESS CAN BRING CLARITY. One of the greatest benefits of a concise historical narrative is the clarity it can bring to a student's understanding of history by focusing on essential knowledge rather than on extensive, confusing, and often-trivial detail. As one of my students put it, "When reading out of a textbook you never know what the important parts are. There is so much information it's hard to tell."

Cognitive psychologist Frank N. Dempster has written that US textbooks are "unrivaled in size and amount of information covered.... Unfortunately, many texts are so packed with facts, names, and details that the real point of the lesson is often obscured."[223] A classroom example may serve to illustrate the professor's point.

One day, as an experiment, I gave my 10th-grade students a standard textbook assignment that consisted of reading a section on the 1815 Congress of Vienna and answering the questions at the end of the section. When the students had finished, I asked them what they had learned. They responded by listing various diplomats who attended the meeting and by identifying several specific changes to international boundaries that resulted from the meeting. These responses were to be expected, since the bulk of the reading was given over to this type of factual detail that few students would remember by dinnertime, and that no students were likely to encounter again during the entire remainder of their lives.

My students completely missed the big picture that the Congress of Vienna was an attempt to undo the egalitarian changes brought about by the French Revolution and Napoleon and to return Europe to the old aristocratic order. Students also missed the more general concept that the Congress of Vienna represented a clash between the perennial political poles of conservatism and liberalism. While these were the most important concepts in the section, and they were relevant to the lives of my students, they were completely lost amid the kind of mind-numbing textbook detail that generates perceptual static and interferes with meaningful understanding.

The textbook used five pages to obscure the important meanings of the Congress of Vienna, whereas the *Student's Friend* used three paragraphs to identify the major concepts involved and, moreover, to relate conservatism and liberalism—the political right and the political left—to the major political parties operating in the United States today.[224] Given what we know about cognition and memory, it seems literally psychotic[‡] to waste time and resources on textbook lessons that teach students the names of European politicians two centuries dead, and the specific changes they made to boundaries of nations long extinct, in the context of a school course that covers the entire history of humanity.

How much is enough? A concise historical narrative such as the *Student's Friend* raises an obvious concern: Does it contain enough information? *Enough* is a concept that, like beauty, may lie in the eye of the beholder, but it's far too important to be left at that. If educators could come to grips with the question of how much is enough, they might make real inroads into dealing with the overstuffed and trivial nature of much history schooling.

The Bradley Commission's report on history in the schools recommended "rethinking" the quantity of content contained in traditional textbooks:

> Has the notion that "less is more" been considered?...
> The amount of time required to achieve student engagement and genuine comprehension of significant issues will necessitate leaving out much that is "covered" by the usual text.[225]

The National Council for History Education took a similar position in the late 1990s, proposing that the "endless store of facts, dates, events, ideas, and personalities" be reduced to an essential core. "Some must be chosen and most left out."[226]

The question of how much is enough was addressed in very different ways by the *Student's Friend* and by the Advanced Placement history program. The AP World History course included 785 required topics by my count, while the US History course specified some 1,274 required topics, which left teachers with substantially less than 6.6 or 4.1 minutes of class time on average, respectively, to cover each required topic.

By contrast, my concise historical narrative had 188 required topics distributed over two courses for an average of 94 topics per course. Using the same assumptions that I used earlier about the length of an academic year and class periods, my curriculum left about 62 minutes on average to cover each required topic.[227]

---

‡ Psychosis: a "fundamental derangement of the mind characterized by defective or lost contact with reality" (*Merriam Webster's Collegiate Dictionary*, 11th edition).

The National Research Council and the Institute of Education Sciences have recommended that students be given the time necessary to achieve deep learning by carefully processing important knowledge through strategies such as distributed practice and exploring underlying principles in multiple contexts. I'll leave it to others to decide if 1,274 required topics are too many in a history survey course or if 94 topics are too few, but one thing seems certain: Deeper understandings are more likely to result from 62 minutes of study than from 4 minutes and 5 seconds.

In reality, the *Student's Friend*—as concise as it is—contains more factual information than a student is likely to remember from taking a single high school course, which is why important historical knowledge should be reemphasized in additional contexts over several years of schooling.

I have taken time here to describe the concise historical narrative that I used in my classroom to demonstrate that it is possible to replace overstuffed textbooks with a more understandable and effective overview of history—a narrative that is consistent with the five commonsense principles of history education featured in this book, including findings from cognitive science about how students learn, retain, and use knowledge.

My classroom experience suggests that such a concise historical narrative can be an effective instructional tool. When tested two years after taking my world history courses, students still retained about 82 percent of the tested *new* learning they acquired in my classes.[228] The *Student's Friend* has been available online since 2001, and a number of other teachers have likewise found it to be a useful educational resource.[229] (The *Student's Friend* is available in book form from Amazon and other booksellers. An online version may be viewed online and downloaded free of charge at studentsfriend.com.)

A CHANGE FOR THE BETTER?

On the surface, the vision of future-focused history education proposed here may look little different from traditional teaching practice. Students and their teachers still examine historical events as they proceed through the chronological record. The big differences lie in the purpose behind instruction and an emphasis on cognitive strategies, both of which are meant to produce learning useful for informing judgment in adult life.

Teachers, like most people, are not generally eager to change their accustomed ways of doing things, and they tend not to enjoy seeing their profession criticized, so teachers may be annoyed or offended by some of the ideas presented in this book. Nonetheless, I hold out hope that teachers might be willing to suspend any negative reactions long enough to consider the benefits that future-focused history education could bring to their teaching and to their students.

Future-focused history education could liberate teachers from the tyranny of content coverage, allowing teachers and students alike to concentrate on deep learning of important historical knowledge that truly matters in people's lives. It would give history education a coherent and worthwhile purpose that the public could understand, value, and support. It could help to elevate historical learning to its rightful place as a fundamental realm of knowledge taught in school alongside mathematics, language, and science.

Future-focused history teaching has the potential to restore to historical learning the kind of power it held when Thycydides wrote his history—not only as a description of events in his own time, but to illuminate enduring principles of history as "a possession for all time."[230] This is the kind of power that history held when our nation's founders looked to ancient Greece and Rome for models of success and failure that could guide their bold experiment in democracy into the future.

Future-focused historical learning might inspire teachers with the sense of mission and pride that comes from knowing they are doing valuable work by helping to improve society's judgment in the crucial realm of human affairs. Perhaps history teachers might even contribute to a new phase of Enlightenment that would assist humanity in saving itself from itself.

To hope that teachers and society will embrace future-focused history education anytime soon might be hoping for too much, but if there is one thing that history teaches us, it's that change is inevitable, and it can sneak up on us when we least expect it. One day we are living in fear of the Soviet Union, and the next day it disintegrates before our eyes. One day black people can't order a sandwich at a lunch counter, and when we look again, a black American has been elected president of the United States. The status quo prevails until it doesn't.

It's true that our contentious political environment would make it difficult to reach consensus on a set of principles of historical knowledge to be taught in American classrooms. So, I say, let a thousand flowers bloom. Let the Republican National Committee put forward its list of principles of history, and let the American Civil Liberties Union submit its list; let Stanford, Harvard, UCLA, Brown, Fordham, and all other interested parties submit theirs.

Lists of general principles proposed by different groups might look quite different from one another, but there might be some areas of overlap. Educators could readily adopt these principles for use in history instruction. Other principles might take longer to hash out, but there's a decent chance that logic and common sense and good scholarship might prevail over the longer term and eventually yield a package of widely accepted principles of historical knowledge suitable for use in American classrooms. Such an effort should probably begin with world history instruction, where nationalistic sensitivities are less pronounced than with US history courses.

As has always been the case, the content of national histories will remain subject to manipulation by governments, who wish to use schooling to indoctrinate the young in a particular worldview. However, the adoption of principles of history might serve to lessen this tendency. Being universal in nature, principles of history are not tied to any particular national history, so let Finland, China, Germany, Saudi Arabia, Ecuador, and any other interested country propose its own list of general principles of historical knowledge, and let the lists compete for credibility and acceptance.

Countries might wish to avoid appearing overly parochial or self-serving in their choices of historical principles, so it's possible that lists might converge toward an honest reflection of reality over time. If such lists were to achieve prominence through their role in schooling, their very presence might promote a wiser and more thoughtful world.

I would think that sets of historical principles should be limited to no more than 20 to 30 of the most important and useful examples—the kind of knowledge that people are most likely to find valuable in the real world of the future. If learned knowledge isn't put to use, it will be forgotten precisely because it's not being used, which makes the teaching of such knowledge essentially pointless.

Limiting the number of historical principles taught in school would help to avoid the tendency to overstuff the history curriculum as we routinely do now. As we have seen, overstuffing leaves insufficient time for students to develop deep understandings of each valuable principle and concept, which prevents the learning from being transferred to adulthood, thereby defeating the fundamental purpose of education.

WIDER APPLICABILITY?

Does a future-oriented vision of history education have anything helpful to say to other school subjects? Unlike history, other subjects already have principles of knowledge that can be applied in the future, so they have no need to overcome the fundamental handicap facing history education.

But other school subjects could stand to benefit from taking a careful look at the *cognition* principle of education, which calls for deep learning of important knowledge. Any school discipline can be guilty of excessive content coverage that produces superficial and trivial learning, especially Advanced Placement courses that appear to be based on a business model that calls for extensive quantity and complexity.

If educators and politicians are concerned about the poor performance of American students on assessments of international learning, they might give consideration to the *scale-to-detail* and *importance* principles of education that can serve to limit excessive content that steals time away from relevant and useful learning. Students and society might be better served by instruction that focuses greater attention on deeper understandings of the most important and useful principles of a school subject, principles that could be helpful to people in living their lives and that also provide a solid foundation for advanced study in the discipline.

David Perkins, professor emeritus at Harvard's Graduate School of Education, questions the tendency of general education to try to turn students into experts in school disciplines. He cites the typical math curriculum as an example of how our schools try to move students toward expertise in a subject with little regard for usefulness. Arithmetic leads to algebra, then to geometry and then to calculus, "an entire subject that hardly anyone ever uses."[231] Perkins values expertise in a subject area but assumes it will be achieved at the college or university level; first, students need to master the fundamentals before deciding where to specialize.[232]

I'll leave the final word on the state of contemporary education to another recognized authority on American schooling: Emma Youngquist, who delivered the valedictory address to the 2015 graduating class at Dolores High School in southwest Colorado, the school where I was doing my student teaching at about the same time that Miss Youngquist was being born.

> I can attest that I have figured out how to work this system....I learned how to memorize names, dates, times, and vocabulary words only to forget them as soon as I turned in the test....
>
> It seems to me that people have forgotten the most important part of our time in high school; being passionate, curious human beings that are excited about learning....
>
> You are more than a number, a statistic, a score on a standardized test, a degree. You are an individual filled with enough innovation and creativity to change the world.

History, history! We fools, what do we know or care?

–William Carlos Williams, *In the American Grain*, 1956

The dance of destiny

E very other Tuesday morning at around eight, Esperanza knocks on the door of our casita in the village of Santiago in northern Mexico. When I open the door, she demurely extends her hand and grants me a beatific smile much as Empress Carlota did—or so I imagine—when greeting a foreign dignitary 150 years ago. Esperanza has arrived to clean our home and leave it smelling of citrus. She spends her days in physical toil; her tools are a broom, a mop, soap, and a bucket of water—all technologies that have existed for well over 150 years.

I spend my days in mental labor. My tool is a sleek, aluminum-clad specimen of 21st-century technology that connects me to the world and its knowledge. Her work and mine could hardly be more different, but when our work is done, our lives are quite similar. We both want to be loved and respected. We are both concerned about the health of our spouses, the happiness of our children, and what we'll be having for dinner.

And thus it has long been. Since the advent of stone tools and language, new technologies have continuously altered the material conditions of life, but these changes sit atop human nature, which remains largely unchanged through the ages. It's not possible to know how new technologies will alter our future lives and labors; it's much easier to predict the human motivations these technologies will serve, and therein lies the power of history.

· · ·

AN ALTERNATIVE MODEL OF HISTORY

For several centuries, beginning at about the time of the Scientific Revolution, the Western world subscribed to a model of history that saw history as a continuous march of progress toward greater enlightenment, freedom, and prosperity, particularly for people in the Western world. This model has unraveled due to the depths of human depravity exposed by recent world wars, genocides, and totalitarian social experiments gone very wrong and by the continued presence of intractable poverty, persistent ethnic violence, and the arrival of technologies that threaten the existence of life on earth.[233]

We may still harbor hope that history will look like a story of human progress when viewed from the perspective of the distant future, but this outcome is by no means assured. Human history could be altered in a flash—like dinosaur history apparently was—by an errant asteroid, but it's more likely to be determined by how humans behave, and at present humans are behaving like self-indulgent and pugnacious adolescents.

If we would prefer a model of history that captures the outlines of our past and the uncertainties of our future, we might consider a model that views human development as a product of the continuous interplay between technology and human nature. Stated as a formula: *History equals human nature times technology* or $H = hn \times t$. While this may be a simplistic model, it's not nearly so simplistic as the notion of unimpeded human progress, and it expresses what might be the central dynamic of historical change.

It has been suggested that the capacity to invent new technologies is the characteristic that most distinguishes humans from other animals,[234] and this unique ability has been altering the material conditions of human life since our species invented its first crude tools and learned to control fire. Humans have since turned these and subsequent technologies to productive uses like agriculture and to destructive uses like warfare.

Technologies owe everything to human nature; they are the product of an unusual spark that is manifested only in the human brain, and they are set in motion by humans responding to the imperatives of their nature. The technologies themselves are disinterested tools that possess neither self-awareness, initiative, nor morality. In deciding whether technologies will be used to build or destroy—to advance good or evil—the thinking falls to us humans.

TECHNOLOGY IS NOT UNDER OUR CONTROL

Although humans have been inventing technologies for millennia, science as we know it is relatively new. Before there was science, there was natural philosophy, which was a human-constructed view of the natural world. Early in the modern era, the introduction of systematic observation, experimentation, and new instruments like the microscope replaced human conceptions of the natural world with empirical findings, and scientists went in search of principles that underlay natural phenomena. Nature was now seen to contain truths waiting to be uncovered by scientists, and scientists displaced philosophers as the bearers of truth.

In the 1500s and 1600s, scientists in their early laboratories pursued basic research that turned into the technologies of the Industrial Revolution. The fruits of scientific discovery were now tied to financial opportunities; there is a direct line from the pioneering experiments of a Robert Boyle to the consumer products of a Thomas Edison.

Technology became the engine of capitalism, each reinforcing the other in what many people saw as a beneficial cycle of prosperity and progress, a perception that suffered a heavy blow in World War I when the nations of Europe turned their technologies on each other in a war of unspeakable horror that decimated a generation of young men. How could Europeans continue to consider themselves the most advanced culture in the history of the world when they had nearly committed suicide? People began to see a link between technology and destruction.

Such misgivings did nothing to prevent humans from employing even more terrible technologies to more devastating effect two decades later in a war that spawned a technology that could end most life on earth. We have some knowledge of what this technology can do because it was demonstrated on two Japanese cities. We know enough to fear it, and society has taken measures to control it, yet it proliferates.

Society has since deployed additional technologies that have the potential to disrupt life on earth, but they are subtler than a thermonuclear bomb. The ultimate impacts of fossil fuel technologies, genetically modified organisms, universal digital surveillance, and artificial intelligence can't be tested on a pair of unfortunate cities, so we don't have a good idea of what these technologies are capable of doing to human life in the future.

Technology is presently conducting experiments on our planet as a whole, the outcomes of which are deeply uncertain. Once set in motion, technologies develop a momentum of their own, and humans are not in control; if a technology promises profit or other advantage, *it will be used*. Technology serves as the powerful hands of society, but the hands are not under control of a brain.

SURVIVING OUR ADOLESCENCE

The unprecedented power and presence of modern technologies impose on humans a responsibility to seek wisdom where it may be found, and there can be no better place to seek wisdom than in the long record of human experience. Religion may tell us that war is bad; science may find in the brain a physiological basis for war; but history *proves* through empirical evidence that war is bad by showing us the appalling results. History, like science, is a bearer of truth—truth in the human realm rather than in the physical realm.

In contemporary society, however, science and technology fill our field of vision, leaving little remaining attention for history, the record of human behavior that can inform society's judgment about important matters, including the uses of science and technology. The wisdom available from history is overlooked because it remains unacknowledged by the history professions, and it lacks profit-making potential.

If history were placed in the service of judgment, its disconnect from the marketplace would be an asset. Whereas science is deeply embedded in commerce,[235] history stands outside the commercial arena, allowing it a more objective view of conditions in society. But if history is to assume its rightful role as an aid to judgment in human affairs, it will need to descend from the creaky third-floor auditorium where it drones away on isolated facts from the past and join the people in the streets, where it can tell us important things we need to know for dealing with the future.

In a large, pluralistic, democratic society such as ours, judgment isn't the exclusive province of leaders or experts. Leaders are just as prone to poor judgment as the rest of us, and an expert can only tell us how to make a nuclear bomb; she can't tell us if the bomb should be dropped on a city full of people. Judgments like this are the responsibility of society as a whole, and society needs all the good judgment it can muster if our species is to survive its adolescence and reach maturity.

Humans have recently arrived at a unique juncture in history, a clear departure from all that came before. Our technologies have achieved the power to affect more than the immediate vicinity—they can harm the entire world and all life on it. The obligation to cope with this changed reality rests with a flawed species that aspires to reach toward the light but too often succumbs to the darker impulses of its nature.

Society can no longer afford to overlook one of the two realms of experience that combine to drive our future. Science and history. History and science. Science is the world we can touch. History is the touching. They are locked in a dance that will determine our destiny.

Appendix

GENERAL PRINCIPLES OF HISTORY
AND
GENERAL PRINCIPLES OF HISTORICAL LEARNING
(mentioned in this book)

GENERAL PRINCIPLES OF HISTORY:
As used in this book, the term general principles of history *refers to tendencies—not invariable rules or laws—derived from observing recurring patterns in the historical record.*

Humans have long manifested an instinctual yearning to explore, to learn, and to develop new technologies to improve their lives.

Humans are a violence-prone species that engages in acts of individual violence and in organized acts of mass homicide, i.e, warfare.

Humans exhibit an instinct to exercise control over others.

Humans exhibit an instinct to resist external control.

Three motives for war are fear, honor, and self-interest. (Thucydides)

Powerful nations tend to prey on weaker nations.

When nations or leaders want to go to war, any excuse will do.

Leaders typically justify foreign invasions by claiming to be helping the people they invade.

Those who promote war tend to disparage those who resist war as cowardly or unpatriotic. (Thucydides)

Rising powers have a tendency to go to war with established powers. (Thucydides)

Even superpowers experience limits to their power.

Many or most military invasions of distant lands fail over the long term.

Democracy is fragile; it has repeatedly fallen to authoritarian rulers.

Leaders try to get their way by appealing to the emotions of their followers.

Power tends to corrupt, and absolute power corrupts absolutely. (Acton)

Government actions tend to have winners and losers.

Government actions tend to produce unintended consequences.

Humans exhibit a propensity to fear, dislike, kill, subjugate, and discriminate against people from groups different than their own.

People tend to promote their self-interest and the interest of their group, so bias is all around us.

Humans tend to position themselves along a political spectrum that ranges from conservative to liberal.

Epidemic diseases have repeatedly claimed countless lives and altered human societies.

Hereditary monarchy is no insurance against civil war and insurrection. (Paine)

Major events usually result from multiple causes, some long-term and some more immediate.

Economies tend to be unstable; they can veer out of control if not carefully monitored.

Major cultures and empires have followed a general pattern of growth, flowering, and decline throughout history.

Historical evidence for representative examples of general principles of history is available at the end of the "Principles of historical knowledge" section of Chapter 5, page 71.

GENERAL PRINCIPLES OF HISTORICAL LEARNING:

The first purpose of historical learning is to foster future judgment in human affairs.

Past experience is the primary indicator of future outcomes.

A single event of the past is not a reliable guide to future judgment and decision-making.

Historical knowledge can reliably serve to inform future judgment only when similar dynamics have been repeated with some frequency over time.

Pretend learning is concerned with memorization of facts for the next exam.

Real learning is concerned with deep learning of relevant and important knowledge, retention of the knowledge in memory, and application of the knowledge in life.

Deep learning is not possible in a curriculum overstuffed with superficial, trivial, and pointless knowledge.

Effective transfer of learning from school to life beyond school is most likely to occur when a limited number of general principles and concepts are learned in multiple contexts over an extended period of time.

Unlike other intellectual disciplines and most productive human endeavors, history (at present) does not officially recognize general principles derived from its subject matter.

Knowledge suitable for general education—internal knowledge carried in our heads—is general in nature, important, and relevant to the future.

External historical accounts of specific events in the past can provide background knowledge when needed for understanding related situations in the present.

Conscious and subconscious bias can interfere with effective judgment and decision-making.

Comparing multiple sources that hold different opinions is a good way to approach the truth.

NOTES

numbered consecutively throughout the book

Chapter Two

1 "Sample Items for World History 2," *Virginia Standards of Learning Assessments, Fall 2011*, Virginia Department of Education, 2011, http://www.doe.virginia.gov/testing/sol/released_tests/2011/history_sample/wh2_history.pdf, accessed Sept. 6, 2011.

These are the two Virginia assessment questions:

Question 2: Which idea best expresses the beliefs of Thomas Hobbes?

A The government should include a separation of powers.

B Government must preserve the people's rights.

C The state must have absolute power.

D Religious toleration should triumph over religious fanaticism.

Question 3:_____?_____ in Africa and Asia

YEAR	EVENT
1857	Sepoy Rebellion in India
1881 – 1898	Mahdi Rebellion in the Sudan
1900	Boxer Rebellion in China

Which phrase completes the title for this table?

A Conflicts Over Religion

B Reasons for Colonization

C Stages of Economic Development

D Responses to European Imperialism

2 Peter N. Stearns, general editor, *The Encyclopedia of World History*, sixth edition, Houghton Mifflin Company, 2001.

As do some historians, I prefer to use the singular term, *Opium War*, referring to the conflict of 1839–42, rather than the plural term *Opium Wars*. Here is an example from *The Encyclopedia of World History*: "Many…historians dated the beginning of 'modern Chinese history' to the Opium War of 1839–42 " (p. 561). The singular term is used again on pages 418, 569, and 575.

When teaching this subject, I found it more expeditious and clearer to discuss the war that began the British–Chinese conflict and makes the essential points, rather than expending time and mental bandwidth on explicating the distinctions between two similar wars or two phases of the same war.

3 William H. McNeill, "Beyond Western Civilization: Rebuilding the Survey," *The New World History*, Ross E. Dunn, ed., Bedford/St. Martin's, 2000, p. 84.

4 "Curriculum Framework 2008: World History and Geography 1500 A.D. (C.E.) to the Present," *History and Social Science Standards of Learning*, Virginia Department of Education, 2008, pp. 23, 34.
The seven are Hobbes, Locke, Montesquieu, Rousseau, Voltaire, Jefferson, and Smith.

5 "Enhanced Scope and Sequence: World History and Geography 1500 A.D. (C.E.) to the Present," *History and Social Science Standards of Learning*, Virginia Department of Education, 2010, p. 59.

6 "Curriculum Framework 2008," p. 23.
This is how the Virginia standards described the philosophy of Thomas Hobbes: "Humans exist in a primitive 'state of nature' and consent to government for self protection." Those fifteen words refer to two of Hobbes's better-known ideas; the *natural state of humans* ("solitary, poor, nasty, brutish, and short") and the *social contract* (rulers rule with consent of the governed). The exam question, however, referred to a third aspect of Hobbes's thinking: "The state must have absolute power." (See Note 1.)

7 "Curriculum Framework 2008," p. 36.
The Mahdi question quizzed students about three uprisings against British rule during the age of European imperialism: the Mahdi Rebellion in the Sudan, the Sepoy Rebellion in India, and the Boxer Rebellion in China. (See Note 1.) But the Virginia content standards specified only one of these three uprisings, the Boxer Rebellion.

8 Fritz Fischer, "The Historian as Translator: Historical Thinking, the Rosetta Stone of History Education," *Historically Speaking*, June 2011, p. 16.

9 Linda Symcox and Arie Wilschut, eds., "National History Standards: The Problem of the Canon and the Future of Teaching History," Information Age Publishing, 2009, p. 6.

10 "Core Purpose and History's Habits of Mind," National Council for History Education, http://www.socialstudies.org/print/121, accessed Nov. 26, 2011.

11 "A Vision of Powerful Teaching and Learning in the Social Studies: Building Social Understanding and Civic Efficacy," National Council for the Social Studies, http://www.socialstudies.org/print/121, accessed Nov. 26, 2011.

12 Joel Sipress and David J. Voelker, "The End of the History Survey Course: The Rise and Fall of the Coverage Model," *The Journal of American History*, Organization of American Historians, March, 2012, pp. 1054, 1056.

13 Searches were made of the following educational materials:
a. History textbooks used in high school, Advanced Placement, and college courses:
Peter N. Stearns, Michael B. Adas, Stuart B. Schwartz and Mark Jason Gilbert, *The Global Experience, Combined Volume*, electronic textbook edition, Pearson, 2015.
Jennifer D. Keene, Saul T. Cornell and Edward T. O'Donnel, *Visions of America: A History of the United States, Combined Volume*, electronic textbook edition, Pearson, 2017.
William Duiker and Jackson J. Spielvogel, *World History*, electronic textbook edition, Cenage Learning, 2016.
b. State curriculum standards in history and social studies:
History and Social Science Standards of Learning for Virginia Public Schools, Board of Education, Commonwealth of Virginia, 2015.
New York State Grades 9–12 Social Studies Framework, New York State Education Department, 2015.
Texas Essential Knowledge and Skills, "Chapter 113, Social Studies, Sub-chapter C. High School," Texas Education Agency, 2011.
c. Curriculum guides that specify required content in Advanced Placement history courses:
AP European History Course and Exam Description, College Board, 2015.
AP United States History Course and Exam Description, College Board, 2015.
AP World History Course and Exam Description, College Board, 2016.

(continued on next page)

These searches yielded no matches for the search terms "principles of historical knowledge," "principle of history," "principles of history," "history's principles," and "historical principles." For good measure, I also searched for terms that might represent synonyms for principles of history: "lessons of history," "history's lessons," "recurring patterns," "historical tendencies," and "historical analogues." I found only two matches, both for the term "lessons of history." One was in the textbook *Visions of America*: "Americans of the revolutionary generation took their cues from the lessons of history, particularly the example of the Roman Republic and its ideal of public virtue" (p. 132). The other match was in the textbook *World History*: "To observant Japanese, the lessons of history were clear. Western nations had amassed wealth and power not only because of their democratic systems and high level of education, but also because of their colonies" (p. 654).

The term *lessons of history* as it appears in these passages does not represent the greater concept of timeless "principles of history" because these mentions are limited to one or two historical events at particular times in the past with no evidence of additional events or eras to which the lessons apply, whereas the term *principles of history* denotes universal principles that have existed for much of human history throughout much of the world and can be expected to extend into the future.

While these materials made no mention of principles of history, they demonstrated wide acceptance of the concept of "principles" in domain knowledge by identifying principles of numerous other fields. The textbook *World History* by Duiker and Spielvogel, for example, discussed principles of research, justice in ancient Egypt, Confucian philosophy, Classical architecture, monarchy, liberty and equality, and Christian morality, among others. The Virginia curriculum standards specified principles of the Scientific Revolution, the Declaration of Independence, American constitutional democracy, citizenship, and market economics, among others. Principles of history were conspicuous by their absence.

Results of these searches of widely used curriculum materials in the field of history confirm beyond any reasonable doubt that principles of history are not part of the official curricula taught to students in American education.

14 Victor S. Navasky, "How We Got into the Messiest War in Our History," *New York Times*, Nov. 12, 1972, http://www.nytimes.com/books/98/03/15/home/halberstam-best.html, accessed June 19, 2014.

In 1972, Pulitzer prize-winning journalist David Halberstam published a book titled *The Best and the Brightest*, a phrase that has since entered popular parlance. His book examined the group of superbly educated, successful, and worldly men who surrounded President John F. Kennedy and how they managed to embroil the United States in the Vietnam War. His conclusion: "They had, for all their brilliance and hubris and sense of themselves, been unwilling to look and learn from the past."

15 John D. Bransford, Ann L. Brown, and Rodney R. Cocking, eds., *How People Learn: Brain, Mind, Experience, and School,* National Research Council, 2000, p. 78.

16 a. Difficult to achieve:
Samuel B. Day and Robert L. Goldstone, "The Import of Knowledge Export: Connecting Findings and Theories of Transfer of Learning," *Educational Psychologist,* American Psychological Association, July 2012, p. 153.

The journal *Educational Psychologist* devoted an entire issue to learning transfer, and the lead article (cited above) observed that a large body of research "finds systematic failures in people's ability to apply their relevant knowledge in new situations," and some researchers have concluded that meaningful transfer of school learning "seldom if ever occurs."

Harry P. Bahrick, "Maintenance of Knowledge: Questions about Memory We Forgot to Ask," *Journal of Experimental Psychology,* American Psychological Association, Sept. 1979, p. 297.

Harry Bahrick of Ohio Wesleyan University is probably the world's foremost researcher in the field of long-term memory of school learning. His landmark findings have been consistently replicated by other researchers, and he has received the American Psychological Association's Distinguished Teaching Award for his international impact on psychological research and education. Based on his findings, Bahrick concluded, "Much of the information acquired in classrooms is lost soon after final examinations are taken."

16 b. Principles learned in multiple contexts:
Bransford, "How People Learn," pp. 20, 238.
"Superficial coverage of all topics in a subject must be replaced with in-depth coverage of fewer topics that allows key concepts in that discipline to be understood....Effective comprehension and thinking require a coherent understanding of the organizing principles in any subject matter."

Bransford, "How People Learn," p. 78.
"Knowledge that is taught in only a single context is less likely to

support flexible transfer than knowledge that is taught in multiple contexts."

Harold Pashler, Patrice M. Bain, Brian A. Bottge, Arthur Graesser, Kenneth Koedinger, Mark McDaniel, and Janet Metcalfe, *Organizing Instruction and Study to Improve Student Learning*, Institute of Education Sciences, US Department of Education, 2007, http://ies.ed.gov/ncee/wwc/Docs/Practice Guide/20072004.pdf, accessed Oct. 22, 2016, pp. 62, 77.

"When a subject is taught in multiple contexts...and includes examples that demonstrate wide application of what is being taught, people are more likely to abstract the relevant features of concepts and to develop a flexible representation of knowledge....The transfer literature suggests that the most effective transfer may come from a balance of specific examples and general principles, not from either one alone."

16 c. Over an extended period of time:

Frank N. Dempster, "Exposing Our Students to Less Should Help Them Learn More," *Phi Delta Kappan*, Phi Delta Kappa International, Feb. 1993, http://www.studentsfriend.com/aids/dempster.html, accessed Oct. 22, 2016.

"The conditions most favorable to [overcoming cognitive interference] involve what learning researchers refer to as 'distributed' or 'spaced' practice....The signature characteristic of distributed practice is that the practice sessions are distributed over a relatively lengthy period of time.... If there is one indispensable key to effective learning, it is distributed practice. But in an overstuffed curriculum, there is little opportunity for distributed practice."

Pashler et al., "Organizing Instruction and Study," p. 35.

"Spacing effects appear to be large in magnitude....It would appear that whenever it is desired that the learner retain information for many years, it is advisable to utilize spacing of at least several months—and spacing even greater than that would seem more likely to improve retention over the longer term."

Bransford et al., "How People Learn," p. 20.

"In-depth study in a domain often requires that ideas be carried beyond a single school year before students can make the transition from informal to formal ideas. This will require active coordination of the curriculum across school years."

17 See Bahrick under Note 16a. above.

Chapter Three

18 "United States Federal, State, and Local Government Spending, Fiscal Year 2017," http://www.usgovernmentspending.com/us_education_spending_20 .html, accessed Feb. 14, 2017.

These figures were confirmed in additional sources including the National Center for Education Statistics and the *Washington Post*.

19 Beverly Thurston, Coordinator for History, Social Science and Textbooks, Division of Standards, Curriculum, and Instruction, Virginia Department of Education, telephone interview with Mike Maxwell, Sept. 28, 2011.

Charles B. Pyle, Director of Communications, Virginia Department of Education, telephone interview with Mike Maxwell, Oct. 6, 2011.

20 Sean Cavanagh, "Demand for Testing Products, Services on the Rise," *Education Week*, Oct. 1, 2013, http://www.edweek.org/ew/articles/2013/10/02/06testing_ep.h33.html?tkn=PSVFKHcN8KakBJQr1YgONoG3PmkTwT2wVDR%2F&cmp=ENL-CCO-NEWS1, accessed Dec. 5, 2013.

21 Michelle R. Davis, "Ed. companies exert public-policy influence," *Education Week*, April 22, 2013, http://www.edweek.org/ew/articles/2013/04/24/29ii-politicalpower.h32.html?r=454773237, accessed June 1, 2013.

22 Philip M. Sadler, "Advanced Placement in a Changing Cultural Landscape," in Sadler, Sonnert, Tai, and Klopfenstein, eds., *AP: A Critical Examination of the Advanced Placement Program*, Harvard Education Press, 2010, p. 3.

23 "AP World History Curriculum Framework," *AP World History Course and Exam Description*, College Board, 2016 pp. 6–104.

The AP World History course is representative; of 99 pages in the course's curriculum framework, 90 pages were devoted to specifying factual content that students were required to know for the single AP exam that would determine the student's eligibility to receive college credit for the course.

24 Sam Wineburg, "Crazy for History," *The Journal of American History*, Organization of American Historians, March 2004, p. 11.

25 James Loewen, *Teaching What Really Happened: How to Avoid the Tyranny of Textbooks and Get Students Excited about Doing History*, Teachers College Press, 2009, pp. 9, 10.

26 Examples:
Jackson J. Spielvogel, *Western Civilization*, ninth edition, Wadsworth Publishing, 2014.
1056 pages, List price $273.95 as listed on Amazon.com, Feb. 15, 2017.

Robert B. Beck, et al., *World History: Patterns of Interaction*, McDougal Littell/Houghton Mifflin, 2007. 1376 pages, 6.8 pounds.

27 "Textbook Weight in California," California Department of Education, May 2, 2010, http://www.cde.ca.gov/ci/cr/cf/txtbkwght.asp, accessed June 12, 2012.

28 Chester E. Finn, "Foreword," *A Consumer's Guide to High School History Textbooks*, Thomas E. Fordham Institute, Feb. 26, 2004, http://208.106.213.194/detail/news.cfm?news_id=329&pubsubid=981#981, accessed May 8, 2012.

29 Pasi Sahlberg, *Finnish Lessons: What Can the World Learn from Educational Change in Finland?*, Teachers College Press, 2011, p. 87.

30 Diane Ravitch, "My View of the PISA Scores," Diane Ravitch's Blog, Dec. 3, 2013, http://dianeravitch.net/2013/12/03/my-view-of-the-pisa-scores/, accessed Dec. 5, 2013.

31 Shortly after the National Standards for History were released in 1994, the United States Senate voted 99 to 1 to reject them. Senators felt that the US history standards were insufficiently traditional and patriotic, that they slighted important (white male) figures in American history in favor of minority groups and women. Senator Slade Gorton, a Republican from the state of Washington, termed the standards "an ideologically driven anti-Western monument to politically correct caricature." Newspaper columnists, radio talk show hosts, and the secretary of education took sides in the conflict, which came to be known as "the History Wars."

32 *National Standards for History, Basic Edition*, National Center for History in the Schools, 1996, pp. 180, 182.

33 Quoted in Linda Symcox, *The Struggle for National Standards in American Classrooms,* Teachers College Press, 2000, p. 121.
The Fordham Foundation's Chester Finn served on the project's National Forum for History Standards.

34 Symcox, *The Struggle for National Standards,* p. 121.

35 Paul Gagnon, "Educating Democracy: Are We Up to It?," National Council for History Education, 2005, p. 3.

36 Robert J. Marzano and John S. Kendall, "Awash in a Sea of Standards," McREL, 1998, p. 1.

Chapter Four

37 *NAEP: National Assessment of Educational Progress,* Institute of Education Sciences, National Center for Education Statistics, US Department of Education, https://nces.ed.gov/nationsreportcard/, accessed Feb. 15, 2017.
Figures are from the most recent assessments available as of February 2017 and identify the percentage of students scoring at proficient or above on the NAEP; scores from all grade levels are averaged to provide an overall proficiency score in each subject area. Figures for mathematics and science are for 2015 assessments in grades 4, 8, and 12. Figures for history are for the 2010 US history assessment, the only history subject tested at this time; 2010 was the last year that all three grades were tested. Figures for language are for the 2015 assessment in reading in grades 4, 8, and 12 (36 percent average proficiency) and the 2011 assessment in writing in grades 4 and 8, the only grades tested in recent years (27 percent proficiency). The reading and writing grades are averaged to yield an overall proficiency of 31.5 percent in the language category.

38 Linda Salvucci, "In the Arena" blog, *Cable News Network,* June 17, 2011, http://inthearena.blogs.cnn.com/2011/06/17/linda-salvucci-history-is-being-crowded-out-of-the-daily-school-schedules-in-many-states-across-the-nation-only-12-minutes-a-week, accessed Nov. 20, 2011.

39 Bruce VanSledright, Kimberly Reddy, and Brie Walsh, "The End of History in Elementary Schools?," *Perspectives on History,* American

Historical Association, May 2012, http://www.historians.org/perspectives/issues/2012/1205/Pedagogy-Forum_The-End-of-History-Education.cfm, accessed Sept. 26, 2012.

40 "A Vision of Powerful Teaching and Learning in the Social Studies: Building Social Understanding and Civic Efficacy," National Council for the Social Studies, http://www.socialstudies.org/positions/powerful, accessed June 29, 2014.

41 Quoted in Richard Rothstein and Rebecca Jacobsen, "The Goals of Education," *Phi Delta Kappan*, Dec. 1, 2006, p. 264.

42 Erik Robelen, "Most Teachers See the Curriculum Narrowing, Survey Finds," *Education Week* blogs, Dec. 8, 2011, http://blogs.edweek.org/edweek/curriculum/2011/12/most_teachers_see_the_curricul.html, accessed Dec. 9, 2011.

43 William H. McNeill, "Beyond Western Civilization: Rebuilding the Survey," in Ross E. Dunn, ed., *The New World History*, Bedford/St. Martin's, 2000, p. 83.

44 Richard J. Evans, *In Defense of History*, W. W. Norton & Co., 1999, pp. 171, 172.

45 Benjamin M. Schmidt, "The History BA since the Great Recession," *Perspectives on History*, The American Historical Association, Dec. 2018, https://www.historians.org/publications-and-directories/perspectives-on-history/december-2018/the-history-ba-since-the-great-recession-the-2018-aha-majors-report, accessed June 10, 2019.

46 Erik Robelen, "Literacy Wins, History Loses in Federal Budget, *Education Week* blogs, January 11, 2012, http://www.edweek.org/ew/articles/2012/01/11/15budget-curriculum.h31.html, accessed Sept. 21, 2012.
In the same year that Congress halted funding for the history grant program, it allocated $180 million to language arts for the Striving Readers Comprehensive Literacy program.

47 Erik Robelen, "White House Issues Inventory of STEM Education Funding," *Education Week* blogs, Dec. 15, 2011, http://blogs.edweek.org/edweek/curriculum/2011/12/amid_all_the_talk_about.html, accessed Sept. 19, 2012. (continued on the next page)

According to the Obama administration, the Department of Education granted STEM education a cool $1 billion. But that wasn't the half of it; STEM education also received about $1.2 billion from the National Science Foundation, $577 million from the Department of Health and Human Services, and $630 million from ten other federal agencies for a total of $3.4 billion. In addition, corporations like Toyota, Google, and Motorola awarded STEM grants of their own.

48 Cheryl Wilkinson, Program Coordinator of the Public History Initiative, UCLA History Department, email communication to Mike Maxwell, Feb. 17, 2017.

Wilkinson wrote: "NCHS [National Center for History in the Schools] is now under the umbrella of PHI [Public History Initiative]. PHI has a new director, so we are in the process of determining how best to move forward with both PHI and NCHS. At present, however, we have no plans to update the current standards."

49 Catherine Gewertz, New Social Studies Framework Aims to Guide Standards," *Education Week*, Sept. 25, 2013, http://www.edweek. org/ew/articles/2013/09/17/05socialstudies.h33.html?qs=national+cou ncil+for+the+social+studies+framework, accessed Dec. 11, 2013.

50 "Review of the 2006 Recommendation on Key Competencies for Lifelong Learning," European Commission, 2017, https://ec.europa. eu/education/initiatives/key-competences-framework-review-2017_en, accessed Dec. 18, 2017.

While history is not identified as a key learning competency, an Annex to the European Parliament action adopting the Key Competencies mentions history briefly alongside current events under the category of civic competence, a category primarily concerned with "democracy, justice, equality, and civil rights." See http://eur-lex.europa.eu/legal-content/ EN/TXT/?uri=celex%3A32006H0962.

51 J. H. Plumb, "The Historian's Dilemma," in J. H. Plumb, ed., *Crisis in the Humanities*, Penguin, 1964, pp. 32, 27.

See also Edward Hallet Carr, *What Is History?*, Vintage, 1967, p. 14.
Carr lamented "a vast and growing mass of dry-as-dust factual histories, of minutely specialized monographs of would-be historians knowing more and more about less and less, sunk without trace in an ocean of facts."

52 Plumb, "The Historian's Dilemma," pp. 27, 28.

53 *Reading Like a Historian*, Stanford History Education Group, Stanford University, http://sheg.stanford.edu/rlh, accessed June 6, 2013.

54 *National Standards for History, Basic Edition*, National Center for History in the Schools, 1996, p. 60.

55 This apt phrase strikes me as reminiscent of something I might have read somewhere. If so, my apologies to the writer, and please contact me for proper credit.

56 *Reading Like a Historian.*

57 Sam Wineburg, "Why Historical Thinking Is Not about History," *History News*, Spring 2016, The American Association for State and Local History, p. 15.

58 Lendol Calder, "Uncoverage: Toward a Signature Pedagogy for the History Survey," *The Journal of American History*, Organization of American Historians, March 2006, p. 1361.

59 Calder, "Uncoverage," p. 1364.

60 Calder, "Uncoverage," pp. 1367, 1368.

61 Calder, "Uncoverage," p. 1359.

62 Teaching students to become "apprentice historians" is commonly identified as a goal of education that emphasizes historical thinking skills; the term has been adopted for use by organizations including the History Association in the UK and the Advanced Placement program in the US.

63 Salvucci, "In the Arena."

64 Evans, "In Defense," pp. 56, 78.

65 Daniel Willingham, *Why Don't Students Like School? A Cognitive Scientist Answers Questions about How the Mind Works and What It Means for the Classroom*, Jossey-Bass, 2009, p. 128.

66 *Occupational Outlook Handbook*, Bureau of Labor Statistics, United States Department of Labor, http://www.bls.gov/ooh/a-z-index.htm, accessed Nov. 13, 2015.

661,400 doctors, 759,800 lawyers, 701,100 auto mechanics, 386,900 plumbers for an average of 627,300 jobs per profession compared to 3,800 historian jobs. 627,300/3,800 yields an average of 165 jobs in each of these other professions for each historian job.

67 "Framework for 21st Century Schooling," P21Partnership for 21st Century Learning, http://www.p21.org/our-work/p21-framework, accessed Dec. 14, 2017.

68 Greg Milo, *Rebooting Social Studies: Strategies for Reimagining History Classes*, Rowan and Littlefield, 2017, p. 16.

If Milo is mistaken about the essential role of subject matter knowledge to thinking, he is nonetheless correct in observing that history schooling as presently taught is largely boring and pointless, and his book offers a number of suggestions for making history courses more interesting to students.

If he and I were to sit down and talk—one high school history teacher to another—I suspect that he wouldn't object to factual knowledge so much as he would object to irrelevant and unimportant factual knowledge.

69 Valerie Strauss, "Why So Many Students Hate History—and What to Do About It," *Washington Post*, May 17, 2017, https://www. washingtonpost.com/news/answer-sheet/wp/2017/05/17/why-so-many-students-hate-history-and-what-to-do-about-it/?utm_term=.e004e9f91ff4, accessed Sept. 9, 2017.

Most of this article was given over to excerpts from Greg Milo's book *Rebooting Social Studies*.

70 F. J. King, Ludwika Goodson, and Faranak Rohani, *Higher Order Thinking Skills*, Center for Advancement of Learning and Assessment, Florida State University, p. 1.

71 Bruce R. Reichenbach, *An Introduction to Critical Thinking*, McGraw Hill, Aug. 9, 2000, http://www.mhhe.com/socscience/philosophy/reichenbach/m1_chap02studyguide.html#2, accessed Sept. 16, 2017.

72 Patricia Armstrong, "Bloom's Taxonomy," Center for Teaching, Vanderbilt University, https://cft.vanderbilt.edu/guides-sub-pages/blooms-taxonomy/, accessed April 27, 2017.

(continued on next page)

Bloom's Taxonomy is named after Benjamin Bloom, who chaired a committee of educators that developed a hierarchical classification of educational learning objectives in the early 1950s. It identified six stages of thinking: knowledge, comprehension, application, analysis, synthesis, and evaluation. A revised version, released in 2001, retained knowledge as the precondition for engaging in five subsequent thinking processes.

73 Willingham, *Why Don't Students Like School?*, pp. 28, 25.

74 Willingham, *Why Don't Students Like School?*, p. 35.

75 "Partnership for 21st Century Skills," National Education Association, 2017, http://www.nea.org/home/34888.htm, accessed Dec. 18, 2017.

76 Daniel T. Willingham, "Critical Thinking: Why Is It So Hard to Teach?," *American Educator*, American Federation of Teachers, Summer 2007, p. 8.

See also Anita Woolfolk, *Educational Psychology*, eleventh edition, Merrill, 2010, p. 293.

"The CoRT [critical thinking] program has been used in over 5,000 classrooms in 10 nations. But Polson and Jeffries (1985) report that 'after 10 years of widespread use we have no adequate evidence concerning the effectiveness of the program.'"

77 David N. Perkins, *Future Wise: Educating Our Children for a Changing World*, Jossey-Bass, 2014, pp. 220, 103.

See also: Willingham, *Why Don't Students Like School?*, p. 29.

"The conclusion from...work in cognitive science is straightforward: we must ensure that students acquire background [content] knowledge parallel with practicing critical thinking skills."

78 *Common Core State Standards for Mathematics*, National Governors Association Center for Best Practices, Council of Chief State School Officers, 2010, p. 7, https://www.mathedleadership.org/docs/ccss/CCSSI_Math%20Standards%20Expanded.pdf, accessed May 30, 2017.

79 *Common Core State Standards for English Language Arts & Literacy in History/Social Studies, Science, and Technical Subjects*, National Governors Association Center for Best Practices, Council of Chief State School Officers, 2010, p. 7, http://www.corestandards.org/wp-content/uploads/ELA_Standards1.pdf, accessed May 30, 2017.

80 Lendol Calder, email communication with Mike Maxwell, Nov. 9, 2011.

Chapter Five

81 Arnold Toynbee, *A Study of History*, abridgement of volumes VII-X by D. C. Sommervell, Oxford University Press, 1987, p. 267.
Toynbee, who perceived patterns in history, applied the phrase disparagingly to historical studies that don't.

82 Ken Burns and Lynn Novik, T*he Vietnam War*, Episode 10 "The Weight of Memory," Public Broadcasting System, Sept. 28, 2017.

83 David N. Perkins, *Future Wise: Educating Our Children for a Changing World,* Jossey-Bass, 2014, pp. 8, 17.

84 Frederick Reif, *Applying Cognitive Science to Education: Thinking and Learning in Scientific and Other Complex Domains*, MIT Press, 2010, p. 138.
"It is important to distinguish between external and internal forms of knowledge organization. The external knowledge organization may be manifest in notebooks, file cabinets, and computers. The internal knowledge organization in a person's head is much less apparent, yet most significant for the person's thinking."

85 Steven D. Levitt, *The Charlie Rose Show*, television broadcast, Public Broadcasting System, May 18, 2014.

86 Nate Silver, *The Signal and the Noise: Why So Many Predictions Fail—but Some Don't*, Penguin Press, 2012, p. 240.

87 Thomas Bayes was a Presbyterian minister in England of the 1700s who devised a mathematical formula for estimating probability. Today an entire branch of statistics is named after Bayes. At its core, Bayes' theorem holds that past experience (what statisticians call "prior probability") is the primary factor in estimating the likelihood of future outcomes. The secondary factor is evidence from the particular case at hand.

(continued on next page)

Here is an illustration of how Bayes' theorem works. Let's say that a friend of yours ran into an acquaintance at the supermarket, and the acquaintance had long hair. What is the probability that the acquaintance was a woman? You know that half of people are women, which represents a prior probability of 50 percent, so this is your baseline prediction. But in the particular case at hand, you have additional information that the acquaintance had long hair, and you believe more women than men have long hair, so probability is weighted in favor of the acquaintance being a woman. This is just common sense so far. If you were to assume that 75 percent of women and 15 percent of men have long hair, Bayes' formula would yield an 83 percent probability that the acquaintance was a woman. (Thanks to Wikipedia for this example.)

If, however, no evidence existed that the acquaintance had long hair, or if you considered the evidence unreliable, you would adjust your estimate of probability back toward the base historical figure of 50 percent. The Bayesian approach calls for forecasts of probability to be updated continually as new evidence becomes available.

In 2009, an Air France passenger jet with 228 people aboard disappeared over the South Atlantic on a flight from Rio de Janeiro to Paris. After a year of surface and underwater searches covering more than a million square kilometers of ocean failed to locate the plane's final resting place, a team of statisticians was called in to help. Using classical Bayesian techniques, they plotted the probable crash site, and within a week of resuming the search, the plane's wreckage was found.

88 "Text-to-Text, Text-to-Self, Text-to-World," *Facing History and Ourselves*, https://www.facinghistory.org/resource-library/teaching-strategies/text-text-text-self-text-world, accessed Feb. 5, 2018.

This is a typical "making connections" lesson: "you can give students the option of writing about one connection they have found between the text and another text, their lives, or the larger world."

89 Human brains are so attuned to recognizing patterns that sometimes we might think we see patterns where none actually exist. Therefore, caution is warranted when choosing principles to teach in history classes. The more often that a pattern has been repeated in the past—and the more people who have recognized it over time—the more likely the pattern is to represent a valid principle of history.

90 Jared Diamond, "The Future of Human History as a Science," in Ross E. Dunn, ed., *The New World History*, Bedford/St. Martin's, 2000, p. 590.

91 I have not capitalized "middle ages" here because I am not using the term as a proper name to designate a particular period of European history, but as a more generic term that applies to the period of history between ancient times and modern times, terms that are likewise not usually capitalized.

92 Diamond, "The Future of Human History as a Science," pp. 588, 590.
    "One cannot deny that it is more difficult to extract general principles from studying history than from studying planetary orbits," but the difficulties facing historians "are broadly similar to the difficulties facing astronomers, climatologists, ecologists, evolutionary biologists, geologists, and paleontologists." These scientific fields—unlike those in which controlled experiments can be conducted—must rely, like history, on observation of the "natural experiments" conducted by Mother Nature and human nature for extracting their general principles.

93 I can't bring myself to use the terms BCE and CE because this nomenclature strikes me as inappropriate on too many levels. The use of BCE and CE is promoted as a means to make non-Christians more comfortable with the worldwide system of dating that originated in the early middle ages in Europe, designated the birth of Christ as year 1, and has been adopted by most of the world for official purposes. In my view, the proposed cure is worse than any problem it is meant to alleviate.
    In the first place, there was no Common Era in history, and if there was one, it began in 1492 when Columbus connected the Eastern and Western Hemispheres, and not in year 1. For historians to pretend that such an era existed is to deny their first responsibility to tell the truth.
    Second, the existing terms BC and AD are more widely known in our culture, and countless historical documents already bear these designations. Introducing a second set of terms with similar letters (and more of them) to designate the very same years is redundant, confusing, anticognitive, and antihistorical.
    Third, designating the Christian era as the Common Era of humankind is a sweeping act of cultural insensitivity that may aggrieve every non-Christian from agnostics to Zen practitioners. It's far better to stick with a simple, centuries-old usage than to intentionally commit a new and greater act of cultural chauvinism.
    Fourth, this whole business could easily have been avoided simply by retaining the original letters and declaring them to represent "**B**efore (year 1) **C**ommon dating" and "**A**fter (year 1) common **D**ating" as in 212 BC and 476 AD. *Before* and *after* provide the helpful cognitive cues that many of us rely on, and common dating *does exist*.

94 Thucydides, *History of the Peloponnesian War*, 423 BC, Perseus Digital Library, Tufts University, http://www.perseus.tufts.edu/hopper/text?doc=Perseus:text:1999.04.0105, accessed March 11, 2018.

This from Book I, Chapter 75: Thucycdes quotes one of the figures in his history as saying, "The subsequent development of our power was originally forced upon us by circumstances; fear was our first motive; afterwards honour, and then interest stepped in."

This from Book III, Chapter 82 [3], [4]: "Reckless daring was held to be loyal courage; prudent delay was the excuse of a coward; moderation was the disguise of unmanly weakness....The lover of violence was always trusted, and his opponent suspected."

95 Carl J. Richard, *The Founders and the Classics*, Harvard University Press, 1994, p. 53.

"Ancient history provided the founders with important, if imprecise, models of personal behavior, social practice, and government form."

96 Graham Allison, "The Thucydides Trap: Are the US and China Headed for War?" *The Atlantic*, Sept. 24, 2015, http://www.theatlantic.com/international/archive/2015/09/united-states-china-war-thucydides-trap/406756, accessed Dec. 6, 2016.

97 G. W. F. Hegel, *The Philosophy of History*, original publication date 1837, Cosimo Books, J. Sibree translator, 2007, p. 6.

98 David Hume, *An Inquiry Concerning Human Understanding*, original publication date 1777, Pearson, 1995, p. 42.

99 Thucydides, *History of the Peloponnesian War*, Book I, Chapter 76.
This, for example: "An empire was offered to us: can you wonder that, acting as human nature always will, we accepted it and refused to give it up again, constrained by three all powerful motives, honour, fear, interest?"

100 Niccolò Machiavelli, *The Historical, Political, and Diplomatic Writing of Niccolo Machiavelli*, translated by Christian E. Detmold, James Osgood & Co., 1882, p. 422.

101 Steven Pinker, *The Better Angels of Our Nature: Why Violence Has Declined*, Viking, 2011, pp. 182, 190.

102 Pinker, *The Better Angels*, pp. xxi, xxiv.

103 David Weinberger, *Too Big to Know*, Basic Books, 2011, p. 1.

104 Richard J. Evans, *In Defense of History*, W. W. Norton & Company, 1999, pp. 53, 52.

105 The Vietnam War could help to illustrate other recurring patterns in history such as the series of proxy wars that were a major feature of the Cold War and that continue to play a role in the Middle East. The Gulf of Tonkin Resolution, which gave President Lyndon Johnson authority to wage full-scale war in Vietnam, could be seen as illustrating a general principle of history: *When nations or leaders want to go to war, any excuse will do*, a pattern prominent in the Roman Empire, where territorial expansion was frequently justified by an imagined slight against the empire, or when the United States declared war on Spain following the sinking of the battleship *Maine* (most likely due to an internal explosion), and again when the US justified invading Iraq because of its nonexistent weapons of mass destruction.

106 Jill Lepore, "The Sharpened Quill," *The New Yorker*, Oct. 16, 2006, http://www.newyorker.com/magazine/2006/10/16/the-sharpened-quill, accessed Feb. 22, 2015.

107 Thomas Paine, *Common Sense*, Jan. 10, 1776, Project Gutenberg, http://www.gutenberg.org/files/147/147-h/147-h.htm, accessed Feb. 22, 2015.

108 *Building a History Curriculum: Guidelines for Teaching History in Schools*, Bradley Commission on History in Schools, http://www.nche.net/content .asp?contentid=160, accessed March 3, 2017.

109 *National Standards for History: Basic Edition*, National Center for History in the Schools, 1996, p. 17.

110 Michael Gazzaniga, "Your Storytelling Brain," *YouTube*, Jan. 27, 2012, https://www.youtube.com/watch?v=3k6P5JiNzrk, accessed June 3, 2015.

Chapter Six

111 *Field of Dreams,* directed by Phil Alden Robinson, Gordon Company, 1989.

112 False research findings can result from a number of factors including psychological biases, errors in research methodology, unsound statistical methods, pressure from funding sources, and outright deception. The following three sources provide some indication of the scope of the problem.

Richard Horton, "What Is Medicine's 5 Sigma?" *The Lancet*, April 11, 2015, http://www.thelancet.com/journals/lancet/article/PIIS0140-6736(15)60696-1/fulltext, accessed May 7, 2017.

Dr. Richard Horton, editor-in-chief of *The Lancet*, one of the world's most respected medical journals, writes, "The case against science is straightforward: much of the scientific literature, perhaps half, may simply be untrue. [It is] afflicted by studies with small sample sizes, tiny effects, invalid exploratory analyses, and flagrant conflicts of interest, together with an obsession for pursuing fashionable trends of dubious importance."

Joseph P. Simmons, Leif D. Nelson, and Uri Simonsohn, "False-Positive Psychology: Undisclosed Flexibility in Data Collection and Analysis Allows Presenting Anything as Significant," *Psychological Science*, Oct. 17, 2011, http://www.haas.berkeley.edu/groups/online_marketing/facultyCV/papers/nelson_false-positive.pdf, accessed June 4, 2017.

"In many cases, a researcher is more likely to falsely find evidence that an effect exists than to correctly find evidence that it does not."

Asher Mullard, "Reliability of 'New Drug Target' Claims Called into Question," *Nature Reviews*, Sept. 2011, http://www.nature.com/nrd/journal/v10/n9/full/nrd3545.html, accessed Feb. 26, 2014.

Bayer Laboratories found that it could replicate only about a third of the claims from 67 research projects published in medical journals.

113 A note about terminology: As cognitive science has appropriated for its use certain terms that have long been in common usage—terms such as learning, perception, and memory—considerable overlap exists between the scientific and common usages of these terms. Science, however, may append specialized elements and meanings to such terms, which may then undergo modification over time as scientific knowledge

develops. Since this book is directed to the general reader and is not specifically directed to a scientific audience, I use such terms as they are understood by the general public and defined in dictionaries.

114 Alan Baddeley, Michael W. Eysenck, and Michael C. Anderson, *Memory*, Psychology Press, 2010, pp. 27, 28, 34.
Baddeley developed a widely used model of working memory.

115 Daniel Kahneman, *The TED Radio Hour*, National Public Radio, Aug. 13, 2013, http://m.npr.org/news/Science/182676143, accessed Sept. 3, 2013.

116 Baddeley et al., *Memory*, pp. 199, 200.
"Over time, experiences accumulate....Adding new memories affects how easily we find things already stored. When memories are similar, this problem should be even worse....Interference arises whenever the cue used to access a target becomes associated to additional memories."

117 Advanced Placement history exams typically ask students to connect inert knowledge to conceptual frameworks of dubious value. See Chapter 8.

118 Harold Pashler, et al., *Organizing Instruction and Study to Improve Student Learning: A Practice Guide*, 2007, National Center for Education Research, Institute of Education Sciences, US Department of Education, p. 1, https://ies.ed.gov/ncee/wwc/Docs/PracticeGuide/20072004.pdf, accessed April 25, 2017.

119 Ulric Neisser, "Interpreting Harry Bahrick's Discovery: What Confers Immunity against Forgetting?" *Journal of Experimental Psychology*, vol. 113, no. 1, 1984, p. 32.
Ulric Neisser, who literally wrote the book on cognitive psychology, termed Bahrick's research "surely the best corpus of data on retention in natural settings that has ever been collected." Bahrick has received the American Psychological Association's Distinguished Teaching Award for his international impact on psychological research and education.

120 Harry P. Bahrick, "Extending the Life Span of Knowledge," in Louis A. Penner, George M. Batsche, Howard M. Knoff, and Douglas L. Nelson (eds.), *The Challenge in Mathematics and Science Education: Psychology's Response*, American Psychological Association, 1993, pp. 65, 66.

121 Moshe Naveh-Benjamin, "The Acquisition and Retention of Knowledge: Exploring Mutual Benefits to Memory Research and the Educational Setting," *Applied Cognitive Psychology*, vol. 4, 1990, p. 306.

Naveh-Benjamin and colleagues studied long-term memory of linguistics and literature. He described Bahrick's research as especially relevant to educational practice, due in part to the long retention interval and because the learning took place in natural settings.

Martin A. Conway, Gillian Cohen, and Nicola Stanhope, "Very Long-term Memory for Knowledge Acquired at School and University," *Applied Cognitive Psychology*, Nov. 1992, p. 479.

The authors studied long-term memory of a cognitive psychology course and the Dickens novel *Hard Times*. They found that students who do not take advanced coursework retain little or no course knowledge 6 to 10 years after instruction.

John A. Ellis, George B. Semb, and Brian Cole, "Very Long-Term Memory for Information Taught in School," *Contemporary Educational Psychology*, vol. 23, 1998, p. 430.

The authors researched long-term knowledge retention among students who took a college child-development course. They said that their findings were "consistent with those of Bahrick (1984), Bahrick and Hall (1991), and Conway et al. (1991)."

122 John D. Bransford, Ann L. Brown, and Rodney R. Cocking (eds.), *How People Learn: Brain, Mind, Experience, and School*, National Research Council, 2000, p. 20.

"In-depth study in a domain often requires that ideas be carried beyond a single school year before students can make the transition from informal to formal ideas. This will require active coordination of the curriculum across school years."

123 Harry P. Bahrick, "Maintenance of Knowledge: Questions about Memory We Forgot to Ask," *Journal of Experimental Psychology*, American Psychological Association, Sept. 1979, p. 297.

124 Bransford et al., "How People Learn," p. 78.

125 M. L. Gick and K. Holyoak, "Analogical Problem Solving," *Cognitive Psychology*, vol. 12, 1980, pp. 306–355.

A classic experiment by Mary Gick and Keith Holyoak illustrated why learning transfer is so difficult to achieve. They presented college students with a problem in which an army commander wanted to capture a fortress located in the center of a country, but the roads leading to the fortress were mined. A large force of soldiers passing over a road would detonate the mines, but a small group could pass safely. The commander solved his problem by dividing his army into smaller groups that traveled over different roads to converge on the fortress simultaneously.

Later, the researchers presented the students with a different scenario. How could a doctor prevent his patient from dying due to a malignant stomach tumor? The tumor could be destroyed with intense radiation, but the treatment would also destroy the surrounding stomach tissue, causing the death of the patient. A smaller dose of radiation would weaken the tumor without harming healthy tissue, but it wouldn't be strong enough to destroy the tumor.

Despite the underlying similarity between the doctor's dilemma and the army commander's problem, few students were able to come up with the idea of focusing several weaker rays on the tumor simultaneously from different directions to produce the intensity needed to destroy the tumor. The surface details of the two situations were different: One involved armies, explosives, and a fortress while the other involved a sick patient, radiation, and cancer. Because we tend to focus on surface details, we can overlook the deeper structure common to similar situations.

126 Samuel B. Day and Robert L. Goldstone, "The Import of Knowledge Export: Connecting Findings and Theories of Transfer of Learning," *Educational Psychologist*, American Psychological Association, July 2012, p. 153.

127 Bransford, et al., *How People Learn*, pp. 239, 238.

128 *Learning and Understanding: Improving Advanced Study of Mathematics and Science in US High Schools*, National Research Council, 2002, p. 177.

129 Pashler, et al., *Organizing Instruction*, pp. 62, 77.

130 Bransford, et al., *How People Learn*, p. 125.
"There is a convergence of many kinds of research on some of the rules that govern learning. One of the simplest rules is that practice increases learning."

131 Pashler, et al., *Organizing Instruction*, p. 35.

132 Pashler, et al., *Organizing Instruction*, p. 21.

133 "Quizzing Works, the Evidence Says," *Teaching Community*, US Department of Education, July 22, 2008, http://teaching.monster.com/benefits/articles/5051-quizzing-works-the-evidence-says?print=true, accessed April 18, 2017.

134 Frank N. Dempster, "Exposing Our Students to Less Should Help Them Learn More," *Phi Delta Kappan*, Phi Delta Kappa International, Feb. 1993, http://www.studentsfriend.com/aids/dempster.html, accessed Oct. 22, 2016.

135 Bransford, et al., *How People Learn*, pp. 173, 20.

Chapter Seven

136 *AP US History Course and Exam Description*, College Board, Fall 2015, p. 6.
AP European History Course and Exam Description, College Board, Fall 2015, p. 6.
AP World History Course and Exam Description, College Board, Fall 2016, p. 6.
Advanced Placement history courses are typical; no purpose or reason for studying history is offered. The following verbiage is as close as the AP courses come: "Students should learn to analyze and interpret historical facts and evidence in order to achieve understanding of major developments in US history" (or plug in "world history" or "European history" in place of US history). Left unspecified is any benefit that might accrue from the acquisition of such learning—any useful purpose to which such knowledge might be applied.

137 Thucydides, *History of the Peloponnesian War*, Book I, Chapter 22, 423 BC, Perseus Digital Library, Tufts University, http://www.perseus.tufts.edu/hopper/text?doc=Perseus:text:1999.04.0105, accessed March 11, 2018.
"But if he who desires to have before his eyes a true picture of the events which have happened, and of the like events which may be expected to happen hereafter in the order of human things, shall pronounce what I have written to be useful, then I shall be satisfied."

138 Niccolò Machiavelli, *The Historical, Political, and Diplomatic Writing of Niccolo Machiavelli*, translated by Christian E. Detmold, James Osgood & Co., 1882, p. 422.

139 Thomas Jefferson, "Notes on Virginia," *The Life and Selected Writings of Thomas Jefferson*, Modern Library, 1998, p. 246.

140 Sam Wineburg, *Historical Thinking and Other Unnatural Acts*, Temple University Press, 2001, pp. ix, 5.

141 *Building a History Curriculum: Guidelines for Teaching History in Schools*, Bradley Commission on History in Schools, http://www.nche. net/document .doc?id=38, accessed Oct. 23, 2014.

142 Jacques Barzun, *Begin Here: The Forgotten Conditions of Teaching and Learning*, University of Chicago Press, 1992, p. 70.

143 Diane Ravitch, *Left Back: A Century of Failed School Reforms*, Simon & Schuster, 2000, p. 14.

144 John Emerich Edward Acton, *Lectures on Modern History*, Appendix I, Macmillan & Co., 1906, p. 315.

145 Barzun, *Begin Here*, p. 140.
"The need for a body of common knowledge and common reference does not disappear when a society is largely pluralistic, as ours has become. On the contrary, it grows more necessary, so that people of different origins and different occupations may quickly find familiar ground, and as we say, speak a common language."

146 David Christian, "The Case for Big History," *The New World History*, Ross E. Dunn, ed., Bedford/St. Martin's, 2000, p. 577.

Chapter Eight

147 "Program Summary Report 2013," *AP Program Participation and Performance Data 2013*, College Board, http://research.collegeboard.org/ programs/ap/data/participation/2013, accessed Oct. 19, 2013.

148 Kristin Klopfenstein and M. Kathleen Thomas, "Advanced Place-ment Participation: Evaluating the Policies of States and Colleges," in Philip M. Sadler, Gerhard Sonnert, Robert H. Tai, and Kristin Klop-fenstein, *AP: A Critical Examination of the Advanced Placement Program*, Harvard Education Press, 2010, p. 168:

"It is now common for upper middle-class parents to evaluate and choose high schools based on the number of AP courses offered at those schools, thereby placing great pressure on schools to expand their AP offerings."

149 Jacques Steinberg, "Head of College Board to Depart Next Year," *New York Times*, March 25, 2011, http://www.nytimes.com/2011/03/26/us/26brfs-HEADOFCOLLEG_BRF.html?ref=advancedplacementprogram, accessed June 14, 2012.

150 The "gold standard" slogan has been used by the Advanced Placement program for a number of years. Here are two references:

A Brief History of the Advanced Placement Program, College Board, 2003, http://www.collegeboard.com/prod_downloads/about/news_info/ap/ap_history_english.pdf, accessed Oct. 24, 2013.

"AP Program to Change AP World History, French and German; Developments Under Way in AP Science," *Connection*, College Board, Nov. 2009, http://www.connection-collegeboard.com/home/programs-and-services/152-apr-program-to-change-ap-world-history-french-and-german-developments-under-way-in-ap-science, accessed May 9, 2012.

151 Maureen Ewing, Kristen Huff, and Pamela Kaliski, "Validating AP Exam Scores: Current Research and New Directions," in Sadler et al., *AP: A Critical Examination*, pp. 102, 103.

An example of this research is the above study, which concluded, "The review suggests that consumers of AP exam scores (i.e. students, parents, teachers, postsecondary institutions, etc.) can be confident in the reliability and validity of AP exam scores when using them to make credit and placement decisions. There is also much to be excited about in terms of the future of AP." The three researchers who compiled this study were employed at the College Board company.

152 Russell T. Warne, Ross Larsen, Braydon Anderson, and Alyce J. Odasso, "The Impact of Participation in the Advanced Placement

Program on Students' College Admissions Test Scores," *The Journal of Educational Research*, May 26, 2015, http://www.tandfonline.com/doi/pdf/10.1080/00220671.2014.917253, accessed Oct. 20, 2015.

153 *Learning and Understanding: Improving Advanced Study of Mathematics and Science in US High Schools*, National Research Council, 2002, p. 176.

154 Saul Geiser and Veronica Santelices, *The Role of Advanced Placement and Honors Courses in College Admissions*, Center for Studies in Higher Education, University of California, Berkeley, 2004, p. 1.

155 Philip M. Sadler, "Key Findings," in Sadler et al., *AP: A Critical Examination*, p. 264.

156 *AP US History Course and Exam Description*, College Board, Fall 2015, p. 6.
AP European History Course and Exam Description, College Board, Fall 2015, p. 6.
AP World History Course and Exam Description, College Board, Fall 2016, p. 6.

157 Christopher Drew, "Rethinking Advanced Placement," *New York Times*, Jan. 27, 2011, http://www.nytimes.com/2011/01/09/education/edlife/09ap-t.html?_r=1&partner=rss&emc=rss, accessed June 15, 2012.

158 Tom Stanley-Becker, "Breaking Free: Opting Out of the AP History Test Is the Smartest Thing I've Ever Done," *Los Angeles Times*, May 8, 2008, http://articles.latimes.com/2008/may/08/opinion/oe-becker8, accessed May 7, 2012.

159 Kevin Levin, "A Short Rant about AP/College Board," *Civil War Memory*, May 9, 2007, http://cwmemory.com/2007/05/09/a-short-rant-about-apcollege-board, accessed May 8, 2012.
Kevin Levin, "Are History Textbooks on Their Way Out?," *Civil War Memory*, April 10, 2009, http://cwmemory.com/2009/04/10/are-history-textbooks-on-their-way-out, accessed May 7, 2012.

160 "AP Program to Change AP World History, French and German," College Board, Nov. 11, 2009, http://press.collegeboard.org/releases/2009/ap174160program-change-ap-world-history-french-and-german, accessed June 15, 2012.

161 *AP World History Course*, pp. 37, 40, 50.

162 *AP World History Course*, p. 49.

163 Frederick Reif, *Applying Cognitive Science to Education: Thinking and Learning in Scientific and Other Complex Domains*, MIT Press, 2010, pp. 44, 46.

164 *AP World History Course*, p. 23:
"The [Concept Outline] framework clearly indicates the depth of knowledge required for each key concept."

165 I began with a typical American school year of 170 instructional days. This number must be reduced by a factor of something like 15 percent due to standard interruptions to instruction including unit exams, final exams, statewide standardized assessments, parent conferences, assemblies, holiday programs, course scheduling, pep rallies, health fairs, homecoming events, professional development sessions, and such. This leaves a high school teacher with approximately 145 teaching days unless she or he is an AP teacher. Because AP exams are administered roughly 10 to 20 days before the end of the school year, the number of days available to teach required AP content is further reduced to about 130.

When high school courses are taught for a full academic year, daily class length usually runs about 45 to 50 minutes. Subtract 5 to 10 minutes for housekeeping tasks such as taking attendance, collecting and returning papers, announcements, and brief meetings with students, and we are left with about 40 minutes of instructional time per class multiplied by 130 class periods for a total of 5,200 minutes of instructional time per course. 5,200 minutes divided by 785 topics equals 6.62 minutes per topic (6 minutes and 37 seconds).

166 *AP World History Course*, p. 14.

167 *AP Biology Course and Exam Description*, College Board, 2012, p. 6.

168 *AP World History Course*, p. 23.

169 Shortly after the National Standards for History were released in 1994, the United States Senate voted 99 to 1 to reject them. Senators felt that the US history standards were insufficiently traditional and patriotic, that they slighted important (white male) figures in

American history in favor of minority groups and women. Newspaper columnists, radio talk show hosts, and the Secretary of Education took sides in the conflict, which came to be known as the "History Wars." A similar history skirmish flared up when the revamped AP United States History course framework was implemented in 2014; it was replaced by a revised version in 2015.

170 *AP United States History*, p. 21.
The AP US History course guide gave teachers this instruction in bold type: "**it is vital that teachers explore the key concepts of each period in depth by using relevant historical evidence of their own choosing**." "In depth" is the vague part. Does this mean that teachers should illustrate each of the required topics included in the key concepts with examples, or does it not?

171 Erik Vincent, Dunwoody High School, DeKalb County, Georgia, AP World History teacher, telephone interview with Mike Maxwell, Aug. 13, 2012.

172 This calculation is based on 130 instructional days available for an AP class taught during a full academic year with a class length of 45 to 50 minutes. Subtracting 5 to 10 minutes for housekeeping tasks like taking attendance, collecting and returning papers, announcements, and brief meetings with students leaves about 40 minutes of instructional time per class multiplied by 130 class periods for a total of 5,200 minutes of instructional time per course. 5,200 minutes divided by 1,274 topics equals 4.08 minutes per topic (4 minutes and 4.8 seconds).

173 This calculation is based on the same assumptions as those immediately above: 5,200 minutes divided by 2,400 topics equals 2.17 minutes per topic (2 minutes and 10 seconds).

174 *AP United States History*, p. 63, Key Concept 8.3,I,A.

175 When I did my counting, for the sake of expediency, I tallied topics serially in the longer entries. In this case, 10 topics are mentioned in order, which is the number used in my tally. However, this entry posits that each of four inputs applies to each of six outputs, which calls for multiplication rather than addition, which means this entry actually specifies 24 topics instead of the 10 that I counted. Therefore, my tally might significantly undercount the number of topics actually required in the AP US History course Concept Outline.

176 *AP United States History*, p. 21.

177 *Learning and Understanding: Improving Advanced Study of Mathematics and Science*, p. 177.

178 Sharon Cohen, Springbrook High School, Silver Spring, Maryland, AP World History teacher, telephone interview with Mike Maxwell, Aug. 1, 2012.
Ted Dickson, Providence Day School, Charlotte, North Carolina, AP US History teacher, telephone interview with Mike Maxwell, Aug. 3, 2012.
Geri Hastings, Catonsville High School, Catonsville, Maryland, AP US History teacher, telephone interview with Mike Maxwell, July 29, 2012.
Erik Vincent, Dunwoody High School, DeKalb County, Georgia, AP World History teacher, telephone interview with Mike Maxwell, Aug. 13, 2012.

179 William Lichten, "Whither Advanced Placement—Now?" in Sadler et al., *AP: A Critical Examination*, p. 238.

180 Stephanie Simon, "Advanced Placement Classes Failing Students," *PoliticoPro*, 8/21/13, http://www.politico.com/story/2013/08/education-advanced-placement-classes-tests-95723_Page2.html#ixzz2dmVT7n8N, accessed Nov. 12, 2013.

181 *9th Annual AP Report to the Nation*, College Board, February 13, 2013, p. 27.

182 Janet Lorin, "Not-for-profit College Board Getting Rich as Fees Hit Students," *Bloomberg* news, Aug. 17, 2011, http://www.bloomberg.com/news/articles/2011-08-18/not-for-profit-college-board-getting-rich-as-fees-hit-students, accessed Oct. 24, 2015.

183 Peter Greene, "Duncan Funnels Millions to College Board," *Huff Post*, Aug. 18, 2014, http://www.huffingtonpost.com/peter-greene/duncan-funnels-millions-t_b_5683016.html, accessed Oct. 24, 2015.

184 Lory Hough, "What's Worth Learning in School?," *Ed: Harvard Ed Magazine*, Harvard Graduate School of Education, Winter 2015,

https://www.gse.harvard.edu/news/ed/15/01/whats-worth-learning-school, accessed Nov. 22, 2017.

David Perkins, professor emeritus at the Harvard Graduate School of Education, questions the value of high-stakes testing: "You end up shooting for the Big contest, the Big test, at the end of the year. It's a distortion...students are asked to learn a great deal for the class and for the test that likely has no role in the lives they will live—that is, a great deal that simply is not likely to come up again for them in a meaningful way."

185 *Merriam-Webster's Collegiate Dictionary*, eleventh edition, 2003, s.v. "rigor."

Rigor is an interesting concept. *Webster's* defines rigor as "stiffness... harsh inflexibility...the quality of being unyielding or inflexible." Rigor is part of the term *rigor mortis*, the rigidity of death. Although rigor has become a popular buzzword in education circles, stiffness and harsh inflexibility hardly constitute good schooling—usefulness does.

186 Tim Lacy, "Examining AP: Access, Rigor, and Revenue in the History of the Advanced Placement Program," in Sandler et al., *AP: A Critical Examination*, pp. 18, 41.

187 Lorin, "Not-for-profit College Board Getting Rich."

188 John Tierney, "AP Classes Are a Scam," *The Atlantic*, online edition, Oct. 13, 2012, http://www.theatlantic.com/national/archive/2012/10/ap-classes-are-a-scam/263456/, accessed Dec. 3, 2012.

Tierney earned his PhD from Harvard and was a professor of American government for 25 years. After he retired from Boston College, Tierney taught AP Government courses at an independent girls school near Boston.

189 Klopfenstein and Thomas, "Advanced Placement Participation," p. 168.

This 2005 study of 539 two-year and four-year colleges and universities found that 91 percent took AP coursework into account in the admissions process.

Sabri Ben-Achour, "More Colleges Stop Giving Credit for AP Exams," *Marketplace*, Feb. 20, 2013, http://www.marketplace.org/topics/

life/education/more-colleges-stop-giving-credit-ap-exams, accessed
June 26, 2015.

This 2015 report identifies a growing trend among colleges to stop
granting credit or to limit credit for AP courses, a trend most pronounced
among selective schools like Harvard, Dartmouth, Columbia, Brown,
and others that have little concern with maintaining student admissions.
Less-selective schools have an incentive to continue to grant credit for
AP coursework so as not to lose prospective students to other institutions that do grant AP credit.

190 Janet Lorin, "College Board Leader Paid More
Than Harvard's," *Bloomberg*, April 25, 2011, http://www.
bloomberg.com/news/2011-08-26/nonprofit-head-of-college-board-
paid-more-than-harvard-s-leader.html, accessed Nov. 12, 2013.

According to *Bloomberg* news, the value of then College Board
president Gaston Caperton's compensation package "was $1.3 million
including deferred compensation in 2009, according to tax filings....
Nineteen executives...got more than $300,000." The *Bloomberg* article
noted that the median compensation for CEOs of nonprofit companies
with budgets over $50 million was $394,508 in 2009, and it quoted
Dean Zerbe, former senior tax counsel for the Senate finance committee
as saying, "This is the kind of salary I would expect from a for-profit
business that is paying taxes."

Chapter Nine

191 Jacques Barzun, *Begin Here: The Forgotten Conditions of Teaching
and Learning*, University of Chicago Press, 1992, p. 54.

192 Steve Rendall, "In Prelude to War, TV Served as Official
Megaphone," *FAIR*, Fairness and Accuracy in Reporting, April
1, 2003, http://fair.org/extra-online-articles/in-prelude-to-
war-tv-served-as-official-megaphone/, accessed Feb. 19, 2015.

Fairness and Accuracy in Reporting (FAIR) looked at nightly news
coverage from ABC, CBS, NBC, and PBS during a two-week period
leading up to the US invasion of Iraq. Of 393 televised interviews about
Iraq, most featured current or former government officials sounding the
drumbeat for war; only three involved people opposed to the impending
war. As these numbers indicate, memories of America's unsuccessful

invasion and occupation of Vietnam were largely forgotten during the run-up to the Iraq War.

193 Anne Kornblut and Charles Sennot, *Boston Globe*, Nov. 22, 2002, http://www.smh.com.au/articles/2002/11/21/1037697805270.html, accessed May 31, 2014.

"In a speech to students [in Prague, capital of the Czech Republic] on the eve of a two-day NATO summit, Mr. Bush compared the challenge of the Iraqi President to the Nazi invasion of Czechoslovakia in 1938, which led to World War II."

194 *Public Papers of the Presidents of the United States: George W. Bush 2004, Book 1*, US Government Printing Office, 2007, p. 560.

At a presidential news conference on April 13, 2004, a reporter noted that public opinion was turning against the war in Iraq, "and some people are comparing Iraq to Vietnam and talking about a quagmire....how do you answer the Vietnam comparison?" President Bush replied, "I think the analogy is false. I also think the analogy sends the wrong message to our troops and sends the wrong message to the enemy."

Michael A. Fletcher, "Bush Compares Iraq to Vietnam," *The Washington Post*, Aug. 23, 2007, http://www.washingtonpost.com/wp-dyn/content/article/2007/08/22/AR2007082200323.html, accessed Nov. 15, 2017.

Interestingly, in 2007, as success continued to elude the United States in Iraq, President Bush pivoted and cited the Vietnam War as an analogy applicable to the war in Iraq. He said that Vietnam demonstrated that the US should not reduce or withdraw its forces from Iraq. Other observers—particularly Democrats—drew the opposite lesson from the Vietnam experience in which the US was unable to achieve victory during 18 years of conflict even with a half million American troops on the ground.

President Bush's opposing positions about the Vietnam analogy illustrate how events from the past may be called upon to provide self-serving "lessons of history" to support virtually any desired position.

195 No doubt, appeasement (by that name or another) has occurred a number of times during the long span of history, but I think it's safe to say that few people know of any instance other than the appeasement situation that occurred in Europe prior to World War II. Historians have yet to determine if that instance represented a net benefit or burden to the Allied (or Nazi) war effort, and I am unaware that any

sort of consensus has emerged regarding previous instances of appeasement. Therefore, the fact that other instances of appeasement may have
occurred does not provide any general principle that might be usefully
applied in future situations.

196 Timothy Geithner, *The Charlie Rose Show*, television broadcast,
Public Broadcasting System, May 11, 2014.

197 Neel Kashkari, *The Charlie Rose Show*, television broadcast, Public
Broadcasting System, March 14, 2016.

198 Noam Chomsky, *Chomsky on Miseducation*, Rowman & Littlefield, 2000, pp. 22, 23.
Walter Lippmann was an influential journalist and author who believed
it was the role of journalism to distill thoughts and actions of the elites
and pass on this information to the general public. He was involved in
a famous debate with John Dewey—the philosopher, psychologist, and
education reformer—who believed that the public should have a more
prominent role in the formation of public policy.

199 Carolyn Y. Johnson, "How an Obscure Drug's 4,000% Price
Increase Might Finally Spur Action on Soaring Health-Care Costs," *The
Washington Post*, Sept. 21, 2015, https://www.washingtonpost.com/news/
wonk/wp/2015/09/21/how-an-obscure-drugs-4000-price-increase-might-
finally-spur-action-on-soaring-health-care-costs/?utm_term=.50ca4085683b,
accessed March 14, 2018.

200 For example, Iran in 1953, Guatemala in 1954, and Chile in 1970.

201 Thomas Jefferson, *The Writings of Thomas Jefferson*, Thomas
Jefferson Memorial Association, 1904, pp. 206, 207.

202 These books include:
How We Know What Isn't So, by Thomas Gilovich, 2008
Predictably Irrational, by Dan Ariely, 2008
Nudge: Improving Decisions about Health, Wealth, and Happiness, by
Richard Thaler and Cass Sunstein, 2008
Thinking Fast and Slow, by Daniel Kahneman, 2011
Incognito, by David Eagleman, 2011
*The Signal and the Noise: Why So Many Predictions Fail—But Some
Don't*, by Nate Silver, 2012

203 Daniel Kahneman, *Thinking Fast and Slow*, Farrar, Straus and Giroux, 2011, pp. 250, 252.

204 World War II: six years; Korean War: three years; Vietnam War: 10 years or 18 years depending on the date chosen as the start of the war. I used the shorter figure of 10 years to calculate an average duration of 6.3 years for the three wars.

205 John Esterbrook, "Rumsfeld: It Would Be a Short War," CBS News, Nov. 15, 2002, http://www.cbsnews.com/news/rumsfeld-it-would-be-a-short-war, accessed Feb. 27, 2014.

206 Rumsfeld's prediction was closer to the duration of the Persian Gulf War (First Iraq War), which lasted seven months, but as an experienced secretary of defense under two presidential administrations, Rumsfeld should have known enough about warfare to recognize that the Gulf War and the Iraq War were not comparable, because they had fundamentally different missions. The mission of the Gulf War was limited to pushing back an invader and reestablishing the status quo that existed prior to the invasion. It was a response to an initial aggression by Saddam Hussein's armies. It had a limited mission, and it was successful.

By contrast, in the Iraq War, the United States initiated hostilities against Iraq, a nation that had done nothing to threaten or harm the United States or its allies. The mission of the Iraq War involved the overthrow of its government, and the replacement of that government with a government more satisfactory to the United States. The mission of the Iraq War was analogous to the mission of the Vietnam War, which the US was unable to win during 18 years of conflict. To use Rumsfeld's terminology, the fundamental differences between the Gulf War and the Iraq War were "known knowns."

207 *Public Papers of the Presidents of the United States: George W. Bush 2002, Book 1*, US Government Printing Office, 2005, p. 2048.

208 Kahneman, *Thinking Fast and Slow*, p. 12.

209 Paul Slovic and Ellen Peters, "Risk Perception and Affect," *Current Directions in Psychological Science*, vol. 15, no. 6, 2006, p. 323.

210 Kahneman, *Thinking Fast and Slow*, p. 139.

211 Sigmund Freud, *The Future of an Illusion*, original publication date 1927, W.W. Norton & Company, 1989, pp. 68, 79.

212 Andrew Campbell, Jo Whitehead, and Sydney Finkelstein, "Why Good Leaders Make Bad Decisions," *Harvard Business Review*, Feb. 2009, https://hbr.org/2009/02/why-good-leaders-make-bad-decisions, accessed March 20, 2015.

213 George Lukianoff and Jonathan Haidt, "The Coddling of the American Mind," *The Atlantic*, Sept. 2015, p. 48.

214 Kahneman, *Thinking Fast and Slow*, pp. 103, 140.
Here Kahneman borrows a phrase from the psychologist Jonathan Haidt, who used it in a different context.

215 Kahneman, *Thinking Fast and Slow*, p. 417.

216 Campbell et al., "Why Good Leaders Make Bad Decisions."

Chapter Ten

217 Daniel Willingham, *Why Don't Students Like School? A Cognitive Scientist Answers Questions about How the Mind Works and What It Means for the Classroom*, Jossey-Bass, 2009, p. 48.

218 Kendall F. Haven, "Your Brain on Stories: Why You Are Hardwired to Think and Learn through Storytelling," Aspen Ideas Festival 2013, http://www.aspenideas.org/session/your-brain-stories-why-you-are-hardwired-think-and-learn-through-storytelling, accessed Feb. 16, 2016.
Haven is author of the book *Story Proof: The Science Behind the Startling Power of Story*. He says human evolutionary history has wired our brains to think in terms of stories: "Information [from] the major sensory organs, the eyes and ears, is converted into story form before it gets into your conscious mind. You can't not think in story terms."

219 Jerome Bruner, *The Process of Education*, Harvard University Press, 1976, p. 33.

220 Grant Wiggins, "The Futility of Trying to Teach Everything of Importance," *Educational Leadership*, Association for Supervision and

Curriculum Development, Nov. 1989, p. 47.

"Questioning is not a context-less skill any more than knowledge is inert content." p. 46.

221 David N. Perkins, *Future Wise: Educating Our Children for a Changing World*, Jossey-Bass, 2014, p. 81.

222 Frederick Reif, *Applying Cognitive Science to Education: Thinking and Learning in Scientific and Other Complex Domains*, MIT Press, 2010, p. 160.

223 Frank N. Dempster, "Exposing our Students to Less Should Help Them Learn More," *Phi Delta Kappan*, Feb. 1993, http://www.studentsfriend .com/aids/dempster.html, accessed April 22, 2017.

I am forever indebted to Dempster of the University of Nevada, Las Vegas for his article that I happened to see tacked to a school bulletin board shortly before I began to teach. The article described cognitive practices useful in education; it strongly influenced my approach to teaching and subsequently this book.

224 "Conservative versus Liberal," *Student's Friend Part 2, Unit 9*, 2016, http://www.studentsfriend.com/sf/sf-online/unit-9-1800s-industrialism-imperialism.html, accessed April 11, 2017.

"Following the Napoleonic Wars, Europe was ready for a period of calm. Leaders representing the "Great Powers" of Europe met in Vienna to hammer out an agreement meant to undo changes brought about by the French Revolution and Napoleon and to maintain a lasting peace by restoring a **balance of power** among European nations. They sought to prevent any nation from becoming stronger than the others as France had done under Napoleon.

Delegates to the Congress of Vienna were members of the **aristocracy** (upper class), who wanted a return to the old order in which monarchs and the upper class controlled a stable society. People who resist change and try to preserve traditional ways are called conservatives. Society's "haves" tend to be conservative because they wish to preserve the system that worked well for them.

Although conservatives were in control in 1815, many common people still believed in Enlightenment ideas. People who support new methods for improving society are called liberals. Because society's "have-nots" desire change, they tend to be liberal. Liberals are said to be on the political "left," while conservatives are on the political "right." (In the United States the Republican Party is considered more conservative than, and to the right of, the more liberal Democratic Party.) Although the Congress of Vienna succeeded in preventing an outbreak of general warfare in Europe for a century, liberal revolts erupted repeatedly as people continued to seek the Enlightenment goals of freedom and equality."

225 *Building a History Curriculum: Guidelines for Teaching History in Schools*, Bradley Commission on History in Schools, http://www.nche.net/document .doc?id=38, accessed Oct. 13, 2012.

226 *Building a World History Curriculum*, National Council for History Education, 1997.

227 That is, 145 instructional days times 40 minutes per day equals 5,800 instructional minutes divided by 94 topics results in an average of 61.7 minutes of time available per topic in the Maxwell curriculum.

228 My state of Colorado did not conduct standardized assessments in history, so I developed a crude measurement of my own. After welcoming students on the first day of class, I handed them a 25-question multiple-choice test that asked the most basic questions about some of the most important topics in world history.

On the last day of class, students encountered these same questions again as part of their final exam. (My high school was on the block plan: 90-minute class periods, five days a week for one semester.) Twelve semesters of results are still accessible on my computer, and they show that students averaged about 12 answers correct on the first day of class compared to about 23 correct on the last day.[i] (Random responses would be expected to produce an average of 6.25 correct answers.)

If it was true, as these results suggested, that students roughly doubled or tripled their knowledge of world history during my courses, I was satisfied with that, but I really wanted to know if their new learning lasted beyond the final exam, so one year I arranged to have my former freshmen students tested again when they were juniors and my sophomores tested again as seniors. On these tests two years later, students averaged over 21 answers correct.[ii]

These brief, multiple-choice tests might not have been the world's finest measurement of historical learning, but they were the measurement I had, and they indicated that students still remembered about 82 percent of the tested new learning that they acquired in my classes.

[i] These tests were conducted between 2001 and 2007 and involved 185 students enrolled in World History 1 and 145 students enrolled in

World History 2 at Mancos High School, Mancos, Colorado.

[ii] The retests involved 28 students enrolled in World History 1 as freshmen and 19 students enrolled in World History 2 as sophomores during the 2001–02 school year. The retests were conducted approximately two years later, during spring semester 2004.

229 The *Student's Friend* has been used in various school settings including home schooling, middle school, high school, and college in locations as diverse as Australia, China and Yemen. Reproduced below is a passage from an information packet supplied by a North Carolina high school teacher to his incoming world history students.

"Welcome to World History," *Mr. Yutzy's World History*, McDowell County Schools, North Carolina, https://sites.google.com/a/mcdowell.k12.nc.us/yutzyworldhistory, accessed Nov. 16, 2013.

"Much of what we do this semester will be based around what I use as our core text. It is called the *Student's Friend*, and I think it is an excellent resource for our class. It offers a very concise overview of world history without getting bogged down with too much trivia that can distract from understanding the general concepts and overall flow of history....I hope that you will keep the *Student's Friend* in mind in the future for other classes in high school or college that may require a working understanding of world history."

230 Thucydides, *History of the Peloponnesian War*, Book I, Chapter 22 (4), 423 BC, Perseus Digital Library, Tufts University, http://www.perseus.tufts.edu/hopper/text?doc=Perseus%3Atext%3A1999.01.0200%3Abook%3D1%3Achapter%3D22%3Asection%3D4, accessed April 18, 2018.

231 Perkins, *Future Wise*, p. 37.

232 Lory Hough, "What's Worth Learning in School?," *Ed.: Harvard Ed Magazine*, Harvard Graduate School of Education, Winter 2015, https://www.gse.harvard.edu/news/ed/15/01/whats-worth-learning-school, accessed Nov. 22, 2017.

Epilogue

233 Richard J. Evans, *In Defense of History*, W.W. Norton & Company, 1999, p. 27.

(continued on the next page)

"The crisis-ridden decades of the 1920s, 1930s, and 1940s with their economic privations, international conflicts, revolutionary upheavals, and, perhaps, above all their revelations...of violence and inhumanity on a scale, and to a degree, previously thought barely possible severely undermined the belief in progress that had sustained the historians of the prewar era."

234 Richard E. Leakey, *The Making of Mankind*, Doubleday, 1992, E.P. Dutton, 1981, pp. 18, 20.

Until the 1960s, it was thought that human life began in Asia, until the husband-and-wife team of Louis and Mary Leakey found older human fossils in the Great Rift Valley of Africa. Their son Richard, also a well-known paleontologist, has written, "Humans are unique because they have the capacity to choose what they do....The most obvious product of our hands and brains is technology. No other animal manipulates the world in the extensive and arbitrary way that humans do."

235 Marcia Angell, "Drug Companies & Doctors: A Story of Corruption," *The New York Review of Books*, Jan. 15, 2009, http://www.nybooks.com/articles/2009/01/15/drug-companies-doctorsa-story-of-corruption, accessed May 7, 2017.

Marcia Angell of the Harvard Medical School provides an example from the pharmaceutical industry of how the marketplace can influence and corrupt science. For 20 years, Dr. Angell was editor in chief of the once-prestigious *New England Journal of Medicine*. She writes, "No one knows the total amount [of money and gifts] provided by drug companies to physicians, but I estimate from the annual reports of the top nine US drug companies that it comes to tens of billions of dollars a year....A study of medical school department chairs (published in the *Journal of the American Medical Association*) found that two thirds received departmental income from drug companies and three fifths received personal income....It is simply no longer possible to believe much of the clinical research that is published, or to rely on the judgment of trusted physicians or authoritative medical guidelines."

Index

Acknowledgments

To my diligent and perceptive first readers, my wife, Sue and my son, Gus,

and to Thucydides, the pioneering historian and spiritual father of this book,

and to the more recent thinkers who contributed much to this book including Harry Bahrick, Daniel Kahneman, Daniel Willingham, and David Perkins,

and to the special people who offered their insights, support, and encouragement along the way (if not always their agreement), Frank N. Dempster, Gary Hill, Heidi Roupp, Dave Kieffer, Sam Wineburg, Joel Allen, Jim Smith, and from Editcetera my wonderful editor Mary Calvez and my eagle-eyed proofreader Paula Dragosh,

and with appreciation to Jeff Bezos, Bill Gates, and Steve Jobs, without whose innovations I could not have researched, written, or published a book from a small village in Mexico or the hinterlands of Colorado,

and, of course, to the smart, shiny, funny, quirky, soulful students who educated me about teaching as I sought to educate them about the past,

thank you.

￼

Thucydides, following the path blazed by Herodotus, had succeeded in creating an entirely new mode of knowledge, independent of philosophical inquiry.... Close attention to human action—society and politics, war and peace—could yield another kind of knowledge. And this knowledge, the result of meditation on the past and close consideration of human affairs, could yield new principles, quite unlike anything established by philosophy or the sciences, to guide humanity into the future.
—Thomas Cahill, *Sailing the Wine Dark Sea: Why the Greeks Matter*

About the author

Mike Maxwell served with the US Army in Vietnam and worked as a broadcast journalist in Columbus, Ohio, before heading west to Colorado, where he held various blue- and white-collar jobs including construction worker, inner-city public housing manager in Denver, and manager of a historic hotel in the mountain town of Telluride.

Mike taught history at Mancos High School for a dozen years, and he has been operating the *Student's Friend* website for world history teachers since 2001. He has a BA in history and an MPA in public affairs, both from the University of Colorado. Mike is married, has two grown children, and resides amid the mountains and deserts of southwest Colorado.

Also by the author:
The Student's Friend Concise World History

Email Mike Maxwell at contactsf@studentsfriend.com

. . .

More information - Join the cause at
futurefocusedhistory.blog

CPSIA information can be obtained
at www.ICGtesting.com
Printed in the USA
LVHW110018270622
722157LV00005B/195

9 781732 120105